D0151180

PQ 4419 .E33 M37 1991
Masciandaro, Franco, 1938-
Dante as dramatist

DEMCO

Dante as Dramatist

Dante as Dramatist

The Myth of the Earthly Paradise and Tragic Vision in the *Divine Comedy*

Franco Masciandaro

upp

University of Pennsylvania Press

Philadelphia

Copyright © 1991 by the University of Pennsylvania Press
All rights reserved
Printed in the United States of America

Library of Congress Cataloging-in-Publication Data

Masciandaro, Franco, 1938–
    Dante as dramatist : the myth of the earthly paradise and tragic vision in the Divine comedy
/ Franco Masciandaro.
        p.   cm.
    Includes bibliographical references (p.   ) and index.
    ISBN 0-8122-3069-8
    1. Dante Alighieri, 1265–1321. Divina commedia. 2. Eden in literature. 3. Tragic, The, in
literature. I. Title.
PQ4419.E33M37   1991
851'.1—dc20   91-2536
                                                                                      CIP

For Laurie

Contents

Acknowledgments

To the specific indebtedness recorded in the pages that follow I must add the expression of my gratitude: to the Northwestern University Press, Rosary College, and Longo Editore, for granting permission to reprint previously published studies; to the University of Connecticut Research Foundation, for contributing to the publications of this volume with a generous grant; to Pia Friedrich, my colleague and friend at the University of Washington, for her interest and generous support during the early stages of my project; to my friend Robert S. Dombroski, of the University of Connecticut, for his perceptive reading and creative criticism of portions of the manuscript; to Sue Brotherton, copyeditor for the University of Pennsylvania Press, for her invaluable suggestions in matters of style; to my children, Anna and Nicola, for their words of encouragement which I found written on the last page of every notebook that I completed; and to my wife, to whom this book is dedicated, for being a patient (and impatient) supporter and interlocutor.

These things are mysteries, not to be explained;
But you will understand when you come there
Alone.

Oedipus at Colonus, 1526–1528

At the place where he had been crucified there was
a garden, and in the garden a new tomb. . . .

John 19:41–42

The joy aroused by the tragic myth has the same origin as the joyous
sensation of dissonance in music.

Nietzsche, The Birth of Tragedy

In the theater man attempts a kind of transcendence, endeavoring both to
observe and to judge his own truth, in virtue of transformation—through
the dialectic of the concealing-revealing mask—by which he tries to gain
clarity about himself. Man himself beckons, invites the approach of a
revelation about himself. Thus, parabolically, a door can open to the
truth of the real revelation.

Hans Urs von Balthasar, Theo-Drama

If we can no longer live the great symbolisms of the sacred in accordance
with the original belief in them, we can, we modern men, aim at a second
naïveté in and through criticism. In short, it is by *interpreting* that we can
hear again. Thus it is in hermeneutics that the symbol's gift of meaning
and the endeavor to understand by deciphering are knotted together.

Paul Ricoeur, The Symbolism of Evil

Introduction

If the dramatic dimension of the *Divine Comedy* is universally recognized, few have made it the object of sustained inquiry. The most notable exception is Francis Fergusson, not only for his *Dante's Drama of the Mind*,[1] but also for the penetrating pages he devotes to Dante in *The Idea of a Theater*.[2] In the latter, from the timeless perspective of analysis, he holds the *Commedia* as a model and touchstone in his interpretation of such landmarks in the history of drama as *Oedipus Rex*, *Hamlet*, and Wagner's *Tristan and Isolde*. "Behind these masterpieces," he notes, "lies the *Divine Comedy*: not written for the stage, yet presenting the most complete imitation of action, and the most developed idea of the theater of human life to be found in the tradition."[3] Jacques Maritain has also called attention to the theatrical component of Dante's poem: "The *Commedia* embraces in its substantial unity forms of poetic creation which demand of themselves to be separate, and which will separate after Dante. . . . The *Divine Comedy* is at the same time and with the same intensive reality poetry of the song, poetry of the theater, and poetry of the tale; the three epiphanies of poetic intuition compose together its single soul or entelechy."[4]

In this study I attempt to bring to light a new measure of the *Commedia*'s poetry of the theater by closely examining Dante's interpretation of the myth of the Earthly Paradise, which is represented in a number of episodes of *Inferno* and *Purgatorio*. These passages constitute crucial stages in the action that emerges in the Prologue and culminates with the fullness of an epiphany at the end of *Purgatorio*, in the episode of Dante's brief stay in the Earthly Paradise. By action I mean not merely an act or deed, but rather—in the Aristotelian sense of the term—the inner motivation from which deeds spring, and which, as Fergusson has pointed out, corresponds to Dante's *moto spiritale*, the movement of the spirit that "never rests until the thing loved makes it rejoice" (*Purg.* XVIII, 32–33).[5]

My principal objective is twofold: to analyze Dante's dramaturgy, especially the creative force of the "tragic rhythm"[6] that the scenes under scrutiny produce as they succeed each other; and to show that Dante stages the action of the pilgrim's journey to the Earthly Paradise as the fundamental conflict between the dream of a future "second innocence"[7] which ignores the irreducible fact of evil, and the recovery of an innocence that is analogous to the innocence of the original myth of Eden. This latter innocence is threatened by the evil that is *already there*, for the serpent is in the garden as the condition or ground for the Fall. Hence, to return to the true garden is, as Dante shows, to discover and to experience the tragic that informs the original Adamic myth. "The serpent," notes Paul Ricoeur, "represents evil that is already there. . . . Man does not begin evil. He finds it. For him to begin is to continue. . . . Adam is older than every man and the serpent is older than Adam. Thus the tragic myth is reaffirmed at the same time that it is destroyed by the Adamic myth."[8]

We will thus learn that the conflict experienced by Dante the pilgrim is one between the denial of the tragic and the acceptance or suffering of the tragic. More important, we will discover that through his suffering of the tragic the pilgrim transcends the tragic and attains tragic vision. Kenneth Burke has given us an important illustration of the dialectical process that engenders tragic vision.

Stated broadly the dialectical (agonistic) approach to knowledge is through the act of assertion, whereby one "suffers" the kind of knowledge that is the reciprocal of his act. This is the process embodied in tragedy, where the agent's action involves an understanding of the act, an understanding that transcends the act. The act, in being an assertion, has called forth a counter-assertion in the elements that compose its context. And when the agent is enabled to see in terms of this counter-assertion, he has transcended the space that characterized him at the start. In this final stage of tragic vision, intrinsic and extrinsic motivations are merged.[9]

Following Burke, I shall treat the language and thought of Dante's text primarily as "modes of action."[10] And like Fergusson's, my analysis will be governed by the principle of analogy, which is especially useful in directing our attention to the relationships between the constitutive elements of Dante's representation.[11] I shall therefore be concerned especially with the poem's literal dimension, whose richness has often been ignored or overshadowed by a concentration on allegory and the problem of Dante's sources. This is not to suggest that the allegorical exegesis and other erudite studies of the *Commedia* are not valuable. Used in excess, however, these approaches tend to become so reductive and mechanical that they prevent us from focussing on the theatrical space of movement and action, where Dante's creative force is most operative. As a result, they neglect what immediately appeals to our imagination and—as Fergusson has observed—"the histrionic sensibility, i.e., our direct sense of the changing life of the psyche."[12] In the spirit of cooperative competition with the allegorists and other erudite *dantisti*, the dramatistic reading I offer below will help both to temper their overindulgence and to build upon their labors.

An important aspect of Dante's poem is the deep relation between drama and ritual, and, correspondingly, between the tragic action of the pilgrim's journey to Eden and the life of the sacred. For example, as I show in Chapters 4 and 6, Dante stages the drama of this return to the garden in a form that is at once reminiscent of Adam and Eve's expulsion from the Earthly Paradise and of the Medieval expulsion rite of Ash Wednesday. The creativity of this rite lies in the fact that the pilgrims, participating in its performance, live their and Adam's expulsion from the garden both as a curse and as a form of expiation and reconciliation—indeed as the necessary *way* back to Eden.

I shall also give special attention to the dialectical opposition between the speculative and the experiential modes of knowing, between the narrow economy of ideas and the expansive economy of the world of action, and, correspondingly, between interpretation and the text, and hence between the tragic as discourse and the tragic as experience or drama.[13] As discourse, interpretation dies the very moment it is formulated, that is, when at the height of its power, as it asserts itself as concept or idea, it leaves the scene or "theater" it is contemplating. As it reaches the apex of its presence to the text (the moment of definition and appropriation of meaning), it withdraws into absence, for it fails to capture the totality or otherness of the experience embedded in the poem. But this is a creative absence and death, for it coincides with the point upon which our attention pivots freely—unencumbered by the "solidity" of interpretation and meaning—to leap again into the sphere of representation.

This is the point of disjunction that helps to create the tragic rhythm which we experience as readers, and that parallels and to some degree reproduces the tragic rhythm lived by Dante the protagonist as he moves from one scene to another. Here Hölderlin's discourse on the transport of tragedy and the *caesura* may be useful: "The transport of tragedy is, in itself, empty and the most unconnected. Thereby, in the rhythmic succession of representations in which the *transport* is portrayed, *that which in prosody is called the caesura*, the pure word, the antirhythmic interruption, becomes necessary, in order to embrace the onrushing alternation of

representations, at its crescendo, in such a way that it is no longer the alternation of representations, but rather the representation itself which appears."[14]

It is this unique interval, this "empty moment," that in the course of the
present study we will repeatedly experience as the privileged moment of
transcendence and tragic vision. This is the paradoxical moment of blindness in which we see, of non-representation when representation appears,
and of expression that dies only to live more deeply in or *as* intuition. This
is akin to T.S. Eliot's "still point":

At the still point of the turning world. Neither flesh nor fleshless;
Neither from nor towards; at the still point, there the dance is,
But neither arrest nor movement. And do not call it fixity,
Where past and future are gathered. Neither movement
from nor towards,
Neither ascent nor decline . . ."[15]

Something like this infinitesimally narrow space—where "the dance
is"—we will also experience with Dante, pilgrim and poet, actor and dramatist, as we shift from representation to performance, or, to borrow
Bachelard's terms, from the *resonances* to the *reverberations* that the poem
produces in us. "The resonances are dispersed on the different planes of
our life in the world, while the repercussions invite us to give greater depth
to our own existence. In the resonance we hear the poem, in the reverberations we speak it, it is our own. The reverberations bring about a change
in being. It is as though the poet's being were our being."[16] Thus, we shall
be concerned at once with tragic vision or tragic wisdom both as an end or
goal of Dante's and of *our* journey to the Earthly Paradise, and as a dialectical process or way—that is, the tragic vision experienced intermittently as
we move with our protagonist from one scene to another.

Our main problem is one of interpretation, not of purely formal elements but of the way the tragic embedded in Dante's representation affects
us, disclosing "existence to existence."[17] In such disclosure something new
and unexpected comes to life: the unutterable takes form and is known, if
only imperfectly and provisionally, within the caesura or empty moment
of which we spoke earlier. Thus, despite the apparent similarities, this
empty moment is not the deconstructionist's moment of "difference" and
différance, that is, of "deferred presence," the ghostly instant that "slides
and *eludes* us between two presences. . . ."[18] In response to and in coopera-

tion with Dante's relentless assertion, throughout the *Commedia*, that truth can be known, this study, in its own fashion, affirms the same belief that truth is attainable, and that we must seek it passionately despite our repeated failures to know it in its totality. In Part III of Hegel's *Encyclopedia* there is this illuminating footnote:

Therefore, when people assert that man cannot know the truth, they are uttering the worst form of blasphemy. They are unaware of what they are saying. Were they aware of it they would deserve that the truth should be taken away from them. The modern despair of truth being knowable is alien to all speculative philosophy as it is to all genuine religiosity. A poet who was no less religious than he was a thinker—Dante—expressed in such a pregnant fashion his belief that truth can be known, that we permit ourselves to quote his words here. He says in the Fourth Canto of the *Paradiso*, verses 124–129:

> Io veggio ben, che giammai non si sazia
>   Nostro intelletto, se 'l *Ver* non lo illustra
>   Di fuor dal qual nessun vero si spazia.
> Posasi in esso, come fera in lustra,
>   Tosto che *giunto* l'ha; e giunger *puollo*—
>   Se non, ciascun desio sarebbe frustra.[19]

Well do I see that never can our intellect be wholly satisfied unless that Truth shine on it, beyond which no truth has range. Therein it rests, as a wild beast in his lair, so soon as it has reached it; and reach it can, else every desire would be in vain.

Significantly, in the tercet that immediately follows, Dante states that because truth can be attained, doubt (and therefore the experience of failure and absence) "springs . . . at the foot of the truth":

> Nasce per quello, a guisa di rampollo,
>   a piè del vero il dubbio; ed è natura
>   ch'al sommo pinge noi di collo in collo.

(Par. IV, 130–132)

Because of this, questioning springs up like a shoot, at the foot of the truth; and this is nature which urges us to the summit, from height to height.

Before turning to discourse as a direct response to the drama that Dante stages in his poem, it is useful to address the question of the apparent contradiction in characterizing a work whose title is *Commedia* with the terms "tragic action," "tragic rhythm," and "tragic vision." In addition, the related question of a "Christian tragedy," which some may consider a paradox, should not be ignored. In *De vulgari eloquentia* Dante defines the tragic style and subject matter:

Now it is clear that we use the tragic style when profundity of thought is harmoniously accompanied by splendor of verses and elevation of construction and excellence of vocabulary. Hence, if we correctly recall that it has already been proved that the highest things deserve the highest, and if that which we call tragic is clearly the highest of styles, those matters which I have distinguished as having to be sung in the highest way ought to be sung in that style only, namely survival, love, and virtue, and whatever we conceive for the sake of these, provided they are not cheapened by anything merely accidental. (II. iv, 7–8)[20]

Although this definition concerns the *canzone*, it can easily be applied to the *Commedia*, whose subject, treated much more deeply and elaborately than in a *canzone*, is indeed *salus, amor et virtus*, and whose style is often the high style of tragedy. One precedent for mixing this style with the low or middle style also appears in a passage of *De vulgari eloquentia*, where Dante advises avoiding "harshness of rhymes unless perhaps [they are] varied by softness: for by the mixture of gentle and harsh rhymes tragic poetry itself shines." (II. xiii, 14)[21]

Let us now turn to the definition of comedy Dante gives in his *Epistle to Cangrande* (paragraph 10):

Comedy begins with sundry adverse conditions, but ends happily, as appears from the comedies of Terence. . . . Tragedy and comedy differ likewise in their style of language; for that of tragedy is high-flown and sublime, while that of comedy is unstudied and lowly. And this is implied by Horace in the *Art of Poetry*, where he grants that the comedian may on occasion use the language of tragedy, and vice versa. . . . And from this it is clear that the present work is to be described as a comedy. For if we consider the subject-matter, at the beginning it is horrible and foul, as being *Hell*; but at the close it is happy, desirable, and pleasing, as being *Paradise*. As regards the style of language, the style is unstudied and lowly, as being in the vulgar tongue, in which even women-folk hold their talk. And hence it is evident why the work is called a comedy.[22]

These two definitions are not as far apart as at first we might have thought, with the exception of course that *De vulgari eloquentia* identifies the tragic action with the subject matter, while the epistle speaks of comedy in relation to plot. For instance, when Dante identifies the style of the *Comedy* with the vernacular of the *muliercule*, he is not really describing the predominant style in his poem. For here he at once appropriates and vies with, among others, Ovid and Lucan, and especially Virgil, whose *Aeneid*, in *Inferno* XX, 113, Dante calls *alta tragedìa* (high tragedy). Significantly, it is the *bello stilo* (the fair style) he learned from Virgil that, at the very beginning of the *Comedy,* he proclaims as the mark of his past achievements as a young poet, and, more important, as a recognition of the master's authority in the new poem (and the new journey) which is about to begin. We also know that he is not identifying his journey to God with the themes of Terence's comedies, except for the generic "happy ending" formula. As he states in *Paradiso* (XXV, 1–2), his is a "sacred poem to which heaven and earth have set hand." Nor can we overlook the significance of the scene in the "noble castle" of Limbo, in which the ancient poets—from Homer to Virgil—honor Dante, making him "of their company," so that he was "sixth amid such wisdom" (*Inf.* IV, 100–102).

If Dante's poem eludes the definition of comedy that he himself has fashioned[23] and appears instead more deserving of the term tragedy, why then did he name it a comedy? Gianfranco Contini's answer is that in the *Commedia* Dante's "intellectual stroke of genius has been to define himself from the lowest level, almost as a sign and measure of the highest exploration. . . . To define oneself from the lowest plane is a proclamation of freedom."[24] And we may also answer with Erich Auerbach:

The *Divine Comedy* is the first and in certain respects the only European poem comparable in rank and quality to the sublime poetry of antiquity. Many passages in the work express Dante's awareness of this; but the word "comedy" and Dante's remarks in his letter to Can Grande show that he never freed himself from the purist views on rhetoric which he sets forth in *De vulgari eloquentia*. There is no point in inquiring here whether it was the vernacular language or the realism of his poem (or its happy ending) that prevented him from assigning it to the highest stylistic class. To me it seems unquestionable that by modern standards he equaled and even surpassed the sublimity of the ancients.[25]

Other critics like Giorgio Petrocchi[26] and Robert Hollander[27]—to mention only a few—have also recognized that the tragic is the predominant style in the *Commedia*. Moreover, Dante's unique synthesis of comedy and tragedy further asserts his freedom by pointing beyond itself, affirming the very life of tragic rhythm and tragic vision of which we spoke above. This may be illustrated by the following passage from *Paradiso*, in which we find Dante struggling with the theme of Beatrice's beauty:

Da questo passo vinto mi concedo
   più che già mai da punto di suo tema
   soprato fosse comico o tragedo:
ché, come sole in viso che più trema,
   così lo rimembrar del dolce riso
   la mente mia da me medesmo scema.
Dal primo giorno ch'i' vidi il suo viso
   in questa vita, infino a questa vista,
   non m'è il seguire al mio cantar preciso;
ma or convien che mio seguir desista
   più dietro a sua bellezza, poetando,
   come a l'ultimo suo ciascuno artista.

(Par. XXX, 22–33)

At this pass I concede myself defeated more than ever comic or tragic poet was defeated by a point in his theme; for as the sun does to the sight which trembles most, even so remembrance of the sweet smile shears my memory of its very self. From the first day when in this life I saw her face, until this sight, the continuing of my song has not been cut off, but now my pursuit must desist from following her beauty further in my verses, as at his utmost reach must every artist.

As he admits defeat, in his attempt to represent the ineffable, Dante is both less and more than the comic or tragic poet: less, because his failure is greater; and more, because his theme is greater. Yet this is also an act of transcendence, the creative "empty moment," which earlier we identified with the *caesura* of tragic rhythm and tragic vision. At this extreme point of "utmost reach" and of failure in the presence of the sublime, Dante unmistakably reveals himself as a tragic poet.

    Another important point to clarify regards the "happy ending" as a reason for naming Dante's poem a comedy, according to the passage cited from the *Epistle to Cangrande*. Despite the view generally held by scholars, Dante did not strictly adhere to this rationale (assuming, of course, that he is the author of the *Epistle*).[28] If he had, he could not have called the *Aeneid* a "high tragedy," for it too ends "happily" (at least from the perspective of the victorious Aeneas). Moreover, a moment's reflection will reveal that in general comedy's happy ending is a temporary or arbitrary reconciliation, usually a marriage,[29] while tragedy's ending is "happy" in a deeper sense—

that of a changed state of being, of transfiguration, such as Oedipus attained at the moment of his death in the sacred grove at Colonus. As Walter Kerr has aptly observed, "whenever the action of tragedy is pressed forward to span its full possible length, whenever it works its way to an irreversible resolution, whenever it insists upon an absolute ending, its ending will be reconciliatory. . . . The tragic action, however, may be curtailed at will by the playwright, depending upon the segment of its arc he most wishes to display."[30]

By showing—though by necessity very succinctly—that we can consider the *Comedy* a tragic poem, we have indirectly shed some light on the related question of whether it is a Christian tragedy. If the *Comedy* is at once essentially tragic and one of the highest expressions of the Christian experience, to call it a Christian tragedy is not inappropriate or contradictory. Yet some may disagree and join Karl Jaspers in asserting that "Christian salvation opposes tragic knowledge. The chance of being saved destroys the tragic sense of being trapped without chance of escape. Therefore no genuinely Christian tragedy can exist."[31] We may refute this view with the help of the same author, who also states: "Christ is the deepest symbol of failure in this world, yet he is in no sense tragic. In his very failure he knows, fulfills, and consummates." Soon after Jaspers adds: "Paradoxically, however, when man faces the tragic, he liberates himself from it."[32] These words (like the famous dictum we find on the same page, "there is no tragedy without transcendence") accurately define what Jaspers has just negated: Christ as a tragic figure and the Christian experience as tragic. Similarly, some have asserted that the Hebrews did not possess a tragic sense of life. George Steiner, for example, states that "tragedy is alien to the Judaic sense of the world."[33] On the other hand, Richard Sewall asserts that "we can see with striking clarity in the writings of the ancient Hebrews the vision which we now call tragic and in *The Book of Job* the basic elements of the tragic form. . . . The suffering, questioning, unanswered Job, is the towering tragic figure of antiquity. More than Prometheus or Oedipus, Job is the universal symbol for the western imagination of the mystery of undeserved suffering."[34]

It is beyond the scope of this introduction, and of this study, to enter into a detailed and systematic defense of the authenticity of the tragic in Christianity and in its matrix, the Judaic tradition. In completing my sketch of the problematic of Christian tragedy and its relation to the *Commedia*, let suffice the words of Roger L. Cox and Hans Urs von Balthasar:

Christianity is so profoundly and uncompromisingly tragic that it ends by seeming to lose its tragic character, by coming out on the other side. That is to say, its catharsis is almost total. But in order to be a Christian, the individual must in turn submit himself to the tragic just as Jesus did. How else may we understand the words, "Whoever does not bear his own cross and come after me, cannot be my disciple"? Christian tragedy *can* exist then, because even if "Christianity stands beyond tragedy," the raw material of literature is experience, and for anyone who accepts Christ's life as the model, experience is fundamentally tragic.[35]

D. Mack[36] is right to point out, with regard to those who reduce Christianity to "an unclouded harmony of God, the world, and man," that "antiquity's *Nemo contra deum nisi deus ipse* found a parallel in the New Testament in Christ's anguished *Eli, Eli, lama asabthani*; the Christian realm still contains the possibility of the most profound doubt, the greatest failure, suffering and conflict, unbelief, the baffling nature of existence this side of the grave and apparent meaninglessness. The Christian is not automatically an optimist; he is exposed to the risk of freedom and hence to the danger of tragic failure."[37]

These and all the preceding remarks do not presume to define the tragic in relation to Christianity in general, and to the *Commedia* in particular. Nor are they offered as a premise for a theory of the tragic to be developed later and systematically applied to our reading of Dante's poem. They are merely tentative assertions whose validity and potentially far-reaching implications must be tested throughout the dramatistic reading I propose. Since my primary concern is to participate in Dante's interpretation and reenactment of the myth of the Earthly Paradise, my interest falls not so much on theory as on the story, without however neglecting the dialectic between theory and experience, between the narrow economy of ideas and the expansive economy of the world of action.

The potential fruitfulness of this investigation lies in its attempt to define the space or stage upon which we move and act as the "chorus" in the presence of Dante the pilgrim. This chorus, which in the course of our reading we must "invent" again and again, includes the diverse "voices" of a number of literary critics and philosophers. As I call upon each of these *auctores* to give greater resonance to the "song" of the chorus, I am not suggesting that I necessarily embrace the school or methodology with which they are generally identified. As a *bricoleur*, or jack-of-all-trades who shares the lot of most literary critics, I use whatever means are at hand (commensurate to the limits of my knowledge) as long as they help us to expand our terminology and sharpen our focus in our field of operation.[38] Despite its obvious limitations, our *bricolage* may prove to be a creative endeavor, in some measure analogous to and coterminus with that of our poet who, reconciling and harmonizing in his vision a myriad of voices—of rationalists and mystics, of poets and philosophers from both the pagan and Christian world—is perhaps the greatest of *bricoleurs*.

As members of the chorus here delineated, and hence as a community that is bound to its hero, with Dante we will catch glimpses of the never completely understood myth of the Earthly Paradise and its deep relation to history. We will learn that myth, in order not to be reduced to a dream, must enter and vivify man's existence and be interpreted anew on the stage of this life; and that drama, if it is not to become only a mirror of fragments, but seeks instead unity in the midst of dispersion and the uniqueness of the individual as a measure of the universal, must recreate myth. Most important, we will experience what Yeats called "tragic joy"[39] as we face with Dante the terrifying reality of the Last Things.

Notes

1. Francis Fergusson, *Dante's Drama of the Mind: A Modern Reading of "Purgatorio"* (Princeton, NJ: Princeton University Press, 1953).

2. Francis Fergusson, *The Idea of a Theater* (Princeton, NJ: Princeton University Press, 1949). See also Piero Boitani's *The Tragic and the Sublime in Medieval Literature* (Cambridge: Cambridge University Press, 1989), a study—as Boitani himself states—of "comparative European literature dominated by Dante."

3. Fergusson, *The Idea of a Theater*, p. 2.

4. Jacques Maritain, *Creative Intuition in Art and Poetry* (Cleveland and New York: World Publishing Co., 1954), p. 278.

5. In his introduction to *Aristotle's "Poetics,"* trans. S.H. Butcher, intr. Francis Fergusson (New York: Hill and Wang, 1961), p. 8, Fergusson writes: "One must be clear, first of all, that *action (praxis)* does not mean deeds, events, or physical activity: it means, rather, the motivation from which deeds spring. . . . It may be described metaphorically as the focus or movement of the psyche toward what seems good to it at the moment—a 'movement-of-spirit,' Dante calls it."

6. Cf. Fergusson, *The Idea of a Theater*, p. 40: "The *Purgatorio* especially, though an epic and not a drama, evidently moves in the tragic rhythm, both as a whole and in detail. . . . Because Dante keeps his eye always upon the tragic moving of the psyche itself, his vision, like that of Sophocles, is not limited by any of the forms of thought whereby we seek to fix our experience—in which we are idolatrously expiring, like the coral animal in its shell." Cf. also Susanne Langer, "The Tragic Rhythm," in *Feeling and Form*, ed. Susanne Langer (New York: Charles Scribner's Sons, 1953), p. 351: "Creatures that are destined, sooner or later, to die . . . hold the balance of life only precariously, in the frame of a total movement . . . the movement from birth to death. . . . That is the tragic rhythm. Tragedy is a cadential form."

7. Cf. Antoine Vergote, "La peine dans la dialectique de l'innocence, de la transgression et de la réconciliation," in *Il mito della pena*, Archivio di Filosofia, ed.

E. Castelli (Padua: Cedam, 1967), pp. 385–386: "Le rêve de la seconde innocence est tout à la fois le désir de ne relever que de soi-même et de retrouver l'harmonie avec soi-même, par la suppression de toute héteronomie. Le désir ne porte pas l'homme à recevoir l'innocence du bon vouloir de l'Autre; il pousse à la conquérir par lui-même."

8. Paul Ricoeur, "Herméneutique des symboles et réflexion philosophique," in *Il problema della demitizzazione*, Archivio di Filosofia, ed. E. Castelli (Padua: Cedam, 1961), pp. 57–58. (Translation mine)

9. Kenneth Burke, *A Grammar of Motives* (New York: Prentice Hall, 1945), pp. 38–39. Cf. Kenneth Burke, *Language as Symbolic Action* (Berkeley: University of California Press, 1966), p. 95: "Most often, perhaps, the tragic principle operates as follows: The hero acts; in the course of acting, he organizes an opposition; then, in the course of suffering the opposition (or 'seeing in terms of' it) he transcends his earlier position—and the audience, by identification with him, undergoes a similar 'cathartic' transformation."

10. Burke, *A Grammar of Motives*, p. xxii. Cf. Kenneth Burke, *The Philosophy of Literary Forms*, 3rd ed. (Berkeley: University of California Press, 1973), p. 107: "The relation between the 'drama' and the 'dialectic' is obvious. Plato's dialectic was appropriately written in the mode of ritual drama. It is concerned with the maieutic, or midwifery, of philosophical assertion, the ways in which an idea is developed by the 'coöperative competition' of the 'parliamentary.' Inimical assertions are invited to collaborate in the perfecting of the assertion."

11. Cf. Fergusson, *The Idea of a Theater*, p. 236: "The concept of analogy (like that of action) is useful, not in making an abstractly intelligible scheme of the art of drama, or of a particular play, but in directing our attention to the relationships between concrete elements. And these elements—actions in various modes—we must perceive directly, 'before predication.' "

12. Ibid., p. 5.

13. We may note with Kenneth Burke (*Language as Symbolic Action*, p. 97) that "though I dare hope that one can distinguish between dialectical transcendence and dramatic catharsis at their extremes . . . , I must admit that the realms covered by the two terms considerably overlap."

14. Friedrich Hölderlin, *Werke und Briefe*, ed. Friedrich Beißner (Frankfurt: Insel, 1969), p. 730; cited by Philippe Lacoue-Labarthe in "The Caesura of the Speculative," trans. Robert Eisenhauer, *Glyph* 4 (1978): 83. On the same page we read this illuminating commentary on Hölderlin's passage: "Such disarticulation of the work and of the process of succession through alternations which constitutes the work as such—and through which we must travel . . . from a melodic conception of the work to a rhythmic one—does not suppress the logic of exchange and alternation. It simply brings it to a halt; it reestablishes the equilibrium; it prevents it, as Hölderlin says, from exhibiting its representations in one sense or another. . . ." Cf. Cyrus Hamlin, "On Tragedy: A Review of Current Research," *Recherches Sémiotiques/Semiotic Inquiry* 4, 1 (1984): 57: "Persuasive to me, as a point of terminological clarification, is the claim that the central dilemma for the meaning of this art form resides within the space or gap that separates tragedy as discourse from the tragic as experience. What is criticism to do in the face of such a space or gap? I

take that silence to be identical with the climactic moment of Sophoclean tragedy, usually termed the catastrophe, which Hölderlin reformulated in his notes to the drama as the cesura in the tragic rhythm, about which everything turns and through which the truth of divinity is revealed. What we need for criticism is a hermeneutics of the ineffable, which would account for the power and authority *per contrarium* of a silence that reveals directly transcendent truth."

15. "Burnt Norton," *Four Quartets* (New York: Harcourt, Brace & World, Inc., 1943).

16. Gaston Bachelard, *The Poetics of Space*, trans. Maria Jolas (Boston: Beacon Press, 1969), p. xviii.

17. Commenting on a passage from Heidegger's *Being and Time* (trans. John Macquarrie and Edward Robinson [Oxford: Basil Blackwell, 1980], p. 205, H. 162), R. Jahan Ramazani writes: "Tragic drama, then, discloses existence to existence. Its ultimate orientation is the tragic affect it produces. Tragedy cannot be considered apart from its 'towards-which,' any more than the actual theater can be considered apart from its orientation towards the experience of drama. Strip the *Wozu* away from the theater and nothing remains but an empty shell—four meaningless walls. Strip the *Wozu* away from the tragic play and nothing remains but a directionless dance of signifiers. In either case, a formalism unbraced by hermeneutics would end in its own deconstruction." R. Jahan Ramazani, "Heidegger and the Theory of Tragedy," *The Centennial Review* 32, 2 (Spring 1988): 108.

18. Jacques Derrida, *Writing and Difference*, trans., intr., and notes Alan Bass (Chicago: University of Chicago Press, 1978), p. 263. Cf. Meyer Howard Abrams, "The Deconstructive Angel," in *Contemporary Literary Criticism*, ed. and intr. Robert Con Davis (New York and London: Longman, 1986), p. 433: "Derrida's chamber of texts is a sealed echo-chamber in which meanings are reduced to a ceaseless echolalia, a vertical and lateral reverberation from sign to sign of ghostly nonpresences emanating from no voice, intended by no one, referring to nothing, bombinating in a void."

19. *Hegel's Philosophy of Mind*, Part III of the *Encyclopedia of the Philosophical Sciences* (1830), trans. William Wallace and A. V. Miller (Oxford: Clarendon Press, 1971), p. 180. Quoted in John Dobbins and Peter Fuss, "The Silhouette of Dante in Hegel's *Phenomenology of Spirit*," *Clio* 11, 4 (1982): 397.

20. Warman Welliver, *Dante in Hell: The "De Vulgari Eloquentia,"* with introduction, text, translation, and commentary (Ravenna: Longo, 1981), p. 101.

21. Ibid., p. 129.

22. *Dantis Alagherii Epistolae*, intr., trans., notes Paget Toynbee (Oxford: Oxford University Press, 1920; rpt. with preface and additional bibliography by Colin Hardy, 1966), pp. 200–201.

23. Cf. Ernst Robert Curtius, *European Literature and the Latin Middle Ages*, trans. Willard R. Trask (New York and Evanston, IL: Harper & Row, 1953), p. 358: "Dante is not consistent in his use of designations for the genres. When he calls the *Aeneid* 'high tragedy' . . . this can only refer to its style. If its action is taken into account, it would have to be called a comedy. The antique system of poetic genres had, in the millenium before Dante, disintegrated until it was unrecognizable and

incomprehensible. Dante's title was a makeshift. Our current title *Divina Commedia* (first appearance in the Venice edition of 1555) was a happy supplement."

24. Gianfranco Contini, "Un'interpretazione di Dante," in his *Varianti e altra linguistica* (Turin: Einaudi, 1970), p. 399. (Translation mine)

25. Erich Auerbach, *Literary Language and Its Public in Late Latin Antiquity and in the Middle Ages*, trans. Ralph Manheim (London: Routledge & Kegan Paul, 1965), p. 225.

26. Giorgio Petrocchi, *Profilo di un'opera: L' "Inferno" di Dante* (Milan: Rizzoli, 1978), p. 110: "La tenuta stilistica abbraccia sovente, e contestualmente, i modi d'uno e d'altro stile, in un registro formale che noi . . . possiam pure designare come comico, ma che è un impasto di comico e tragico, una lingua 'mediana' ma *spostata continuamente sul tragico*." (Italics mine)

27. Robert Hollander, *Il Virgilio dantesco: Tragedia nella "Commedia"* (Florence: Olschki, 1983), p. 125: "Per valutare lo stile che risulta nella *Commedia*, ritengo che la logica e l'esperienza del testo dantesco portino a concludere che lo stile è in effetti misto, con *il tragico in posizione predominante*." (Italics mine)

28. Whether or not the *Epistle to Cangrande* is spurious is still not certain. The most recent argument against the *Epistle*'s authenticity has been presented by Professor Henry Ansgar Kelly in his *Tragedy and Comedy from Dante to Pseudo-Dante* (Berkeley: University of California Press, 1989). I must note that despite what the title of that work suggests, its focus, unlike that of the present study, is on the definition of tragedy and comedy as found in Dante's *De vulgari eloquentia*, in the *Epistle to Cangrande*, in Dante's possible sources for such definitions, and in a number of the early commentaries of the *Commedia*.

29. Cf. Walter Kerr, *Tragedy and Comedy* (New York: Da Capo Press, 1985), p. 64: "There is very good reason why all comedies should end in marriages. Cornford long ago pointed out—persuasively, I think—that Aristophanic comedies generally end in arbitrary Sacred Marriages not because there is any logical or literary need for such marriages but because the form of comedy had derived from that portion of Greek ritual which sang 'the hymeneal hymn' of fertility."

30. Ibid., p. 55.

31. Karl Jaspers, *Tragedy Is Not Enough*, trans. Harald A.T. Reiche, Harry T. Moore, and Karl W. Deutsch (Boston: Beacon Press, 1952), p. 38.

32. Ibid., pp. 40–41.

33. George Steiner, *The Death of Tragedy* (New York: Hill and Wang, 1963), p. 4.

34. Richard Sewall, *The Vision of Tragedy*, 2nd ed. (New Haven, CT: Yale University Press, 1980), p. 9.

35. Roger L. Cox, *Between Earth and Heaven: Shakespeare, Dostoevsky, and the Meaning of Christian Tragedy* (New York, Chicago, San Francisco: Holt, Rinehart and Winston, 1969), p. 25. Cf. R.B. Gill, "The Forms of Christian Tragedy," *Bucknell Review* 26, 2 (1982), 80: "To exclude Christian tragedy from tragedy because it includes a resurrection is to forget that high tragedy from the ancient Greeks on has included very similar things."

36. Dietrich Mack, *Ansichten zum Tragischen und zur Tragödie* (Munich: Fink, 1970), p. 128.

37. Hans Urs von Balthasar, *Theo-Drama: Theological Dramatic Theory*, trans. Graham Harrison (San Francisco: Ignatius Press, 1988), p. 428. "The words used by Mack," the author adds (p. 429), "such as 'doubt' and 'unbelief' should not be applied to the abandonment of Jesus on the Cross (which can show certain parallels in the destinies of Christians and human beings generally: 'being handed over to evil'), even though this abandonment is more profound than anything we can imagine and, according to the Christian understanding, underpins everything in the world that can be termed 'tragic.' This mystery eludes all literary categories and relativizes them."

38. Cf. Jacques Derrida's discussion of *bricolage* (based on Lévi-Strauss' and G. Genette's use of the term), in his "Structure, Sign, and Play in the Discourse of the Human Sciences," *Contemporary Literary Criticism*, op. cit., p. 486.

39. W.B. Yeats, "The Gyres," in *The Collected Poems of W.B. Yeats* (Toronto: Macmillan, 1956), p. 291. Cf. George Santayana, "Tragic Philosophy," *Essays in Literary Criticism of George Santayana*, select., ed. Irving Singer (New York: Scribner, 1956), p. 276: "The individual souls in Dante's hell and heaven speak the language of tragedy, either in desperate pride or in devout self-surrender. . . . In Dante the hurly-burly is rounded out into a moral tale, into a joyful tragedy, with that sense of finality, of eternity, which Christian eschatology had always preserved."

I. The Prologue: The Nostalgia for Eden and the Rediscovery of the Tragic

Nel mezzo del cammin di nostra vita
  mi ritrovai per una selva oscura,
  ché la diritta via era smarrita.

(*Inf.* I, 1–3)

Midway in the journey of our life I found myself in a dark wood, for the straight way was lost.[1]

The poetic force of the first line of the *Divine Comedy* lies less in the fact that it tells of Dante's age at the time of the fictional journey, or that it echoes Isaiah 38:10 ("I said: In the midst of my days I shall go to the gates of hell"),[2] than in the scene that it brings forth. From a dramatistic viewpoint there is an interrelation or ratio between scene and act, because "cammin" means at once "way" and "journey." Allen Mandelbaum has captured both meanings, in his translation: "When I had journeyed half of our life's way."[3] There are of course other ratios, such as scene-agent, scene-purpose, and so on, which are implied by the first, especially if we consider the two dimensions that further define the scene evoked by "cammin": "nel mezzo" and "nostra vita."[4]

Here *cammin* is the essential term because it seems to contain or imply all the others. As "way" and "journey," as both scenic and kinetic, it calls forth and helps define agent and purpose. The agent is at once collective, choral, as the adjective "nostra" suggests, and individual, as "mi ritrovai" declares. The purpose is to attain the proper end of the journey, which has its new inception in the wayfarer's action of finding himself in the dark wood. "Nel mezzo" speaks of a discrete, crucial point or moment, which by its very position brings into focus both the beginning and the end of our life's journey. Its special force is further revealed by "mi ritrovai," which tells of the action of sudden awakening, of becoming conscious of going through a dark wood.[5]

Dante enlarges the first scene of his poem, creating an opposition between the journey that might have been undertaken, the "diritta via" that was lost, and the dark wood that marks both the middle of that journey and a deviation from it. If at first glance this opposition seems to emphasize the negative aspect of the dark wood, a closer reading reveals that as a constitutive part of the entire journey it possesses, at least potentially, a positive value. Dante does not say "mi ritrovai *in* una selva oscura," but "*per* una selva oscura," and—as Antonino Pagliaro notes—"this choice of preposition, which expresses motion, shows how the wood is substantially a part of the journey itself, that is, of being in this life."[6] The preposition "per" also emphatically declares what was implicit in "cammin": the creative ambivalence of motion (and action, which is conscious motion), and therefore of the fundamental condition of being in the scene of this life. As we read in the *Epistle to Cangrande*, "Everything which has motion moves because of something which it has not, and which is the terminus of its motion. . . . Everything, then, which has motion is in some respect defective, and has not its whole being complete."[7] And conversely, to move presupposes being: *movere praesupponit esse*.[8]

The dialectical interrelation of the two scenes—of our life's journey and the dark wood—represents the necessary condition for change, and therefore for the wayfarer's awakening. As such, these scenes also help to define the conscious direction of his desire and will towards a goal, "that which he has not and which is the terminus of his motion."

According to the conventional reading, the dark wood symbolizes the wayfarer's sinful state and the political and spiritual decay of the world in Dante's time. This interpretation fails to capture the full symbolic force of the "selva oscura," because of the questions it does not ask. What is a wood for us, and for Dante the wayfarer? And, more important, what makes it the appropriate place, the *necessary* scene[9] for his awakening, for his finding himself at once as *lost* and as *homo viator*?

In terms of an elementary phenomenology, we may note that we generally think of immensity when we think of a forest or when we move through one. In his *The Poetics of Space*, Gaston Bachelard, examining what is meant by the "immensity of the forest," writes: "This 'immensity' originates in a body of impressions which, in reality, have little connection with geographical information. We do not have to be long in the woods to experience the always rather anxious impression of 'going deeper and deeper' into a limitless world."[10] Another essential attribute of the forest is that it is "ancient." Let us again turn to Bachelard's reflections:

But who knows the temporal dimension of the forest? History is not enough. We should have to know how the forest experiences its great age: why, in the reign of the imagination, there are no young forests. . . . In the vast world of the non-I, the non-I of the fields is not the same as the non-I of forests. The forest is a before-me, before-us, whereas for fields and meadows, my dreams and recollections accompany all the different phases of tilling and harvesting. When the dialectics of the I and the non-I grow more flexible, I feel that fields and meadows are with me in the with-me, with-us. But forests reign in the past.[11]

Significantly, Charles S. Singleton, glossing Dante's "selva oscura," cites two passages from the *Aeneid* (VI. 179, 185–188) which contain references to the forest being *immense* and *ancient*:

itur in antiquam silvam, stabula alta ferarum . . . atque haec ipse suo tristi cum corde volutat, aspectans silvam immensam, et sic forte precatur: "si nunc se nobis ille aureus arbore ramus ostendat nemore in tanto!"

They pass into the forest primeval, the deep lairs of beasts . . . And alone [Aeneas] ponders with his own sad heart, gazing on the boundless forest, and, as it chanced, thus prays: "O if now that golden bough would show itself to us on the tree in the deep wood!"[12]

Singleton then reproduces Bernard Silvestris' gloss on the passage, from which I extract the following:

In silvam, in collectionem temporalium bonorum. *Umbrosam* [sic] et *immensam*, quia non est nisi umbra. Antiquam, ab inicio temporis natam.

In silvam (in the woods), in the totality of the things of this world. *Umbrosam* (shadowy) and *immensam* (immense), because the shadows are everywhere. *Antiquam* (ancient), born in the beginning of time.[13]

These glosses will constitute, in the end, a mere display of erudition, if we ignore what they suggest: namely, that the forest's primeval immensity and darkness have the power of creating within the wayfarer deep reverberations whereby he may be transformed, and the immense, dark forest is thus the appropriate condition or scene for his awakening to the possibility of beginning a new journey.

To begin to measure the creativity of this scene-act ratio, we should ask: if in the realm of imagination "forests reign in the past," and they are both within and beyond history, does not the "selva oscura" speak of the mythical "first scene" of the human race, and therefore not only of Dante the wayfarer but of all who move and act in this life's journey? How can we, then, unhesitatingly identify it with sin alone and not instead with life's formless, original chaos, what has been aptly called "the slumberous vitality of the cosmic substrate, awaiting development"?[14] Is not the "selva oscura" an amalgam of good and evil "awaiting development" by one who, like our wayfarer, awakens to its immensity and darkness?

It is premature to answer with the gloss to the "selva oscura" that Dante himself offers later in his poem, when he calls the Earthly Paradise a "divina foresta spessa e viva" ("divine forest green and dense," *Purg*. XXVIII, 2), and a "selva antica" ("ancient wood," *Purg*. XXVIII, 23), where the water of a stream flows "bruna bruna / sotto l'ombra perpetua" ("quite dark under the perpetual shade," *Purg*. XXVIII, 31–32). All that the text requires of us now is that we see in the "selva oscura" at once the sinful life and the "slumberous vitality" of the mythical forest that may "develop" into a garden or even a plurality of gardens, and perhaps into the "divine forest," the "ancient wood" at the summit of Purgatory.

Another important dimension characterizing the forest and, by analogy, Dante's "selva oscura" is the *sacred*. Commenting on a poem about the forest written by Pierre-Jean Jouve,[15] Bachelard observes: "Thus, Pierre Jouve's forest is *immediately sacred*, sacred by virtue of the tradition of its nature, far from all history of men. Before the gods existed, the woods were sacred, and the gods came to dwell in these sacred woods."[16] To further illustrate the nature of the sacred in (analogical) relation to the scene of Dante's awakening in a dark wood—"far from history"—let us turn to Mircea Eliade:

Man becomes aware of the sacred because it manifests itself, shows itself, as something wholly different from the profane. To designate the *act of manifestation* of the sacred, we have proposed the term *hierophany*. It is a fitting term, because it does not imply anything further; it expresses no more than is implicit in its etymological content, i.e., *that something sacred shows itself to us*. It could be said that the history of religions—from the most primitive to the most highly developed—is constituted by a great number of hierophanies, by manifestations of sacred realities. From the most elementary hierophanies—e.g., manifestation of the sacred in some ordinary object, a stone, a tree—to the supreme hierophany (which, for a Christian, is the incarnation of God in Jesus Christ) there is no solution of continuity. In each case we are confronted by the same mysterious act—the manifestation of something of a wholly different order, a reality that does not belong to our world, in objects that are an integral part of our natural "profane" world.[17]

The full significance of these observations will become clear as our investigation progresses.

Considering the scene-act, scene-agent, and act-agent ratios of the scene of the "selva oscura," we now note that the figure of Dante the wayfarer takes on the traditional features of the tragic hero. This is borne out first by the phrases "cammin di nostra vita" and "era smarrita," whose intrinsic power of "symbolic action" reveals the connection of the wayfarer to the community, and his role as both its victim and its representative, as one who is expelled by his community and at the same time embodies it. The impersonal form of the phrase "la diritta via *era* smarrita" ("The straight way *was* lost") defines the objective condition of sin shared by everyone. This is for the pilgrim the unexplainable larger scene which he has not created, but within which he nevertheless finds himself—a scene symbolizing a sinfulness much greater than his own. Like Oedipus or Lear he is, in Lear's own words, "more sinned against than sinning." Moreover, as he ventures from the profane world of "our life's journey" into the sacred world of the "dark wood," he begins to discover in himself the confluence of life's historical and mythical dimensions: he is called to be at once Dante the Florentine of 1300 and Everyman, or, more accurately, a new Adam. Robert Hollander offers us the following illuminating remarks on Dante as the new Adam:

Before Exodus is present in the poem, in a few large strokes which are neither inappropriate nor particularly surprising, we are presented with the figures of the first two great events of Genesis which concern our race. We can sense them in the dark wood that Dante metaphorically relates to dangerous waters, thus suggesting that the Fall and the Flood are the historical analogues to the Pilgrim's dire situation, which is, after all, causally related to Adam's sin. It would be unlike Dante not to begin at the Beginning. His journey to God begins in memory of the beginning of the race's journey—Adam cast forth from the Earthly Paradise, his offspring shortly after to be confronted by a flood—and all of this is present in and behind the first thirty lines of the poem.[18]

In the scene of the "selva oscura," the wayfarer is an Adam who awakens to the duality of the garden at the time of the Fall. Like Adam, in the crucial moment of differentiation, when the *principium individuationis* emerges for the first time, he experiences the harshness and terror of the immense, primeval forest as a manifestation or correlative objectification of sin, and at the same time as the creative ground, the original condition, the "totality of the things of this world," as Bernard Silvestris defined it. This is the forest or garden to which he, like all men, wishes to "return."

But how can the pilgrim undertake such a journey? How can he move from the world of the profane into the world of the sacred, transforming the "slumbrous vitality" of the "selva oscura" into the full, manifest vitality of the forest of the Earthly Paradise, if there is no solution of continuity between the profane and the sacred? The poet invites us to seek the answers to these questions by becoming his companions in his journey, that is, his attentive, sympathetic readers:

> Ahi quanto a dir qual era è cosa dura
>   esta selva selvaggia e aspra e forte
>   che nel pensier rinova la paura!
> Tant'è amara che poco è più morte;
>   ma per trattar del ben ch'i' vi trovai,
>   dirò de l'altre cose ch'i' v'ho scorte.

(*Inf.* I, 4–9)

Ah, how hard it is to tell what that wood was, wild, rugged, harsh; the very thought of it renews the fear! It is so bitter that death is hardly more so. But to treat of the good that I found in it, I will tell of the other things I saw there.

At first we are surprised, or puzzled by the shift from evil to good, from the terrifying dark wood to the good of the "other things." Yet, if we recollect the dialectical coexistence of good and evil we have earlier discerned as virtually present in the first scene of the dark wood, we discover that what here seems to be incongruous, in the light of discursive reasoning, is quite coherent and meaningful from the dramatistic viewpoint. This viewpoint allows us to move from one assertion to another, or from one scene to another, and to experience at once the break, the discontinuity from the "selva" as evil to the "selva" as good and the connection, by contrast and contiguity, of the two. In other words, we learn to discover gradually what this mysterious, immense, primeval dark forest *is*, by what it *is not*, that is, by what is not immediately perceived by us as a constitutive part of the wood—its *otherness*.

Significantly, the poet speaks of the good he found, not by identifying its intrinsic quality, but in the "metonymic way," as Jakobson[19] would say, by "telling" of "other things" he discovered in the dark wood.

The poet's assertion calls forth questions that have not yet been given convincing answers.[20] What is this "good" found in the "selva oscura"?

Many commentators identify it with Virgil, or specifically with Virgil's saving action. Singleton reproposes this reading in his commentary: "This 'ben' will be the wayfarer's rescue by Virgil after the she-wolf thrusts him back into the dark wood."[21] The inaccuracy of this interpretation is quite evident. On the one hand, we can easily object that Virgil's rescue does not take place in the dark wood but on the desert slope of the hill that lies outside the wood; on the other hand, Dante speaks of this "good" in terms of other things, not of one thing (or action) alone. Virgil's action of rescuing the wayfarer—though the most crucial—must be seen as one among a plurality of "things," such as the leopard, the lion and even the she-wolf. For each of these, with its respective actions and scenes, constitutes, as we shall soon see in greater detail, an essential link in the long chain of events that lead to the scene of Virgil's intervention.

In order to capture some measure of the fullness and integrity of the original good found in the "selva oscura," the poet must necessarily point to other things. The text suggests that this good, which is innately present in the "selva oscura," manifested itself in the moment of the wayfarer's awakening, the timeless moment expressed by "nel mezzo," that is, the point of which Dante spoke in the *Convivio* (IV. xxiii, 9) as "lo punto sommo di questo arco [de la vita]" ("the highest point of this arch [of life]").[22] This is the moment of vision, "the point of intersection of the timeless / with time,"[23] where the sacred crosses the profane. It is a hierophany. Its very nature defies definition. It is ineffable. Yet—the "ma" of Dante the poet ("Ma per trattar del ben . . .")—he can attempt to reveal its vitality and creative force by *telling* of other things, that is, by creating through analogy a play of correspondences between his words, the "other things" and the good. *Sub specie aeternitatis*, the privileged moment of the wayfarer's vision "contains" all the "other things." Thus the poet can say that he saw these where he found the good. In the temporal perspective of both the narration and the fictional journey, however, they can only be expressed and experienced as *other*, and therefore as occurring *outside* that privileged moment and place of the wayfarer's awakening.[24] Dante's apparently incongruous words are a clear example of disjunction, which, according to its technical meaning in logic, expresses the following relation: the truth of A is in B or in C or in D. . . . This relation, like the one between the "good" of the "selva oscura" and the "other things," is a constitutive element of drama, and specifically, of the "dialectic of tragedy."

We are again at first puzzled and then reassured of the coherent, meaningful representation offered to us by the poet, when we continue reading and find a series of sudden shifts and breaks paradoxically connecting a variety of opposite scenes. Having announced the good found in the "selva oscura" in terms of "other things," Dante attempts to define the forest by recalling the undefined point where he entered it:

> Io non so ben ridir com'i' v'intrai,
>   tant'era pien di sonno a quel punto
>   che la verace via abbandonai.
>
> (*Inf.* I, 10–12)

I cannot rightly say how I entered it, I was so full of sleep at that moment I left the true way.

Then we witness another sudden shift in the action:

> Ma poi ch'i' fui al piè d'un colle giunto,
>   là dove terminava quella valle
>   che m'avea di paura il cor compunto,
> guardai in alto e vidi le sue spalle
>   vestite già de' raggi del pianeta
>   che mena dritto altrui per ogne calle.
>
> (*Inf.* I, 13–18)

But when I had reached the foot of a hill, there at the end of the valley that had pierced my heart with fear, I looked up and saw its shoulders already clad in the rays of the planet that leads men aright by every path.

As the pilgrim looks up to the sunlit hill, the action comes to a halt. But even this pause, if analyzed closely, reveals an underlying dramatic structure of opposition and disjunction. Dante tells of the present "somewhat quieted" fear and at the same time links it to the past fear that he had experienced in the wood the night before (I, 19–21). Then, in the famous simile of the shipwrecked, he speaks of his mind that, as it was fleeing toward the hill, "turned back to gaze upon the pass that never left anyone alive":

> . . . l'animo mio, ch'ancor fuggiva,
>   si volse a retro a rimirar lo passo
>   che non lasciò già mai persona viva.
>
> (*Inf.* I, 25–27)

. . . my mind which was still fleeing turned back to gaze upon the pass that never left anyone alive.

In this pause of external action, we witness another dramatic shift as we glance for a moment at the inner action, the movement of the mind which is turned at once towards the dark wood and the hill. Thus the beginning and the end are paradoxically linked by the very distance that separates them. Here we discern the essentially dramatic structure of correlation by disjunction.

This dramatic form continues to assert itself in the scenes that follow. As the wayfarer resumes his climb, the sudden irruption of a leopard ("almost at the beginning of the steep"), creates a new action and a new scene. The way is now barred. All action stops, or rather there is only a semblance of action, a kind of "inert motion," an "immoto andare . . . delirio . . . d'immobilità" ("immobile going . . . a delirium . . . of immobility"),[25] to say it with words of a modern poet:

. . . i' fui per ritornar più volte vòlto.

(Inf. I, 36)

. . . more than once I turned around to go back.

Suddenly the focus changes, as this terrifying, nightmarish scene of "immobile motion" is followed by an expansive scene that at once embraces the present time and the time of creation:

Temp'era dal principio del mattino,
   e 'l sol montava 'n sù con quelle stelle
    ch'eran con lui quando l'amor divino
mosse di prima quelle cose belle;
   sì ch'a bene sperar m'era cagione
    di quella fiera a la gaetta pelle
l'ora del tempo e la dolce stagione. . . .

(Inf. I, 37–43)

It was the beginning of the morning, and the sun was mounting with the stars that were with it when Divine Love first set those beautiful things in motion, so that the hour of the day and the sweet season gave me cause for good hope of that beast with the gay skin. . . .

Once again we witness a kind of leap, or transcendence, brought about by the juxtaposition of two scenes. Hence, the movement, the progression of the action, is the product not of a linear, continuous development of events, which could be translated into the discursive logic of cause and effect, but of the series of *caesurae*, of dislocations produced by the mere contiguity of scenes. The scene of the threatening leopard is radically transformed by the scene that immediately comes into being the moment the protagonist discovers that the temporal frame is the mythical *illud tempus*, the very beginning of time, coinciding with God's creation of the "beautiful things." The historical time (spring of 1300) and the mythical time are represented as one. Hence, against this background or scene, is the wayfarer not acting as Adam, as we have already glimpsed at the very beginning of the Prologue, that is, as Adam before the Fall? And, in this perspective, can we still find it incongruent that the protagonist not only no longer feels threatened by the leopard, but, as the poet clearly states, also experiences "good hope"? Can we, like most commentators, be silent here, or merely express bewilderment?

The protagonist cannot but find cause for good hope at the sight of the leopard. He *must* feel that he is in harmony with it, as Adam was in harmony with all the beautiful things of creation before the Fall. (Note that this beauty is also echoed in the "gay skin" of the leopard.)[26] "Friendship with the wild animals," writes Mircea Eliade, "and their spontaneous acceptance of men's authority are manifest signs of the recovery of a paradisiac situation."[27] Yet the wayfarer's sudden recovery of the paradisiac state is annulled by the equally sudden appearance of a lion (*Inf.* I, 44–48), and, most decisively, by the irruption of a she-wolf "that in her leanness seemed laden with every craving" (I, 49–50). She brings on such fear that the wayfarer loses all hope of reaching the summit of the hill, of "returning" to Eden.

Before we examine the next scene, we should pause a moment to take stock of what has just preceded. One compelling question arises that requires our immediate attention: why do the lion and the she-wolf destroy the wayfarer's hope of attaining his goal at the hill's summit? Why, instead, do they not reinforce the hope he had gained at the sight of the leopard? How does the paradisiac scene of the leopard suddenly cease to exist? At this point, like the wayfarer, we see but without understanding. We experience the sudden shifts from misery to joy and then back to misery again, without knowing why. Hence, we have before us a dramatic coexistence of scenes which are antithetical, and whose sequence exhibits no solution

of continuity. All we can do now is to try to apprehend their inner motivational force, that is, their intrinsic value as ground for the scenes that
follow. We can begin by observing that the "paradisiac scene" that the wayfarer seems to have recovered, soon after the appearance of the leopard,
serves him well only for a moment, a timeless instant which transcends or
annuls the time of fear and misery, the time of fallen man. In dramatistic
terms, the correlation among scene, act, and agent that the wayfarer had
found proves to be an illusory, false recovery of the paradisiac state. In fact,
his perception of the scene itself is false. For as he discovers the propitious
confluence in his time of the mythic time of creation, and acts as if he had
suddenly attained the Earthly Paradise, he fails to see that he is still outside
the "garden," that he is on a desert slope ("la piaggia diserta"; I, 29), separated both from the dark wood (which, as we have seen, "contained" or
prefigured the garden of Eden) and from the sunlit hill ("another" figure
of Eden, as we shall later see more distinctly). We can tentatively interpret
this failure to perceive the correct scene-act-agent ratio as a sign of what
we may call the "narcissism of the mind," which had already been expressed
by the mind's "flight" toward the summit of the hill ("l'animo mio ch'ancor
fuggiva . . . ," I, 25),[28] a flight from the world of conflict, of drama, and
therefore a flight from history. Seeing the summit of the hill with the
mind's eye produces the reflexive, mirror-like effect of possession, of "being already there" (the mind's goal being always appropriation), for by its
very nature the mind, the moment it beholds its object, has the illusion of
possessing it.

At the appearance of the leopard, the wayfarer experiences first the terror of separation from the natural order; this triggers the mechanism of
flight, which in turn becomes a nostalgia for Eden. This return to the
Earthly Paradise proves to be illusory as it clashes with the reaffirmation of
an unsurmountable evil, manifested this time by the appearance of the terrifying lion and, finally, of the ravenous she-wolf that thrusts the wayfarer
back to the wood "where the sun is silent" (I, 60).

A new scene emerges the moment when the pilgrim is completely powerless, alone with his terror:

Mentre ch'i' rovinava in basso loco,
    dinanzi a li occhi mi si fu offerto
    chi per lungo silenzio parea fioco.
Quando vidi costui nel gran diserto,

> "*Miserere* di me," gridai a lui,
> "qual che tu sii, od ombra od omo certo!"
>
> (*Inf.* I, 61–66)

While I was running down to the depth there appeared before me one who seemed faint through long silence. When I saw him in that vast desert, I cried to him, "Have pity on me whatever you are, shade or living man!"

It is important to note that here Dante does not say that Virgil appeared to him or that he saw Virgil coming to his rescue. Such a reading does violence to the text and almost destroys its poetic force, which comes from its eminently dramatic structure. Here we find two separate and distinct scenes that are dialectically related. In the first the new action that intersects the wayfarer's retreat towards the dark wood is initially represented as something autonomous in its objectivity. Dante writes: "dinanzi a li occhi mi si fu offerto" ("before my eyes was offered to me"), *suddenly,*[29] we might add, "chi per lungo silenzio parea fioco," that is, one who appeared to be faint both to the eye and to the ear because of a long absence and a long silence.

In the scene that follows, the act of seeing is expressed by the verb "vidi" ("I saw"). This reveals the subject's deeper awareness of the object, which, significantly, is intimately related to a keener perception of the background, the scenic dimension, within which the object appears—"lo gran diserto" ("the vast desert"). Of even greater consequence is the deep connection of this seeing with the assertion of the subject as he utters the words "*Miserere* di me." These three words mark a new beginning, a moment of heightened awareness, of awakening to a new dimension of reality analogous to the very first awakening through the dark wood. The fundamental difference is that now the pilgrim's hope to escape the danger and terror of the dark wood rests not on himself and on his perception of the journey, but on his total surrender to one whom he sees essentially as Other, as the words "qual che tu sii" ("whatever you are") clearly express.

But how does he reach this new state? Once again, we have noted no causal relation between the various scenes through which we have seen him move. Yet each scene has constituted, dialectically, the ground for the scene following it, and linked together they have created a larger scene which acts as background to the new scene we are now examining. If each step that the wayfarer took toward the hill finally led him back toward the dark wood, each step also proved to be salutary by forcing him to see, face to face, and objectified before his eyes, various manifestations of disorder, and of evil as a constitutive dimension of reality, a given state of things against which he is totally powerless. Only when he has reached this degree zero of his strife, of his tragic condition, is he prepared to be part of a new scene and to apprehend the objective presence of the Other, seeing and hearing him, at first faintly, and then with greater accuracy.

The expression "chi per lungo silenzio parea fioco" represents the pivotal, creative moment through which the wayfarer moves into this new scene. Singleton has offered the following gloss:

The verse seems deliberately ambiguous, since "fioco" can mean "faint" either to the eye or to the ear, and "silenzio" can have meaning with respect both to space and to time. If the one who comes is faint to the eye, then he appears dim because he is seen "through long silence," i.e., "nel gran diserto" of the following verse; if faint to the ear, then it is because Virgil's voice, as the voice of reason, had not reached the wayfarer for a long time—for as long, in fact, as he had wandered from the path of virtue. The voice of reason contributes to the temporal meaning of the "long silence," and the "gran diserto" to its spatial meaning.[30]

This illuminating note helps us to define the crucial moment of ambiguity in which the wayfarer's inner, subjective awareness interacts with the objective presence of the one who appears to him. Yet, to merely identify the ambiguity, as this note does, is not to disclose its resources, its creative force. The question that the text provokes is: what vitality (and hence poetic validity) does this ambiguity possess in relation to what immediately precedes and follows it? This vitality can be greatly diminished if, like Singleton, we overlook the distinction between the scene of the object's first "dim" appearance and the scene of the wayfarer's more distinct apprehension of it. If we merge the two into one scene, reading it in a timeless perspective, we will fail to see what Dante places before our eyes. Like Singleton, we will anachronistically interpret "lungo silenzio" in terms of "gran diserto," and "Chi" and "qual che tu sii" already as Virgil. This mode of reading destroys the temporalization and dramatization of the timeless, eternal "now." A striking example is the reduction of Virgil to Reason and subsequent explanation of "the temporal meaning" of "lungo silenzio" in the light of this reading.

I propose instead the following dramatistic interpretation. As the wayfarer is pushed by the she-wolf back towards the dark wood, there suddenly appears before his eyes one whose voice has not been heard. (Here I would add: not only by the wayfarer but also by many others, for there is still a strong objective, universal dimension inherent in the scene we are studying.) In this crucial moment the wayfarer transfers his own failure to hear this voice, and, of course, to have an inner "vision" of this "one" who speaks but goes unheeded, to the object that is before him, and thus perceives him as one who has been silent for a long time and for a long distance. In other words, the wayfarer begins (indeed, *only begins*) to link—and therefore to understand—his inner silence (for, having not heard, there is no resonance within him), with the silence of both the agent (the "one" who comes to him) and the space, the scene within which he appears. This scene is yet to be clearly defined; hence, all that could be said of it now is that it is a "desert slope" (the "piaggia deserta" of line 29), and not yet a "vast desert" ("gran diserto"). In this flash of intuition, he may very well be seeing him, given the elements of scene-act-agent (and their ratio) that he now has at his "disposal," as one whose voice has been for a long time a *vox clamantis in deserto*, that is, "silent" only because no one would go to such a barren, terrifying place—a place of death—to hear him (as Dante the wayfarer is learning to do) in this scene.[31]

As the wayfarer discovers in his "desert" a ground or condition shared by *Another*, he is prepared to *see* at once this one, this *Other*, no longer in the ambiguous light within which he first saw the leopard—when the "piaggia deserta," for a moment of nostalgia for Eden, was transformed into a paradisiac scene—but in a real desert. At this point we cannot fail to grasp the importance of the shift from the "piaggia deserta" to the "gran diserto." And, more important, we cannot ignore the *necessity* of the wayfarer's cry *"Miserere* di me" once this desert is felt as real, as the scene of misery. Perceiving the desert as a space that he shares with another, he puts to flight (if only temporarily, as we shall soon see) all solipsistic constructs of reality, all false nostalgias for an easily accessible paradise.[32] Like the dark wood toward which he is being thrust by the she-wolf, this is a place of absolute fear, the absolute fear of death. By the intrinsic motivational force of the scene, here, as soon as one, or rather anyone appears ("qual che tu sii . . ."), the first words—the only words that can be uttered by one who is lost—are "have mercy on me" (*"Miserere* di me"). These are words of humility, the ground for "service and obedience," to use Hegel's terms. "Without the discipline of service and obedience," we read in *The Phenomenology of Mind*,

fear remains formal and does not spread over the whole known reality of existence. Without the formative activity shaping the thing, fear remains inward and mute, and consciousness does not become objective for itself. Should consciousness shape and form the thing without the initial state of absolute fear, then it has a merely vain and futile "mind of its own"; for its form or negativity is not negativity *per se*, and hence its formative activity cannot furnish the consciousness of itself as essentially real. If it has endured not absolute fear, but merely some slight anxiety, the negative reality has remained external to it, its substance has not been through and through infected thereby. Since the entire content of its natural consciousness has not tottered and shaken, it is still inherently a determinate mode of being; having a "mind of its own" (*der eigene Sinn*) is simply stubbornness (*Eigensinn*), a type of freedom which does not get beyond the attitude of bondage. As little as the pure form can become its essential nature, so little is that form, considered as extending over particulars, a universal formative activity, an absolute notion; it is rather a piece of cleverness which has mastery within a certain range, but not over the universal power nor over the entire objective reality.[33]

We could thus reread the scenes preceding that of the "gran diserto" as expressions of the wayfarer's consciousness "shaping and forming the thing *without the initial state of absolute fear*," the fear he had first experienced in the dark wood. That consciousness had a "merely vain and futile 'mind of its own'," as it fashioned for itself an illusory "return to Eden," when, at the sight of the leopard, it transformed fear into hope. As it shaped this "pure form" of a leopard that gave him "cause for good hope" (*Inf*. I, 41), it proved to be "a piece of cleverness which has mastery within a certain range, but not over the universal power nor over the entire objective reality." The moment the wayfarer is thrust back to the initial, absolute fear (of death) of the dark wood, he discovers the presence of the Other, and with this presence the creative function of "service and obedience," that is, the "formative activity shaping the thing." The *other* journey—"l'altro viaggio"—has now its true beginning. Allen Mandelbaum, who led me to Hegel's passage on fear, writes:

[Dante] needs to begin his journey from a state *as like* to death as one can get while still alive. He needs to read his Hegel well (just as Hegel must read him) to understand that not only the Christian but the Hegelian—or the Heideggerian—poet can gather ultimate energy from only one sure fount: the fear—the absolute fear—of death, a wood "so bitter—death is hardly more severe" (*Inf*. I, 7). . . . Hegel's formulation of that fear couples it, of course, with service and obedience (functions Dante fulfills most immediately in relation to Virgil and Beatrice—and, ultimately, to his God).[34]

As we hear the words "*Miserere* di me" and pronounce them "with" the wayfarer, just as we first pronounced the words "nostra vita" at the start of our journey as readers, we know that we are evoking, in the company of the poet, a "space" into which entered a manifestation of the sacred, a hierophany. And as the poet invites us to recall that these are the first words of the most famous of the Penitential Psalms (number 50 of the Vulgate), and that they are addressed by the psalmist to God ("Miserere mei Deus . . ."), we begin to grasp the richness, the full force of the sacredness of this scene and its inner dramatic structure. Against the starkness of the "gran diserto" we see two equally stark figures, standing one before the other in absolute "nakedness," as that of the "I" and the "Other," one essentially, absolutely defined by his misery; and the other, correspondingly, by the pity, the *misericordia* which such misery calls into being. The power of the words "*Miserere* di me" is directly dependent on this essential, elementary or primordial perception of this "shade or living man" *as Other*, and therefore, I repeat, not as Virgil. Given the scene whose components we have identified, this "Other" reveals himself as the appropriate *dramatis persona*, the mask without a name who can best represent the Other in an absolute sense, the One whom the psalmist addresses with the words "Miserere mei Deus."[35]

This entire scene would collapse, proving to be futile, if we imagined that these words were addressed to Virgil, or worse to Virgil-as-Reason! The absoluteness or fundamental state of the wayfarer's misery calls forth an equally absolute, fundamental invocation for help from *anyone* ("*qual che tu sii*") who can *act as* God, that is, the only One who can fully (infinitely) know and be present to that misery. In fact, if we pause to reflect upon this fine distinction, we realize that if the wayfarer had said "*Miserere*" to one whom he had immediately identified as Virgil, this cry for mercy might not have come from the depth of his being, and from the profound awareness of the despair, the desolation of the desert, that he was experiencing. His might very well have been merely a call from one man to another, and from one poet to another, across the "desert" of the centuries that separate them. This we could interpret as being, at best, a significant, enriching, yet "profane" recognition of Virgil as a wise man, a literary *auctoritas*, and at worst as a "sentimental" or "nostalgic" recovery of an "ancient voice"—a kind of sterile, "neoclassical" restoration. And if his cry to be saved had not been ultimately directed to God, if it had not expressed— if only inchoately, mysteriously—his deepest anguish for being separated from himself, from the community (the civitas) and from God, how could he later, as we shall soon see, ask Virgil to lead him away from the desert and to prepare him, through the journey through Hell and up the mountain of Purgatory, for the "flight" to the Celestial City and the vision of God?

We see now, at least in part, why it is that Dante the wayfarer says *"miserere"* to the "one" who appears to him in the "gran diserto." I find, *mutatis mutandis*, particularly illuminating for our discourse the following excerpt from Karl Kerényi's essay, "Theos and Mythos":

Helen, in the homonymous tragedy by Euripides, exclaims: ὦ θεοὶ θεὸς γὰρ καὶ τo γιγνώσκειν φίλους: O Gods! For this also is God, that friends are recognized. The event of recognizing friends is *theos*. Another example has come down to us in Latin from Pliny the Elder, translated, I believe, from a saying by Menander: *deus est mortali iuvare mortalem*. The fact that man helps another man, is God for man.[36]

It is of special interest to us to note that if the manifestation of God through human action implies on the one hand a continuity and a merging of the human with the divine, on the other hand it is characterized by discontinuity and even conflict, and hence by an essentially dramatic form. For the person who, by friendship and solidarity with another, makes God manifest, is neither a mannequin moved by God nor God's emanation. Like the one who appears to the wayfarer in Dante's desert scene, such a one is a person who freely moves and acts and who, by the very status of being mortal (or of having been mortal, as in Virgil's case), is finite, imperfect, and thus only partially, imperfectly can manifest God's presence and action.

In the very moment that a human event asserts itself as a manifestation of the divine, it in fact reveals the distance that separates it from God's infinite action, a distance which in a sense is itself infinite. This paradoxical union and separation of opposites, of infinite closeness and infinite distance between the human and the divine is at the very root of the dramatic forms we are discovering in Dante's Prologue. These are further defined in Virgil's speech:

"Poeta fui, e cantai di quel giusto
    figliuol d'Anchise che venne di Troia,
    poi che 'l superbo Ilïón fu combusto.
Ma tu perché ritorni a tanta noia?
    perché non sali il dilettoso monte
    ch'è principio e cagion di tutta gioia?"

(*Inf.* I, 73–78)

"I was a poet, and I sang of that just son of Anchises who came from Troy after proud Ilium was burned. But you, why do you return to so much woe? Why do you not climb the delectable mountain, the source and cause of every happiness?"

The two major scenes represented here are at once joined and separated by the pivotal "Ma" ("But"). How is the first scene creatively related to the second? That is, how does one constitute the ground for the definition and interpretation of the other? And how can the meaning of the latter be transformed through this definition and interpretation? We may answer that the two scenes are characterized by striking similarities, with one functioning as a "model" for the other. The first scene that Virgil evokes is that of Aeneas' departure from his destroyed city and of his journey to Italy (note the force of "venne," which brings this journey "near" to both Virgil and Dante). The construction of this scene constitutes an assertion against which the scene of the wayfarer's "running back toward the dark wood" is measured. Here the motivational force inherent in the scene evoked by Virgil "invites" the wayfarer to view his own departure from the dark wood as something similar to Aeneas' departure from burned Ilium—a departure that excludes a return to the woe left behind.

The very moment Virgil is suggesting to the wayfarer a way out from the scene of woe and destruction, however, he points not to a new action and scene—such as Aeneas' journey to the shores of Latium—but to a journey to the "dilettoso monte," which the wayfarer has already attempted and which has ended in failure. This failure to climb the "delectable mountain," that is, according to our interpretation, to "return to Eden," is brought about and made manifest the moment the reality of evil and of fallen nature reveals itself—without ambiguity and with all its force—with the irruption of the she-wolf. But why does Virgil exhort Dante to climb the "delectable mountain"? Why does he not immediately announce the journey to God through the three realms of the beyond?

If we now join the allegorist, who "knows" that Virgil is the providential guide who soon will begin to lead Dante the pilgrim through Hell and then up the mountain of Purgatory, and that he represents Reason, which cuts through all that is illusory, thus revealing reality in its nakedness, we cannot but react with puzzlement to Virgil's exhortation. We might experience a certain embarrassment as we fail to explain away this incongruence, an embarrassment which we can discreetly hide under silence. As the dramatistic readers that the text keeps enjoining us to become, however, we cannot be silent as we witness the very "rupture" or dislocation that the scene before us exhibits. We must speak only by virtue of what we have gathered in the previous scenes and what the present scene offers us. And so we ask what is the "dilettoso monte" for Virgil?—the persona who has just introduced himself with the words "Non omo. . . . Nacqui sub Iulio. . . . Poeta fui. . . ."

In the light of what we have already said of this mountain, we can tentatively interpret it as a kind of Eden. We do not have to search far and wide to find that while to the wayfarer the "dilettoso monte" evokes the Judeo-Christian myth of Eden, to Virgil it must evoke, analogously, the myth of the Golden Age, and that both myths may be characterized by the idea of nostalgia, of return.

We may add another important note to this characterization if we return to the text for a moment and observe that a significant component of the scene preceding Virgil's exhortation to the wayfarer is Virgil's definition of himself as poet. It cannot escape our attention that, by virtue of the dramatic ratio of agent-scene and agent-act, when he enjoins the wayfarer, a fellow-poet, to climb the "delectable mountain," he seems to be suggesting that this return to Eden, or its pagan equivalent, the return of the Golden Age, may coincide with the poet's ascent of Mount Parnassus. In other words, the Virgil we find represented in this scene, that is, the persona that, with his actions and words, coherently fills this space, at once defining and being defined by it, proposes to another poet, whom he can only see in his own perspective, a salvation from sin and strife through poetry, and therefore, essentially, by an act of evasion from conflict, from drama. We can better understand this journey of the poet, this "return" to Eden-Parnassus[37] proposed by Virgil, as soon as we note that Virgil's own identification of his poetry contains the implication that one can indeed climb the "delectable mountain" *as poet*, that is, as one who sings the deeds of a persona, of a hero like Aeneas, without being one with his creation. The poet can therefore maintain a "safe" distance from his hero's journey, and the suffering and tragic conflicts which ensue, not to mention his descent to the underworld. As we look closely at our text and follow its built-in dramatic logic, we see a Virgil who, contradictorily, moves within two opposing scenes which are not reconciled into unity: the scene of his poetry *as poetry*, leading to the delight of "Eden-Parnassus"; and the scene of his poem, Aeneas' journey of suffering and strife. And we see him "act out" this opposition, this contradiction, when we hear him utter the words "perché non sali il dilettoso monte?" after he has spoken of Aeneas' coming to the shores of Latium. In terms of this scene, we would expect him to invite the wayfarer (consistent with his exhortation to leave behind, like

Aeneas, the old scene of woe) to imitate the Trojan hero's journey to the underworld, and, specifically, the journey to the father (clearly echoed by the words "il giusto figliuol d'Anchise"), and, like Aeneas, to embark on a quest for a new city.

Being "separated" from his work and his hero, Virgil transfers this separation to the wayfarer's scene, failing to see that this persona is at once poet and character, dramaturge and actor, and that the mountain he must reach cannot be merely a fiction of Eden or a fictional Parnassus, but it must be at once fictional and real and must be experienced as it is represented. The word must be wedded to the flesh: it must be rooted in reality and suffering, or in the reality of suffering. In other words, the wayfarer cannot take flight towards the summit of the mountain either by virtue of a nostalgia for the pristine innocence and bliss or by the power of a poetry that would give expression to such a flight, such a nostalgia. He must face the she-wolf. Significantly, Virgil ignores her presence, true, as we have noted, to his own perspective, to his own "scene."

Note that it is the wayfarer who points to the presence of the she-wolf, awakening Virgil to the reality of evil, to its being a condition of this life's journey. We must observe, however, that he does this only after he has recognized Virgil as his author and teacher, and as one who is at once poet and sage:

> "Or se' tu quel Virgilio e quella fonte
>   che spandi di parlar sì largo fiume?"
>   rispuos' io lui con vergognosa fronte.
> "O de li altri poeti onore e lume,
>   vagliami 'l lungo studio e 'l grande amore
>   che m'ha fatto cercar lo tuo volume.
> Tu se' lo mio maestro e 'l mio autore,
>   tu se' solo colui da cu' io tolsi
>   lo bello stilo che m'ha fatto onore.
> Vedi la bestia per cu' io mi volsi;
>   aiutami da lei, famoso saggio,
>   ch'ella mi fa tremar le vene e i polsi."
>
> (*Inf.* I, 79–90)

"Are you, then, that Virgil, that fount which pours forth so broad a stream of speech?" I answered him, my brow covered with shame. "O glory and light of other poets, may the long study and the great love that have made me search your volume avail me! You are my master and my author. You alone are he from whom I took the fair style that has done me honor. See the beast that has turned me back. Help me against her, famous sage, for she makes my veins and pulses tremble."

The wayfarer does not give a direct answer to Virgil's question, "Why do you not climb the delectable mountain?" He instead first turns his attention to Virgil, and specifically to Virgil-as-poet, emphasizing his "stream of speech" and his "fair style," and then, shifting the focus to Virgil-as-sage (and thus to the poet-as-sage), he points to the threatening presence of the she-wolf. This, finally, constitutes his answer, an answer which emerges not from a discursive process but from one that is essentially dramatic, for it is embedded in actions and scenes and comes into being through a movement, a rhythm created by the antithetical relation, or the disjunction of those actions and scenes as they succeed each other in a dynamic play of similarity and opposition.

As we closely observe this rhythm and this play, let us choose as a starting point the words "lo bello stilo" ("the fair style"). They possess a special force, for they reassert, in synthesis, what has characterized the scene we have previously studied: the power of poetry as pure form, as a unique manifestation of beauty, and hence of poetry that can be quite alluring to the wayfarer-poet, as alluring as the "lonza" with the attractive "gay skin" had earlier been to him after he had just emerged from the dark wood. This recollection of the "fair style" awakens in him a "figure" of the poet with which he has already identified, and with this recollection the desire to interpret and transform his present scene of return to the dark wood by the power of the "fair style," which he has learned from Virgil, and which "has done him honor."[38] This desire still betrays a retrospective gaze, a return to the past, a nostalgic movement of the soul toward what must now appear, in contrast with the present time of misery dominated by the she-wolf, as a time of innocence and bliss, a figure of Eden that in the perspective of a purely aesthetic experience easily merges with a figure of Parnassus.

Yet as this scene attains its full actualization, as it is *represented*, it dialectically calls forth a new scene. As soon as the wayfarer recognizes Virgil in terms of his "stream of speech" and "fair style," that is, as soon as he has internalized this "figure" or this "mask" of the poet Virgil, linking it to his own experience as poet, a contrasting assertion emerges, and with it the possibility to construct a new scene. This new assertion begins with the wayfarer's definition of Virgil as "famous sage," a definition that, significantly, is directly proportional to the new definition of the scene, which is now unmistakably one in which the she-wolf is again in focus as a dominant, real presence. In this moment of awakened attention to the dramatic ratio of agent-scene-action (and purpose), both the wayfarer and Virgil (as well as the reader) know that no "stream of speech" or "fair style," no "flight" to Parnassus or nostalgia for Eden can, *by itself,* exorcise this presence, this manifestation of evil. There is nothing ambiguous about this beast. She does not have the beautiful coat, the "fair skin" of the "lonza" which could stir the aesthetic sensibility of the wayfarer-poet, luring him into the illusion that Eden-Parnassus was within reach. And she is much more threatening than the lion, whose presence had been perceived still with some degree of detachment, I would even say *aesthetic* detachment, as the image of the "air that seemed to tremble at it" suggests. The she-wolf's presence is felt in the very fibers of the wayfarer's being; she makes his "veins and pulses tremble." This is much more than a mere image that appears to the mind's eye and kindles the imagination. She is *there, now.* Her presence permits no escape towards the sunlit "delectable mountain." The dramatic ratio of scene-agent, scene-action, and so forth, is now decisively defined, and it is apprehended and experienced by both the wayfarer and Virgil in its integrity and objectivity. The she-wolf is no longer ignored, and, most important, the one whose help the wayfarer had earlier invoked with the words "*Miserere* di me" is, appropriately to this scene of terror and anguish, the one who, "re-entering" the scene as both poet and sage, points to another scene, another journey:

> "A te convien tenere altro vïaggio,"
>   rispuose, poi che lagrimar mi vide,
>   "se vuo' campar d'esto loco selvaggio;
> ché questa bestia, per la qual tu gride,
>   non lascia altrui passar per la sua via,
>   ma tanto lo 'mpedisce che l'uccide . . . ."

(Inf. I, 91–96)

"It behooves you to go by another way if you would escape from this place," he answered when he saw me weep, "for this beast, the cause of your complaint, lets no man pass her way, but so besets him that she slays him . . . ."

Virgil announces this "other journey" the moment he correctly interprets the present scene as that of a "loco selvaggio" ("savage place") and as a place of impending death because of the evil presence of the she-wolf. The word "selvaggio" obviously harks back to the scene of the "selva selvaggia," where death was also near ("Tant'è amara che poco è più morte"; *Inf.* I, 7). But now, as then, by their very finality this savageness and death constitute dialectically, dramatically, the ground for transformation and transcendence, by pointing, as the only salvation, to all that is *other*—"l'altro viaggio."

As we speak of this *other*, we recall the poet's words of *Inferno* I, 8–9: "ma per trattar del ben ch'i' vi trovai / dirò de l'*altre* cose ch'i' v'ho scorte"—words whose creative ambiguity we have earlier discovered and discussed. As we were prompted to do then, now again we ask about the otherness of the journey which Virgil announces. What does it mean? Or rather, more realistically, what measure of meaning does it now reveal, or what intimations of greater, deeper meaning that awaits us in the pages (the "journey") that follow? Why does Virgil abandon his earlier exhortation to climb the "delectable mountain" for the present exhortation to embark on another journey? What are the implications of such a sudden shift, such a reversal of assertions? To these questions there are answers which, however tentative and incomplete, are embedded in the "grammar" created by the contiguity and the resulting opposition of actions, agents, scenes, and so on, each of which constitutes both an assertion and a counter-assertion, as one succeeds the other. We notice, thus, that Virgil's new invitation to another journey immediately follows the act of the pilgrim's weeping: "he answered when he saw me weep" (*Inferno* I, 92).

The opposition between Virgil's invitation to climb the delectable mountain and the wayfarer's pointing to the she-wolf as the insurmountable obstacle to that climb is now resolved. Significantly, Virgil introduces the new perspective of the "other journey" not when Dante the pilgrim shows him the evil presence of the she-wolf, but when, fully aware of that presence, he has reacted with weeping. This weeping reasserts his previous cry of "*Miserere*" at the appearance of Virgil (or Virgil-as-the-Other). There is, obviously, a certain complexity and ambiguity in this weeping, absent in the act of pointing to the threatening presence of the she-wolf. It is obviously a sign of suffering, of *passio*. But what is the nature and reason for this suffering? Is it a recognition of one's own limitations before the overpowering force of evil represented by the she-wolf, or even of remorse for one's own share of that evil, or, finally, all of these things experienced at once? These are questions that for the moment remain unanswered. All we know is that Virgil responds to the pilgrim's act of weeping, and not merely to the condition, or "scene," in which the she-wolf is the center. Here we find, again, distinctive signs of a pattern, a dramatic form, which Kenneth Burke has called the "tragic grammar":

We can discern something of the "tragic" grammar behind the Greek proverb's way of saying "one learns by experience": "ta *pathemata mathemata*," the suffered is the learned. . . . A *pathema* (of the same root as our word, "passive") is the opposite of a *poiema* (a deed, doing, action, act; anything done; a poem). A *pathema* can refer variously to a suffering, misfortune, passive condition, state of mind. The initial requirement for a tragedy, however, is an *action*. Hence, by our interpretation, if the proverb were to be complete, at the risk of redundance, it would have three terms: *poiemata, pathemata, mathemata*, suggesting that the act organizes the opposition (brings to the fore whatever factors resist or modify the act), that the agent thus "suffers" this opposition, and as he learns to take the oppositional motives into account, widening his terminology accordingly, he has arrived at a higher order of understanding. However, this statement may indicate more of a temporal sequence than is usually the case. The three distinctions can be collapsed into a single "moment" so that we could proceed from one to the others in any order.[39]

Thus, the pilgrim's act of crying out to Virgil *"Miserere* di me" "organizes the opposition," "bringing to the fore" Virgil's response that he should climb the "delectable mountain" if he wishes to escape from the "gran diserto." This opposition objectifies for the wayfarer his own conflict experienced earlier when, indeed, he had hoped to flee from the evil of the "selva selvaggia" by climbing that mountain. Only when he "suffers" this opposition is he ready to transcend his initial state. This solution implies not an "escape" from conflict, a mirage of an ascent of the delectable mountain, an almost instantaneous "return to Eden," but a return to conflict, to drama. This is the perspective that Virgil opens to Dante the pilgrim as he points to the "altro viaggio"—a perspective within which the she-wolf, with the evil she represents, is now redefined.

Virgil can expound on the reality and the nature of the she-wolf—whom earlier he appeared to have ignored—when he sees objectified before him its effects on the pilgrim, as he notices his weeping. As he "suffers" with the pilgrim the opposition (which he has contributed to create) between an easy conquest of the "delectable mountain" (as we have seen, an Eden-Parnassus) and the impossibility of such a conquest brought about by the irruption of the she-wolf, he does not merely acknowledge her terrifying presence, but transcends this awareness by evoking a "scene" that is much larger and richer in meaning:

> "Molti son li animali a cui s'ammoglia,
>   e più saranno ancora, infin che 'l Veltro
>   verrà, che la farà morir con doglia.
> Questi non ciberà terra né peltro,
>   ma sapïenza, amore e virtute,
>   e sua nazion sarà tra feltro e feltro.
> Di quella umile Italia fia salute
>   per cui morì la vergine Cammilla,
>   Eurialo e Turno e Niso di ferute."
>
> (*Inf.* I, 100–108)

"Many are the beasts with which she mates, and there will yet be more, until the Hound shall come who will deal her a painful death. He will not feed on earth or pelf, but on wisdom, love, and virtue, and his birth shall be between felt and felt. He shall be the salvation of that low-lying Italy for which the virgin Camilla and Euryalus, Turnus, and Nisus died of their wounds."

It is evident that now, for Dante the pilgrim and Virgil, and of course for the reader as well, the she-wolf's reality, or rather the reality of evil she symbolizes, is not confined to the individual scene within which she first moved. She now represents a universal condition and is part of a story that has a beginning and an end. As such, she is a constitutive part of the human drama throughout the ages, of course as Dante could envisage. She is, though mysteriously, an irreducible component and hence a tragic dimension of that drama.

We now discern the familiar pattern, the inner dialectical structure we have learned to identify with this vision. The she-wolf's action in the world is defined in terms of the opposite action of the Hound. Evil thus acquires meaning by virtue of the conflict that ensues when an opposing force is called forth, significantly, at the height of the power of the former, when the she-wolf will mate with more beasts ("e più saranno ancora"). Through this dialectic of good and evil, the figure of a hero emerges, asserting himself as the savior of the community. This agon, to which Virgil draws attention, in turn acquires special meaning, metonymically, by its contiguity with the drama played out by the heroes who died for Italy. It is particularly significant that Dante the poet unites the warriors of the opposing camps—Euryalus and Nisus with Camilla and Turnus. In his vision, which can best be described as tragic, there are no enemies. Their conflict has been transcended, as their wounds and their death are remembered as a common suffering for Italy. They are all heroes, the victims and their oppressors.

Dante gives form to this tragic vision by the very order in which the names of these heroes are mentioned. He breaks the conventional opposition between "heroes" and their "enemies." We may say with Tibor Wlassics: "why not 'Euryalus and Nisus' (inseparable in their author's conception) 'and Camilla and Turnus'? How can mortal enemies be mixed in the phrase that seems to break the inner logic of history? The answer is implicit in the question; but only the reading of Ungaretti, the reading of a poet, could extricate the implication. 'We see the fallen adversaries united in the same glory.'[40] . . . Friends and enemies united in glory—, joined also, we might add, in the common tragedy: their names are co-mixed in the line of the poet, like the ashes of the fallen on the battle-field."[41] Dante fashions a new order, that of alternating, or uniting by contiguity the warriors of opposing camps. Here René Girard's remarks on the "alternating movement" and the tragic spirit are especially useful:

If the tragic heroes are all compared, their distinctive traits vanish, for they all successively assume the same roles. Oedipus is an oppressor in *Oedipus the King*, but the oppressed in *Oedipus at Colonus*; Creon is oppressed in *Oedipus the King* but becomes the oppressor in *Antigone*. Nobody, in short, incarnates the true oppressor or the true oppressed; and the modern ideological interpretations seriously misconstrue the tragic spirit. They relegate the plays to the company of romantic melodrama or American westerns. A static Manichaean confrontation of "good guys" and "bad guys," an unyielding rancor that holds fast to its victims, has replaced the revolving oppositions of real tragedy and completely overshadowed the concept of the tragic peripeteia. . . . It is clear that alternation constitutes a *relationship*. In fact, alternation is a fundamental fact of the tragic relationship—which is why it can scarcely be considered characteristic of any single individual.[42]

In the light of these observations, we can better apprehend the creative force of Virgil's recollection of the heroes who died for "low-lying Italy." As his words shatter the conventional opposition, the accepted order, they create, as we have seen, a new opposition, a new order that transforms and transcends the old. If Euryalus and Nisus are now "separated," they are, however, reunited on a higher plane, one that, by virtue of alternance, includes (introduces in their "midst") their former enemies. We must note that the creative moment when the tragic vision asserts itself, touching us directly, making us experience an expansion of meaning, coincides with the shift of perspective. It is in this "narrow space," this *caesura* that the two perspectives become visible, so that we see at once the separation and the unity, in other words, the disjunctive relation we have already encountered in the preceding analyses as a distinctive inner structure of drama, and specifically, of tragic vision.

Most important, beyond these abstractions we see that the vision of Dante's Virgil—and therefore of the Virgil through whom Dante lives, making his own vision manifest—as it speaks of Italy and, by implication, of the Roman *imperium*, is not celebrating the violence and suffering that is indissolubly linked with its existence and destiny. The longing for the Hound who "will not feed on earth or pelf, but on wisdom, love, and virtue" leaves no doubt about the condemnation of violence. Through the scene of "the virgin Cammilla and Euryalus, Turnus, and Nisus" Dante has helped us to see in the *Aeneid* a measure of the tragic truth that he has seen in it, something very much like that which Allen Mandelbaum has seen "through Ungaretti": ". . . the underground denial—by consciousness and longing—of the total claims of the state and history: the persistence in the mind of what is not there, of what is absent, as a measure of the present."[43] This vision is at once Virgil's and Dante's, though the latter, as we are gradually discovering, goes much further and deeper, as he learns from his *maestro* and surpasses him. In the scene of the "gran diserto," Dante invites us to recover this vision and to start from it, for it constitutes the ground for the journey which he is about to begin and which he will share with us.

Another important expansion of meaning created by a "leap" from one view, or one scene, to another is inscribed in the last tercet of our passage. Here we find the "Hound's" action (and scene) of thrusting the she-wolf back to Hell linked, again by contiguity, to the original act (and scene) of "envy," the "invidia prima" (of the serpent, but also, of course, of Adam and Eve) sending her forth from Hell. The act of vanquishing the evil of the she-wolf evokes the first act that introduced it into the world. Put in other terms, the history of the human struggle with evil, when viewed in its totality, as its end is announced, is closely connected to the original "story," the original conflict between good and evil. Drama is inseparable from myth. As we shall see more clearly in the course of this work, one engenders the other, one interprets and is, in turn, interpreted by the other, following a movement, a rhythm of "alternance" or "tragic rhythm" which by definition excludes the reduction of one or of the other to a fixed form. The myth of Eden and the drama of history live side by side, perpetually interacting, with history alternately "reading" the myth as a story of pristine innocence and as a story of the Fall, rarely, however, reading it as the story of innocence and of misery. Only if we are open to tragic vision is it possible to discover at least a measure of the myth's creative force, with its tensions and conflicts. This is the vision that Virgil offers to Dante the pilgrim as he points to the "other journey."

The "new scene" that Virgil constructs, and that we have attempted to define in the preceding pages, contains the deepest justification, the crucial "motivational force" for the scene of this "other journey" that the wayfarer is now being enjoined to enter. We cannot lose sight of this connection, for upon it rests the innermost meaning of this journey, and correspondingly, the poetic form that will best make this meaning manifest. As we have already observed, the wayfarer's "other journey" is closely dependent on the inescapable presence of the she-wolf in the world. But, we must ask, how can this journey take place, and what will be its nature? In other words, what is the full meaning of the words Virgil utters immediately after the passage we have just analyzed?

> "Ond'io per lo tuo me' penso e discerno
> che tu mi segui, e io sarò tua guida,
> e trarrotti di qui per loco etterno. . . ."

(Inf. I, 112–114)

"Therefore I think and deem it best that you should follow me, and I will be your guide and lead you hence through an eternal place. . . ."

How is Virgil's "therefore" justified? Again, the answers, though necessarily sketchy, as they must be at the threshold of the poem, are given to us by the very sequence of scenes (and acts and agents) that precede this pivotal point marked by "therefore." As we have noted, these sequential scenes say much more than the conventional reading has so far extracted from them. Dante the pilgrim must undertake the "other journey," moving in the "other" scene of the "eternal place" not merely because the she-wolf blocks his otherwise easy access—which Virgil will later call "the short way" (Inf. II, 120)—to the sunlit "delectable mountain." This is only one component of a larger scene or more spacious "ground," which calls forth the "other journey." And this ground, as we have at least in part discovered, is constituted dynamically as movement or rhythm (that of the alternance of tragic vision) that comes into being when Virgil, like a dramatist, brings together the she-wolf and the Hound, and their conflict with the conflict that "separates and unites" the Trojans and their enemies.

The fundamental motivation inscribed in these scenes and actions is offered by the conflict and reconciliation of the tragic vision and *through* the resolution of reconciliation, which is contrasted with the evasion from conflict, the annulment of the tragic spirit that the nostalgia for Eden earlier experienced by the wayfarer clearly represents. In fact, to this very nostalgia for Eden is juxtaposed the one that speaks (as Virgil now, though obliquely, speaks) of the "first envy" and therefore of the original conflict between good and evil, between Adam and Eve and the serpent, and consequently between God and man. The two "myths" are thus defined, if only tentatively, as they oppose each other, or rather, as they "alternate" each other. The original myth, as Virgil's reference to "invidia prima" decisively shows, is characterized by the presence of the serpent, and therefore of evil as the inescapable human condition; the other myth is characterized by the absence of evil, and thus represents a false interpretation or "recollection" of the original myth.

This crucial distinction, and its profound implications, we shall see more clearly in the pages that follow, in a measure that, to my knowledge, no reader of the *Commedia* has yet perceived. More important, what has escaped the critics' attention is the interaction, the dramatic (dialectic) coexistence of the two myths. To shed further light on the idea of myth, but only by way of introduction (we are still in the Prologue scene), let us turn for a moment to these observations of Antoine Vergote on the "original myth" or the "true myth":

The true myth, in fact, is a discourse on the origins; it speaks precisely of the original separation that brings beings to their manifestation. The dream of a future that satisfies and pacifies beings in an unchanged transparency and ex-stasis, expresses the nostalgia to erase the manifestation displayed by the original mythical discourse. The myth of Paradise is mythical only by virtue of its retrospective reference to the true myth which ex-poses the rupture of the origins. The myth of innocence, because it projects into the future the annulment of the ruptures that the myths of the origins describe to us, is therefore rather an anti-myth.[44]

From the moment the wayfarer finds himself moving through the dark wood—that is, when he awakens to the reality of evil (and good)—to the moment when Virgil invites him to undertake the "other journey" through

an "eternal place," these two myths have been alternately present, constituting one of the fundamental structures underlying the pilgrim's drama of
conversion. From that first moment we have seen him gradually become
aware of the decisive choice that one must make when facing the reality of
evil, whether this takes the form of a dark wood or of a leopard or of a she-
wolf—a choice that can be essentially translated into these terms or
"roads". One is the short road, really a "flight" of the mind towards an
illusory Eden, or garden of delight that knows only peace and happiness;
the other is the road through time and history, and therefore through the
life of conflict. In other words, the choice is, finally, between the idyllic
vision and the dramatic (tragic) vision, between the immobility of the one
and the dynamism of the other, between evasion of suffering and full acceptance of suffering.

Notes

1. This and all subsequent quotes of the text and translation of the *Commedia*
are taken from *The Divine Comedy*, trans. with a commentary by Charles S. Singleton, 3 vols. (Princeton, NJ: Princeton University Press, 1970–1976). References to
the commentary are hereafter cited as *Commentary* 1, 2, or 3. A portion of this chapter has appeared under the title of "The Good in Dante's *selva oscura*: A Dramatistic
Reading," in *Studi di Italianistica in onore di Giovanni Cecchetti*, ed. Paolo Cherchi
and Michelangelo Picone (Ravenna: Longo, 1988), pp. 67–73.

2. Singleton, *Commentary* 1, n. 1, p. 3.

3. *The Divine Comedy of Dante Alighieri, Inferno*, trans. with intr. by Allen Mandelbaum, notes by Allen Mandelbaum and Gabriel Marruzzo, with Laury Magnus
(Berkeley: University of California Press, 1980; Toronto: Bantam Books, 1982),
p. 2.

4. Now, and in the course of this work, I shall focus only on those ratios that
seem most meaningful because of their creative tension, or I shall emphasize one
term alone—scene, act, or agent, etc. If with each choice I necessarily exclude or
obscure other terms and their various combinations and ratios, by virtue of the
overlap of these terms, when I give prominence to one I also implicitly point to the
others. Thus, when I temporarily treat one of them as the "essential" term, I consider the others as being distinct yet convergent toward or originating from it. Cf.
Kenneth Burke, *A Grammar of Motives*, p. xx: ". . . it is by reason of the pliancy
among our terms [the pentad: Act, Scene, Agent, Agency, Purpose] that philo-
sophic systems can pull one way and another. The margins of overlap provide op-
portunities whereby a thinker can go without a leap from any one of the terms to
any of its fellows. . . . Hence no great dialectical enterprise is necessary if you would
merge the terms, reducing them even to as few as one; and then, treating this as
the 'essential' term, the 'cause' or 'ancestor' of the lot, you can proceed in the reverse
direction across the margins of overlap, 'deducing' the other terms from it as its
logical descendants."

5. In his *Commentary* I, n. 2, p. 4 Singleton has aptly observed: "The form with *ri* (*ritrovai* instead of *trovai*) stresses inwardness, awareness ('I came to myself')." For a review of the various interpretations of "mi ritrovai," see Anthony K. Cassell, *Lectura Dantis Americana: Inferno I*, foreword by Robert Hollander (Philadelphia: University of Pennsylvania Press, 1989), pp. 8–14.

6. Antonino Pagliaro, *Nuovi saggi di critica semantica*, 2nd, rev. ed. (Messina—Florence: G. D'Anna, 1963), p. 255. (Translation mine)

7. *Dantis Alagherii Epistolae*, intr., trans., notes Paget Toynbee, p. 207.

8. St. Thomas Aquinas, *Super libr. de Causis*, Lect. XVIII.

9. "The central paradox of the theater," writes Jacques Maritain (*Creative Intuition in Art and Poetry*, p. 252), "is the fact that on the one hand . . . human agents are endowed with free will and can change, to some extent, the course of the events, while, on the other hand, the work itself, which has no free will, is all the more perfect as everything in it results from necessity, so that the action must also develop with unbending necessity. This paradox is but an effect and a sign of the *transposition* or recasting which nature inevitably undergoes when it passes into the work of art."

10. Bachelard, *The Poetics of Space*, p. 185.

11. Ibid., p. 188.

12. Singleton, *Commentary* I, n. 2, p. 4.

13. Ibid., pp. 4–5. In the *Convivio* (IV. xxiv, 12) Dante speaks of "la selva erronea di questa vita" ("the wandering wood of this life").

14. I borrow this phrase from Pascual Jordan ("Die Stellung der Naturwissenschaft zur religiösen Frage," *Universitas* [Jan. 1947]), as cited by Ernst Robert Curtius in his discussion of Bernard Silvestris' description of the condition of matter (*silva*), in *European Literature and the Latin Middle Ages*, trans. Willard R. Trask (New York and Evanston, IL: Harper & Row, 1963), p. 109.

15. Pierre-Jean Jouve, *Lyrique* (Paris: Mercure di France, n.d.), p. 13; quoted in Bachelard, p. 186.

16. Bachelard, p. 186.

17. Mircea Eliade, *The Sacred and the Profane*, trans. Willard R. Trask (New York: Harcourt, Brace & World, Inc., 1957), p. 11.

18. Robert Hollander, *Allegory in Dante's "Commedia"* (Princeton, NJ: Princeton University Press, 1969), p. 80. On p. 260 we read: "Dante is the new Adam, looking up at the place from which he fell (for surely that is the hill [the 'dilettoso monte' of *Inf.* I] which has Eden at its top)."

19. "The development of a discourse may take place along two different semantic lines: one topic may lead to another either through their similarity or through their contiguity. The m e t a p h o r i c   w a y would be the most appropriate term for the first case and the m e t o n y m i c   w a y for the second, since they find their most condensed expression in metaphor and metonymy respectively. . . . A competition between both devices, metonymic and metaphoric, is manifest in any symbolic process, either intra-personal or social. Thus in an inquiry into the structure of dreams, the decisive question is whether the symbol and the temporal sequences used are based on contiguity (Freud's metonymic 'displacement' and synecdochic 'condensation') or on similarity (Freud's 'identification and symbolism')." Roman

Jakobson and Morris Halle, *Fundamentals of Language* (The Hague: Mouton, 1956), pp. 76, 80–81.

20. From a psychoanalytical perspective Egidio Guidubaldi offers an interpretation of *altre cose* that is close to mine: "Nella particolare coloritura interiore cui soggiacciono queste 'altre cose' (ci suggerirebbe Dante) man mano che vengono passate al filtro delle 'coupures' d'inconscio . . . i tanti piccoli 'a' [i.e., 'altri'] con cui ci imbattiamo nella nostra vita quotidiana non stentano a trasformarsi in veri volti dell''Altro' . . . , ad operare come autentici messaggi d''altra scena' trasportatasi, con sempre maggior violenza, nella 'scena' in cui agiamo noi." Egidio Guidubaldi, "*Paradiso* XXXIII: Rassegna di ponti semantici analizzati con J. Lacan," in *Psicoanalisi e strutturalismo di fronte a Dante*, Atti dei mesi danteschi 1969–1971, vol. II (Florence: Olschki, 1972), p. 366.

21. Singleton, *Commentary* I, n. 8, p. 6.

22. For an elaborate discussion of this passage see F. Masciandaro, *La problematica del tempo nella "Commedia"* (Ravenna: Longo, 1976), pp. 38–47.

23. T. S. Eliot, "The Dry Salvages," *Four Quartets* (New York: Harcourt, Brace & World, Inc., 1943).

24. I am not suggesting that this awakening coincides—in the wayfarer's journey as represented by Dante—with what Fernando Figurelli has described as a full moment in which the pilgrim has "redeemed *himself*" ("Il canto I dell'*Inferno*." *Inferno*: *Letture degli anni 1973–76. Casa di Dante in Roma. Nuove Letture* [Rome: Bonacci, 1976], pp. 21–22). I agree with Cassell's comment that this is a "modern Pelagian or semi-Pelagian" interpretation (Cassell, *Lectura Dantis Americana: Inferno* I, p.10). What I am saying is that the wayfarer awakens to the reality both of sin and of good, and that, as the poet declares, to "treat" of that good he will "tell" of the "other things found" in the "selva oscura." Thus Dante begins the narration or articulation in time (and space) of a timeless experience—a *vision* of evil and good, of Hell, Purgatory, and Paradise. But the moment or *point* of the first scene *represented* in *Inferno* I (like the "primo punto" when Virgil felt compassion for Dante, in which converges Breatrice's intervention, and therefore God's grace; *Inf.* II, 50 ff.) is an image or *sign* of what lies outside time and space. The entire *Comedy*, as poem and as journey, is an attempt to represent and discover the *good* of Dante's timeless, ineffable vision, and therefore a measure and manifestation of the *Summum Bonum* that granted such vision. And this good must also include that partial, initial good inherent in the wayfarer's awareness that he is a sinner and that the world is sinful. Hence I disagree with Cassell's assertion, "there is nothing positive in the letter of the verse 'mi ritrovai per una selva oscura'—'I found myself again within a dark wood'—when we first come upon it in the poem; it signifies a return to sin and sadness, a fact essential to the theology and narrative structure of the *Commedia*" (*Lectura Dantis Americana: Inferno* I, p. 9). Another measure of the good found in the "selva oscura" is revealed to us (as Virgil awakens Dante's memory)—later, of course—by the poet's "telling" of one more *altra cosa* in *Inferno* XX, 127–129:

e già iernotte fu la luna tonda:
ben ten de' ricordar, ché non ti nocque
alcuna volta per la selva fonda.

and already last night the moon was round. You must remember it well, for it did you no harm sometimes in the deep wood.

25. Eugenio Montale, "Arsenio," *Ossi di seppia*, 8th ed. (Milan: Mondadori, 1966).

26. From the perspective of time, I pointed out the Adam-Dante correspondence and the momentary recovery of Eden in *La problematica del tempo*, pp. 102–104.

27. Mircea Eliade, *Myths, Dreams and Mysteries*, trans. Philip Mairet (New York and Evanston, IL: Harper & Row, 1967), p. 68.

28. Cf. John Freccero, "Dante's Prologue Scene," *Dante Studies* LXXXIV (1966): 5: "The phrase 'l'animo mio ch'ancor fuggiva,' has an unmistakable philosophical ring. For one thing, the word *animo* is decidely intellectual, rather than theological in meaning, quite distinct from the more common *anima*. For another, the phrase recalls, or at least would have recalled to the Church fathers, the flight of the soul from the terrestrial to the spiritual realm according to the Platonists, and especially to Plotinus." Rprt. in his *Dante: The Poetics of Conversion*, ed. and intr. Rachel Jacoff (Cambridge, MA: Harvard University Press, 1986), p. 6.

29. "E' probabile," writes Franca Brambilla Ageno, "che in questo passo il trapassato abbia un valore aspettivo perfettivo, indichi cioè il rapido e immediato compiersi dell'azione, pur se non entrano in giuoco avverbi indicanti appunto immediatezza temporale. Il significato sarebbe quindi, 'mi si offrì improvvisamente dinanzi agli occhi uno.' " "Annotazioni a passi della *Commedia*," *Studi danteschi* XLII (1965): 352.

30. Singleton, *Commentary* 1 n. 63, p. 14.

31. My reading is corroborated by Robert Hollander's interpretation of Virgil as figurally related to John the Baptist, which I find on p. 261 of his *Allegory in Dante's "Commedia"*: "Virgil is figurally related to John the Baptist, whose desert voice leads to Christ, and who performs the first baptism. What are Dante's first words in describing Virgil? 'Quella fonte / che spandi di parlar sì largo fiume' (lines 79–80). Virgil is a fountain which pours forth a river of speech. Is his 'water' figurally related to the baptism in Jordan (Mark 1:5; John 1:28) given by John the Baptist, the first baptistm which is then completed in the baptism offered by Jesus in that same river? The last words of Dante to Virgil (*Purgatorio* XXX, 51) are these: 'Virgilio a cui per mia salute die' mi' ('Virgil, to whom I gave myself up for salvation')."

32. Cf. Giuseppe Mazzotta, *Dante Poet of the Desert: History and Allegory in the "Divine Comedy"* (Princeton, NJ: Princeton University Press, 1979), pp. 12, 37–38: "In the dramatics of the poem the desert is the locus of encounters and radical decisions." "The desert contains a conceptual ambivalence. In a sense, the desert is where you are, where you fall into idolatry, or where you discover God's presence, or better, man's presence to God."

33. G.W.F. Hegel, *The Phenomenology of Mind*, trans., intr., and notes J.B. Baillie, 2nd ed. (London: George Allen & Unwin, Ltd.; New York: Macmillan, 1955), pp. 239–240.

34. Allen Mandelbaum, *The "Divine Comedy" of Dante Alighieri, Inferno*, Introduction, p. xviii.

35. Cf. von Balthasar, *Theo-Drama*, p. 19:

If God is to deal with man in an effective way and in a way that is intelligible to him, must not God himself tread the stage of the world and thus become implicated in the dubious nature of the world theater? And however he comes into contact with this theater—whether he is to take responsibility for the whole meaning of the play or is to appear as one of the cast (in which case one can investigate his connection with the other *dramatic personae*)—the analogy between God's action and the world drama is no mere metaphor but has an ontological ground: the two dramas are not utterly unconnected; there is an inner link between them. . . . On the human stage . . . [God] "plays" through human beings and ultimately *as* a human being; does that mean that he goes completely incognito behind the human mask? Is he only to drop this mask in death, when the play reveals who the actor in reality was ("This man was truly the Son of God" [Mt 27:54])? And surely only a human being can die; and if God was this human being, is not God really and truly dead? Thus, by entering into contact with the world theater, the good which takes place in God's action really is affected by the world's ambiguity and remains a hidden good. This good is something *done*: it cannot be contemplated in pure "aesthetics" nor proved and demonstrated in pure "logic." It takes place nowhere but on the world stage— which is every living person's present moment—and its destiny is seen in the drama of a world history that is continually unfolding.

36. Karl Kerényi, "Theos e Mythos," trans. from German into Italian, in *Il problema della demitizzazione*, ed. E. Castelli (Padua: Cedam, 1961), p. 39. The passages quoted are, respectively, from Euripides' *Helen*, 560, and Pliny's *Nat. Hist.* 2.18. (Translation mine)

37. I am borrowing this expression from Franco Ferrucci, who, in his *The Poetics of Disguise* (Ithaca, NY and London: Cornell University Press, 1980), pp. 118 ff., applies it to the Earthly Paradise.

38. A similar interpretation has been proposed recently by Rachel Jacoff and William A. Stephany in the *Lectura Dantis Americana: Inferno II* (Philadelphia: University of Pennsylvania Press, 1989). On p. 72, commenting on *Inferno* I, 82–87, they write:

Dante's hope that his long study of and great love for Virgil's poem would somehow deliver him from his spiritual wilderness is touching and moving, but it is also, in terms of a rhetoric of conversion, patently vain: philology and literary affiliation may be important human activities, but they cannot on their own terms fill Dante's spiritual void. His praise of Virgil as the sole source of his own honor as a poet shows in retrospect how imperfectly he understands at the poem's beginning what he will come to learn during its course: the true nature of honor and of poetry, as well as the transformed role Virgil will come to play in his life and his writing.

39. Burke, *A Grammar of Motives*, pp. 39–40.

40. Giuseppe Ungaretti, "Il Canto I dell'*Inferno*," in *Letture dantesche*, vol. I, ed. Giovanni Getto (Florence: Sansoni, 1968), p. 22.

41. Tibor Wlassics, *Dante narratore: Saggi sullo stile della "Commedia"* (Florence: Olschki, 1975), pp. 110–111.

42. René Girard, *Violence and the Sacred*, trans. Patrick Gregory (Baltimore: Johns Hopkins University Press, 1984), p. 150.

43. Allen Mandelbaum, trans., *The Aeneid of Virgil* (New York: Bantam Books, 1961), p. vii.

44. Antoine Vergote, "La peine dans la dialectique de l'innocence, de la transgression et de la réconciliation," in *Il mito della pena*, Archivio di Filosofia, ed. Enrico Castelli (Padua: Cedam, 1967), p. 386. (Translation mine)

II. The Garden of the Ancient Poets

The motif of the garden and correspondingly the drama of the pilgrim's return to Eden take on new significance in *Inferno* IV. Between lines 106 and 120, the poet portrays a "noble castle" rising in the midst of a "meadow of fresh verdure," which is encircled by seven walls. Here dwell the souls of the famous virtuous men and women of antiquity, eminent among them the poets—from Homer to Lucan. This castle occupies the privileged place earlier described as defined by a fire that overcomes "a hemisphere of darkness" (IV, 69). "Here," notes A. Bartlett Giamatti "Dante gives the pagan poets a dwelling place which approximates the best they portrayed in their poems. They live in an Elysium because Elysium was the highest state they could conceive."[1] Yet, we must add with the same critic, this is more than an Elysium, more than a garden. "This benign landscape blends, for the first time, the twin notions of City and Garden, later tentatively reconciled in Eden (*Purg.* XXXII) and finally luminously integrated in the rose of the City of God (*Par.* XXXIII)."[2]

If this reconciliation of the antinomy of city and garden constitutes a significant counter-assertion to the assertion represented by the pilgrim's illusory recovery of Eden inscribed in the Prologue, it is also significant as an unforeseen counter-assertion to the more recent scene of Dante's and Virgil's entrance into Hell. This scene begins to take shape the moment the wayfarer sees the inscription above Hell's portal:

> PER ME SI VA NE LA CITTÀ DOLENTE
> PER ME SI VA NE L'ETTERNO DOLORE
> PER ME SI VA TRA LA PERDUTA GENTE.
> GIUSTIZIA MOSSE IL MIO ALTO FATTORE;
> FECEMI LA DIVINA PODESTATE,
> LA SOMMA SAPÏENZA E 'L PRIMO AMORE.
> DINANZI A ME NON FUOR COSE CREATE
> SE NON ETTERNE, E IO ETTERNO DURO.
> LASCIATE OGNE SPERANZA, VOI CH'INTRATE.

Queste parole di colore oscuro
   vid'io scritte al sommo d'una porta;
   per ch'io: "Maestro, il senso lor m' è duro."

(Inf. III, 1–12)

THROUGH ME YOU ENTER THE WOEFUL CITY,
   THROUGH ME YOU ENTER ETERNAL GRIEF,
   THROUGH ME YOU ENTER AMONG THE LOST.
JUSTICE MOVED MY HIGH MAKER:
   THE DIVINE POWER MADE ME,
   THE SUPREME WISDOM, AND THE PRIMAL LOVE.
BEFORE ME NOTHING WAS CREATED
   IF NOT ETERNAL, AND ETERNAL I ENDURE.
   ABANDON EVERY HOPE, YOU WHO ENTER.

These words of obscure color I saw inscribed over a portal; whereupon I said, "Master, their meaning is hard for me."

Appropriately, as these words communicate the message of the eternity of both the portal and of Hell, they enter the wayfarer's and our field of vision abruptly. This unannounced presence is the presence of eternity under the negative sign of sin and despair, marking the entrance into the city of the dead. It should not surprise us that as they speak of the eternal existence of the suffering of punishment, and correspondingly of evil (by "eternal" here we of course mean "perpetual" or "everlasting," for, in a strict sense, "eternal" can be said only of God), they appear unintelligible to the wayfarer. We may interpret the pilgrim's response with the question that is asked through the ages: why is there evil and the corresponding punishment? And as we read the declaration that God, moved by justice, created the gateway and the infernal city, the place and instrument of everlasting pain, we find new ground for the wayfarer's perplexity, which prompts us to ask: what is this justice that at once permits evil to exist and punishes its perpetrators for eternity? How can the Power of the Father, the Wisdom of the Son, and the Love of the Holy Spirit create an infernal machine that inflicts eternal pain and yet is just? As we read the final statement of the portal's inscription, we ask: if the city of everlasting torment, destined to receive Satan and the other fallen angels, was created after the heavens, primal matter and the angels (cf. Par. XXIX, 22–48), and therefore before the creation of Adam and Eve, did this not already constitute a scene of transgression, of sin, and of corresponding punishment which we have inherited and thus could not avoid "entering"? In other words, does not the very creation of Dis, resulting from Satan's fall, constitute the ground, or the "scene" preordained as the place of punishment for future sinners, before man was created and before he sinned? What is, then, the meaning of such preparation by God? Has He, like a dramaturge, set the stage on which we act in a drama whose text is unknown, and in which we must choose or fashion a role, experiencing the freedom of each individual choice, and yet being governed by the necessity dictated by the total design of the drama in which we move and act? This setting, this stage is *already there*, as the serpent is already there in the Garden of Eden. As Paul Ricoeur has observed,

the inscrutable, I believe, consists precisely in the fact that evil which always begins by virtue of freedom is always there *for* freedom, that it is act and habitus, sudden appearance *and* antecedent. It is for this reason that Kant makes expressively of this enigma of evil for philosophy the transposition of the mythical figure of the serpent; the serpent, I think, represents the "always already there" of evil, of that evil which, meanwhile, is beginning, act, determination of freedom by itself.[3]

It is this inscrutability of evil and its being "always already there" that the portal's "obscure words" reveal as an essential component of the very reality of evil, a reality whose finality, equalled by the finality of the infernal punishment, and therefore of God's judgment, becomes most intensely present, and hence is most terrifying, in the last words of the inscription: "Abandon every hope, you who enter." As we pronounce these words, perplexed and fearful as the wayfarer (for is there not the danger that *we* also may not fare well through our experience of reading the *Inferno*, that we may not find a way out, and also that, in some proportion with our reading, we may not find a way out in the journey of our life?), we ask: how can one embark on a journey through Hell if this means entering a world without hope? How can one hope to find salvation through this journey?

Once again, we must look for our answers in the play of assertions and counter-assertions and hence in the tragic rhythm created by the very sequence of scenes. Let us begin with Virgil's response to his disciple's statement that he does not understand the portal's inscription:

Ed elli a me, come persona accorta:
    "Qui si convien lasciare ogne sospetto;
    ogne viltà convien che qui sia morta.
Noi siam venuti al loco ov'i' t'ho detto

che tu vedrai le genti dolorose
c'hanno perduto il ben de l'intelletto."
E poi che la sua mano a la mia puose
con lieto volto, ond'io mi confortai,
mi mise dentro a le segrete cose.

(Inf. III, 13–21)

And he to me, as one who understands, "Here must all fear be left behind; here let all cowardice be dead. We have come to the place where I
have told you you will see the wretched people who have lost the good of
intellect." And when he had placed his hand on mine, with a cheerful look
from which I took comfort, he led me among the secret things.

Virgil replies, not with an explanation of the "words of obscure color"
(III, 10), not with discursive reasoning, but with an exhortation to leave all
fear behind and letting "all cowardice be dead." These words are followed
by the comforting action of placing his hand on the hand of the wayfarer
and then by the action of leading him "among the secret things." Thus
Virgil cuts through the "surface" of the wayfarer's awareness of and response to the gateway's words, reaching a deeper area of perception. What
he awakens is not a mere preoccupation of the mind to grasp immediately
the meaning of the words that appear before it, which could produce a
kind of mirage of easy conquest, of easy possession of a truth, but rather
the pilgrim's attention to the state of his being in the form of fear and
cowardice, as he faces these mysterious, frightening words. The movement
from mind to passion, or from seeing to suffering, which Virgil has helped
bring to light, is striking. The scene created by the obscure words is unintelligible to the mind's eye, yet it is now present to the whole being of the
protagonist as something integrally experienced within as inscrutable, as
other, and yet as real. There is thus a marked shift from words, obscurely
perceived as difficult and harsh, to the inner action of self-awareness, and
finally to the action of entering the world of "le segrete cose." This action
promises an interpretation of those obscure words through drama, with its
disjunctive, tragic structure and rhythm, and with its own logic—the logic
of events as they succeed one another, drawing to them the wayfarer and
his guide (as well as, of course, the sympathetic reader).

Virgil and Dante move in a world that is at once relatively familiar and
absolutely *other*, as we have seen announced by the words inscribed on
Hell's portal. The pilgrim (and, again, the reader) has some understanding

of the words "eternity," "eternal grief," "supreme wisdom," and so forth. Yet this is an understanding of words having a very limited range and resonance, separated as they are from the world of experience and action. It is to this world we find represented in Dante's journey that we must direct our attention to gain deeper understanding of those "obscure words," namely by following and defining the tragic rhythm created by the contiguity and interrelation of words and actions, and specifically, by the ever-changing proportion between what appears as a segment of a known reality—something that the mind already possesses—and what reveals itself as totally other in actions and events. This is also the tragic rhythm of our journey as readers. This is also *our* drama. We recognize certain allusions, certain features of a scene, distinguishable at first as literary or experiential, but in the end forming one integral experience. Yet at the same time we feel, as the wayfarer does, that our head is "circled with error" (*Inf.* III, 31).

With him we are now led by Virgil "among the secret things," as we turn to the beginning of Canto IV:

Ruppemi l'alto sonno ne la testa
    un greve truono, sì ch'io mi riscossi
    come persona ch'è per forza desta;
e l'occhio riposato intorno mossi,
    dritto levato, e fiso riguardai
    per conoscer lo loco dov'io fossi.
Vero è che 'n su la proda mi trovai
    de la valle d'abisso dolorosa
    che 'ntrono accoglie d'infiniti guai.

(*Inf.* IV, 1–9)

A heavy thunderclap broke the deep sleep in my head, so that I started like one who is awakened by force; and, standing up, I moved my rested eyes around, gazing intently to make out the place where I was. True it is that I found myself on the brink of the chasm of pain, which holds the clamor of endless wailings.

Dante the pilgrim is awakened to the reality of a new scene by a thunderclap whose force is as mysterious as it is terrifying. He now finds himself on the edge of the infernal abyss and therefore on the other shore of the Acheron, without having experienced the crossing. We recognize the form of this movement, of this passage, perceiving in it echoes of the shifts and ruptures that characterized the succession of scenes in the Prologue, beginning with the wayfarer's first movement from the dark wood to the foot of the "delightful mountain," which occurred without his awareness of the passage from one to the other scene. How has the wayfarer crossed the Acheron? Neither he nor the reader knows. All that the text suggests, paralleling what the wayfarer himself may infer, is that, as Charon had earlier shouted to him, he has crossed to the shore "by another way, by other ports" (III, 91).

Significantly, the force that now awakens the wayfarer is similar to the one that, in the closing scene of Canto III, had acted upon him in the opposite manner, overcoming his senses and making him fall "like one who is seized by sleep" (III, 136). This was the violent tremor that "shook the gloomy plane," and the ensuing flash of lightning (130–131). Once again we witness the unfolding pattern of tragic rhythm and therefore of transformation which, paradoxically, is produced by the interruption of movement, by the rupture that an outside power—the power of an incomprehensible act and scene—causes within the wayfarer. The first rupture introduced in the wayfarer's consciousness, in the form of a tremor and a lightning-like flash, brings on a kind of death, the death of the "I" facing an act and a scene of overwhelming force, one that, as we have said earlier, is perceived as *totally other*. Yet this very death constitutes the ground for the wayfarer's transformation, what allows him to "suffer the opposition," that is, to internalize the "otherness" of what at first was apprehended as being "out there," as a merely "scenic" reality, and then to transcend his original "blindness" to the scene through this "suffering," attaining a higher plane of awareness.

The poet gives form to this tragic rhythm of death and rebirth by placing side by side acts and scenes that are distinct yet related, as the flash of crimson light is related to the violent tremor of the plane (Canto III) and as the thunderclap (Canto IV) is in turn related to that tremor and that flash. This relation clearly exhibits a metonymic structure and hence the essentially disjunctive inner form of all dramatic art. As we follow closely the further development of this form in Canto IV, in search of the creative movement that this form engenders within the wayfarer's soul (and in ours), we observe that the "thunderclap" that broke the wayfarer's deep sleep was really the sound of Hell's endless wailings. The pilgrim's awakening to the reality of this scene is clearly marked by the tercet that, significantly, begins with the words "Vero è" ("True it is").

Once again, it is the reality of pain that gains focus, and with it the problematic enunciated by the inscription above Hell's portal. The poet articulates this conundrum through eminently dramatic forms. Virgil's summons to "descend now into the blind world here below" (*Inf.* III, 12), which is punctuated by his growing "all pale" (III, 13), is interpreted by the wayfarer as an incongruent message that prompts him to say:

> . . . "Come verrò, se tu paventi
> che suoli al mio dubbiare esser conforto?"
>
> (*Inf.* III, 17–18)

. . . "How shall I come, if you are afraid, who are wont to encourage me when I hesitate?"

Here the wayfarer's perceived opposition between words and act, between Virgil's exhortation and his pallor, causes him to suspend movement, to refuse to act. Yet in this moment of inertia he finds the space, the creative platform, upon which he represents his inner conflict, his inner fear as he, mistakenly, attributes Virgil's pallor to fear. Transformation is thus born of the ambiguity initially present in Virgil's message, for this ambiguity enables the wayfarer to objectify his inner conflict, his inner battle between the desire to embark on the journey through Hell and the fear of facing its endless evil and pain. The moment he has externalized this inner conflict, seeing it mirrored in his guide, he is ready to make the leap from the scene of fear he has constructed in the presence of Virgil to the scene of pity that the latter reveals to him with these words:

> . . . "L'angoscia de le genti
> che son qua giù, nel viso mi dipigne
> quella pietà che tu per tema senti."
>
> (*Inf.* III, 19–21)

. . . "The anguish of the people here below paints my face with the pity that you take for fear."

Dante the pilgrim can experience this "leap" when he completely "suffers" the opposition he has created or organized with the help of Virgil's ambiguous "scene," when he sees side by side, in dialectical relation, fear and pity. In this moment of awakened attention, he faces both his own suffering and the suffering of others, both passion and compassion.

If for a moment we return to consider the problematic of pain that, with the wayfarer, we found inscribed over Hell's portal, we cannot fail to note that the scene we have just interpreted constitutes to a certain degree a kind of counter-assertion, and therefore a dramatic shift from that which the inscription affirmed. The most significant element of this counter-assertion is of course pity, of which there is no mention in the gateway's "words of obscure color." But more of this later. We must now turn our gaze to the central theme of Canto IV, the main action of Dante's "return to Eden."

Having seen on Virgil's face a measure of the anguish of those who dwell in Limbo, the wayfarer enters with his guide "the first circle that girds the abyss" (IV, 24), where he encounters with greater immediacy the nature as well as the mystery of that anguish:

> Quivi, secondo che per ascoltare,
>   non avea pianto mai che di sospiri
>   che l'aura etterna facevan tremare;
> ciò avvenia di duol sanza martìri,
>   ch'avean le turbe, ch'eran molte e grandi,
>   d'infanti e di femmine e di viri.
>
> (*Inf.* IV, 25–30)

Here there was no plaint, that could be heard, except of sighs, which caused the eternal air to tremble; and this arose from the sadness, without torments, of the crowds that were many and great, both of children and of women and men.

The image of the eternal air that trembles with sighs arrests our attention, as it calls to mind the series of similar images we have encountered earlier: from the violent earth tremor and crimson flash at the end of Canto III, to the thunderclap at the beginning of Canto IV, which is later identified with the thunder of all the wailings of Hell. But what is the meaning of this correspondence? We may also ask: since each of these images represents a condition that provokes fear, are they perhaps related to the fear that the wayfarer had experienced at the sight of the portal's inscription? And are they also connected with the fear that permeates the first scenes of the *Comedy*, beginning with that of the "selva oscura"? And, finally, is the present scene related to that of the lion, who so terrified Dante that "the air seemed to tremble"? (*Inf.* I, 48). If they are not directly linked, do they nevertheless independently express the same fundamental conundrum, the same conflict?

We shall attempt to answer these questions beginning with some reflections along the lines sketched earlier when we first apprehended the creative contiguity and dialectic of fear and pity. Let us start at the beginning. The fear of which Dante speaks in the first scene of *Inferno* coincides with the wayfarer's awakening to the reality of the "selva oscura," and therefore to its evil (which, we recall, is yet to be differentiated from the other dimension of the "selva"—the good). Yet the very terror by which the wayfarer is seized as he finds himself in the midst of this place of darkness, where there is no path, no sign of a way out, constitutes the ground for escape from such condition. For this terror puts him in touch with himself and the unknown reality that surrounds him. While he does experience the separation from a creative order, from the "diritta via," this is better than being blind to such separation. It is here that the journey begins. And it is here that the new passion, pity, begins to stir within the pilgrim. But first it is akin to fear; it is what we may call the pain of fear, or the tremor—the reverberation of fear—which Dante calls "pièta," as we find in this tercet:

Allor fu la paura un poco queta,
   che nel lago del cor m'era durata
   la notte chi'i' passai con tanta pièta.

(Inf. I, 19–21)

Then the fear was somewhat quieted that had continued in the lake of my heart through the night I had passed so piteously.

The moment fear is experienced and "suffered" in the "lake of the heart," it dialectically calls forth a new sentiment, or a new form of suffering, "pièta," that is, suffering that implies a keener self-awareness and a self-commiseration which lives side by side with fear, and in opposition to it. Thus there is an inner drama whereby fear is transformed into suffering, or "pièta." Once this drama is lived within the wayfarer's soul, and its form, with its inherent creativity, is made manifest in this inner space, he is prepared to enter the outer drama of fear and pity such as the drama whose first scenes we have encountered in *Inferno* IV, and to which we must now return.

As we fix our gaze upon the scene of the eternal air that trembles with the sighs of the souls in Limbo, we must reiterate the observation we made earlier about the counter-assertion that Virgil's pity constituted vis-à-vis the assertion inscribed above Hell's portal, adding that, similarly, the suffering in Limbo "sanza martìri" ("without torment") stands in opposition to that assertion, and specifically, to the "eternal grief" of the souls in Hell it announces. This opposition is given further expression in the ensuing dialogue between Virgil and Dante concerning the nature and cause of the virtuous pagans' suffering in Limbo. In a form that is obviously dramatic, Virgil directly confronts the wayfarer's silence at the sight of these souls with the words:

> . . . "Tu non dimandi
> che spiriti son questi che tu vedi?"
>
> *(Inf.* IV, 31–32)

. . . "Do you not ask what spirits are these that you see?"

Here Virgil calls attention to what we can easily construe as the wayfarer's perplexity which, much like our own, arises from not understanding the particular status of the virtuous pagans in Hell, especially, as we have already noted, in the light of the "eternal grief" announced by the inscription above Hell's portal.

Having thus identified Dante's tacit perplexity or questioning, hence "organizing the opposition" according to the dialectical movement of the action, Virgil offers the following "answers":

> "Or vo' che sappi, innanzi che più andi,
> ch'ei non peccaro; e s'elli hanno mercedi,
>   non basta, perchè non ebber battesmo,
>   ch'è porta de la fede che tu credi;
> e s'e' furon dinanzi al cristianesmo,
>   non adorar debitamente a Dio:
>   e di questi cotai son io medesmo.
> Per tai difetti, non per altro rio,
>   semo perduti, e sol di tanto offesi
>   che sanza speme vivemo in disio."
>
> *(Inf.* IV, 33–42)

"I will have you know that they did not sin; but if they have merit, that does not suffice, for they did not have baptism, which is the portal of the faith you hold; and if they were before Christianity, they did not worship God aright, and I myself am one of these. Because of these shortcomings, and for no other fault, we are lost, and only so far afflicted that without hope we live in longing."

These are not really answers for the rationalist who lives in the wayfarer and in each one of us, for they do not reveal the deep, ultimate cause of the suffering of the virtuous souls in Limbo. To give as reason the lack of baptism or for those who lived before Christianity, the imperfect worship of God, is not to increase understanding. Rather it is merely to speak of the obscure, unfathomable correlation between the realm of reason and the realm of faith, and correspondingly, between the realm of law or ethics and the realm of grace. In other words, here Virgil gives his disciple answers or clarifications phrased in opposing assertions that, again, within the perspective of the rationalist, are irreconcilable, and whose meaning lies in the very correlation and tension created by those assertions.

In short, this meaning lies in an essentially dramatic structure, whose underlying or organizing principle is that of the tragic. For how else can we characterize these assertions that speak of the punishment of the virtuous—a punishment that must be accepted as just, for it is God's judgment? How can these same assertions not produce pity in the heart of Dante the wayfarer and in the heart of the reader? But, we must hasten to ask, what is the nature of this pity? At first, I think that this sentiment or passion is born of the spectator's opinion or conventional view of the worthiness of the souls punished in Limbo. This is clearly expressed in the pilgrim's response to Virgil's words quoted above:

> Gran duol mi prese al cor quando lo 'ntesi,
>   però che gente di molto valore
>   conobbi che 'n quel limbo eran sospesi.
>
> (*Inf.* IV, 43–45)

Great sadness seized my heart when I heard him, for I recognized that people of great worth were suspended in that Limbo.

Having "suffered" this pity—first, objectively, as we found in lines 19–21, by seeing it "painted" on Virgil's face, and now, subjectively, by experiencing it within his heart—the wayfarer has to reconcile it with his faith: he must resolve the opposition between the logic of reason and law and the logic of faith and grace. He must therefore experience it as pity for a suffering that, although imparted to the virtuous souls, is nevertheless merited and hence must be accepted not as an arbitrary but as a just retribution. In a sense, the wayfarer is now ready to transcend or to transform the pity born of the somewhat conventional view of the incomprehensible, if not altogether unjust suffering of the innocent. This is not to say that he wishes to erase such pity, or correspondingly, that he will fathom the ultimate reason for this suffering, but rather that he now seeks to experience it on another plane, in another perspective, by shifting his focus, just as earlier, with the help and in the presence of Virgil, he had shifted his focus from fear to pity. The wayfarer's search for this new plane, this new perspective, is expressed by the following question he addresses to Virgil:

> "Dimmi, maestro mio, dimmi, segnore,"
>   comincia' io per volere esser certo
>   di quella fede che vince ogne errore:
> "uscicci mai alcuno, o per suo merto
>   o per altrui, che poi fosse beato?"
>
> (Inf. IV, 46–50)

"Tell me, master, tell me, sir," I began, wishing to be assured of the faith that conquers every error, "did ever anyone go forth from here, either by his own or by another's merit, who afterwards was blessed?"

This question concerns actions, events, and their logic. The wayfarer does not ask *why* being virtuous before Christianity or being without baptism is not sufficient to merit salvation. His attention is directed to the fundamental scene, that is, to the condition of souls being confined to the enclosed space of Limbo and to the action that such a scene by its intrinsic motivational force calls into being: to be free, whether by one's own efforts or by those of another. Virgil readily understands to what scene and action Dante alludes:

> E quei che 'ntese il mio parlar coverto,
> rispuose: "Io era nuovo in questo stato,
>   quando ci vidi venire un possente,
>   con segno di vittoria coronato.
> Trasseci l'ombra del primo parente,
>   d'Abèl suo figlio e quella di Noè,

di Moïsè legista e ubidente;
Abraàm patriarca e Davìd re,
    Israèl con lo padre e co' suoi nati
    e con Rachele, per cui tanto fè,
e altri molti, e feceli beati.
    E vo' che sappi che, dinanzi ad essi,
    spiriti umani non eran salvati."

(Inf. IV, 51–63)

And he, who understood my covert speech, replied, "I was new in this condition when I saw a Mighty One come here, crowned with sign of victory. He took hence the shade of our first parent, Abel his son, and Noah, and Moses, obedient giver of laws, Abraham the patriarch and David the king, Israel with his father and his children and with Rachel, for whom he did so much, and many others; and He made them blessed. And I would have you know that before these no human souls were saved."

To capture the full significance of these words and their creative power—their power to move and to transform both the wayfarer and his companion the reader—we must weigh them, and therefore the action and scene that they evoke, in relation to the original suffering and pity experienced by the wayfarer. In other words, we must recall that scene of pity which has called forth the present scene and action. And as we perceive the contiguity of these scenes, we should ask: is it the same pity, or is it not modified, transformed by the event of Christ's descent to Limbo? Does not this event stand in opposition to the condition that called into being the wayfarer's pity? True, the wayfarer learns that not all the virtuous souls of Limbo were freed and made blessed. But before Christ's descent to Hell, did the chosen (who, it is understood, had the implicit faith in the advent of a Redeemer) not share the status or fate of Virgil and of all those like him? Were they not equally *lost* until such time? And the words inscribed over Hell's gate, "LASCIATE OGNE SPERANZA, VOI CH'INTRATE," were they not also intended for them? If we now recall the scene of the wayfarer's reaction to that inscription, can we not construe, by an implicit analogy, that like him each one of those souls found those same words and the divine judgment they express obscure and terrifying? Yet, as the wayfarer now learns from Virgil, the extraordinary event of the coming of the Savior shattered that "scene" of despair experienced by those souls when they entered Hell, and in a certain sense (the one that is inherent in the temporal dimension, the horizontal line of history), it transformed the initial condemnation and the original punishment prescribed by Divine Justice. Again, in the company of the wayfarer, we witness another shift, another break, which appears to be incongruent in the light of discursive reasoning, but is meaningful, if mysterious, in the light of the logic of action.

We can now attempt to answer our question concerning the transformation of the wayfarer's pity the moment we recall that the event of Christ's descent to Hell is directly dependent on the passion of the Cross— as the sign of victory (the cruciform nimbus) itself represents—and is therefore the most dramatic expression of God's pity for sinners. We cannot now think of the wayfarer's pity in the same way we first apprehended it. Aware of God's pity—and therefore of His suffering—the pity that Dante the pilgrim experiences at the sight of the sad souls of Limbo must take on a larger meaning. As we have hinted earlier, the wayfarer's pity is reaffirmed on a higher plane—that of God's *oikonomia*, whose center is the Cross.

We are now proceeding by hints and guesses as we try to fathom the underlying meaning of the scenes that the poet places before our eyes. Now we can only speak of what such scenes suggest to us. What they *declare*, of course, in the eventuating words of Virgil, is the entrance into Limbo of Christ "crowned with sign of victory." We cannot ignore the force of this focus. Here there is no manifest reference made to Christ's Passion, and therefore to the question of pity. With a swift movement Virgil introduces into the wayfarer's consciousness an *event*: Christ's coming to Limbo to set free the souls of those who had implicitly believed in Him and in His coming. This is the action that cuts through the wayfarer's pity for the souls in Limbo and redefines it by revealing that Limbo, contrary to what the inscription over Hell's portal announced, is *not* an eternal prison, because some of the souls dwelling there were once freed.

Is there not an unspoken, secret analogy at play here between the descent of Christ into Limbo evoked by Virgil and Beatrice's descent into the same region, which Virgil related to the pilgrim in the Prologue? (*Inf.* II, 52–117). And did not Beatrice, like Christ, also "free" a soul from Limbo, namely Virgil, as she, "moved by Love," enjoined him to help free Dante from the bondage of sin by guiding him through Hell and up the mountain of Purgatory? And though temporarily and imperfectly (for, within the context of the *Commedia*, he will return to Limbo when Beatrice appears to Dante in the Earthly Paradise), is this not a tangible sign of a possible, future salvation of Virgil? How can we ignore—as many critics have done—the implications of Beatrice's promise to Virgil that "before God" she will often praise him? ("Quando sarò dinanzi al segnor mio, / di te mi loderò sovente a lui," *Inf.* II, 73–74). Are we to take this promise as false, or as another *captatio benevolentiae*? If not, can we consider Beatrice's praise of Virgil as ultimately ineffectual and therefore as not pointing to a future event? Can we say this of one whom Lucy called "loda di Dio vera" ("true praise of God," *Inf.* II, 103), not to mention other, all too obvious proofs of Beatrice's authority? And if Virgil is excluded from the City of God because he "was rebellious to His law" (*Inf.* I, 124–126), can we be certain that this exile is final, eternal? If we recall that Virgil has been obedient to Beatrice's command and, through her, to God's command to help save Dante ("your command so pleases me, that had I obeyed already it would be late," *Inf.* I, 79–80), how can we not see that this obedience is the salutary medicine for his former rebellion to God's law, and therefore a form of expiation and preparation for God's grace which might make Virgil one of the elect? Is there any evidence in the entire *Commedia* that Dante the poet views Virgil's destiny as one of eternal exile from the Celestial City? Can we be certain that Dante did not envision for Virgil the kind of salvation which, as we read in *Paradiso* XX (106–117, 118–124), God granted to the Emperor Trajan and to Aeneas' companion Ripheus,[4] not to mention Cato and Statius, who are found in Purgatory?[5]

Many critics have expressed this certainty of perpetual exile for Virgil. Professor Hollander, for example, who has addressed the problem of Virgil's fate with thoroughness and acumen, asserts that Dante saw and portrayed Virgil as one who is condemned to remain in Limbo for eternity, despite the fact that, if only temporarily, he is freed from Limbo and is allowed to enter Eden and that, as Beatrice promised him, he will often be praised by her before God.[6] Fr. Kenelm Foster, who has also studied in great depth the problem of Virgil's salvation, comes very close to finding a basis for such salvation, but in the end conludes that Virgil, with all the other souls of Limbo, is condemned to eternal exclusion from Heaven.[7]

I shall return to this question in the course of this study. Meanwhile, let us resume our analysis of *Inferno* IV.

With another touch that betrays the hand of the dramatist, Dante introduces a series of tightly knit scenes:

Non lasciavam l'andar perch'ei dicessi,
 ma passavam la selva tuttavia,
 la selva, dico, di spiriti spessi.
Non era lunga ancor la nostra via
 di qua dal sonno, quand'io vidi un foco
 ch'emisperio di tenebre vincia.
Di lungi n'eravamo ancora un poco,
 ma non sì ch'io non discernessi in parte
 ch'orrevol gente possedea quel loco.

             (*Inf.* IV, 64–72)

We did not cease going on because he spoke, but all the while were pass-ing through the wood, I mean the wood of thronging spirits; nor had we yet gone far from the place of my slumber when I saw a fire, which over-came a hemisphere of darkness. We were still a little distant from it, yet not so far but that I might in part discern that honorable folk possessed this place.

The focus, once again, is on action and movement. Here we are invited to ask the meaning of the poet's note that he and Virgil did not "cease going" while the latter spoke. Or, what does the note assert in relation to the pre-ceding actions and to those that follow, that is, to its immediate context or scene? In strict dramatistic terms, we can easily observe that this action, this "going," if seen as contiguous to the main action evoked earlier by Virgil—the coming of Christ the Victor—reveals an emphasis on action itself. This meaning is reinforced and sharpened by contrast, the moment we recollect the equally dramatic note we have encountered earlier, the one concerning the pause of which Virgil spoke when he told the wayfarer of the state of the virtuous in Limbo:

 "Or vo' che sappi, *innanzi che più andi*,
ch'ei non peccaro . . . ."

           (*Inf.* IV, 33–34; italics mine)

"Before you go farther, I will have you know that they did not sin . . . ."

This moment of stasis dramatically parallels and underscores, on the one hand, the state of the souls in Limbo, which Virgil portrays as unchanging, and having the finality of fate ("for no other fault, we are lost"). On the other hand, it highlights the moment of reflection, the "state" of the wayfarer as he learns of these souls and internalizes this experience, feeling pity for them, before turning to Virgil to ask about an action that may have brought about a change in the state of those souls, and implicitly, as we have observed, a change in his pity.

We thus perceive a certain tension created by the opposition of this static scene to the dynamic scene of the coming of Christ evoked by Virgil, which is then echoed in the movement of the wayfarer and his guide through Limbo. The meaning of this movement is then expanded by Dante the dramatist, as he introduces the image of the "selva," of the wood, first in the literal and then in the metaphorical sense, which harks back to the first scene of the poem, that of the "selva oscura." As in that scene, here the emphasis is on *moving* through a dark place that is perceived as immense, and where there is no path, indeed as in a wood or a crowd. This correlation between two scenes—the Prologue and Limbo—becomes more significant as the poet, in one continuous movement, gives form to the scene of the wayfarer's discovery of the "fire, which overcame a hemisphere of darkness." As the text clearly suggests, Dante has created a distinct opposition between the "wood" of spirits (or rather we should now say the "dark wood" of spirits), and the luminous area possessed by the "honorable folk" of Limbo. This opposition seems to echo the one between the "selva oscura" and the luminous hill of the Prologue scene. We recall that, in that scene, the wayfarer had acted as one who, having just awakened to the reality of sin, had experienced a nostalgia for Eden, for the luminous life of a pristine innocence and bliss. And we also remember that it was Virgil who, after the wayfarer's failure to reach the summit of the sunlit hill, had enjoined him to climb the "mountain of delight," adhering for a moment to the vision of the pagan world and its nostalgia for the Golden Age—a vision that he, after being reminded by the wayfarer of the presence of the she-wolf, soon abandoned, pointing to the other journey, "l'altro viaggio."

The drama of the return to Eden, which here is obliquely announced, becomes manifest in the scenes that follow, especially in the representation of the noble castle. Before the wayfarer and his guide enter this castle, they are first spectators and then actors in a series of scenes that prepares the way for the scenes with which the drama of Dante's and Virgil's journey through Limbo comes to a close. The main action or theme of these scenes is the honor that a community bestows on its poets—in Dante's perspective, on those who, through their creative activity, in turn honor "scïenzïa e arte." This action is clearly defined by the words the wayfarer and his guide exchange, in which the notion of honor is reiterated:

"O tu ch'onori scïenzïa e arte,
    questi chi son c'hanno cotanta onranza,
    che dal modo de li altri li diparte?"
E quelli a me: "L'onrata nominanza
    che di lor suona sù ne la tua vita,
    grazïa acquista in ciel che sì li avanza."

(*Inf.* IV, 73–78)

"O you who honor science and art, who are these that have such honor that it sets them apart from the condition of the rest?" And he to me, "Their honored fame, which resounds in your life above, wins grace in Heaven, which thus advances them."

An important, if not indeed the most important facet of this action is the divine grace merited by those who earned honor on earth—especially the poets—so that they occupy the privileged, luminous space of Limbo. This privileged state of the noble souls of Limbo acquires greater significance the moment we see it juxtaposed to the first scenes of *Inferno*, especially that of the inscription upon Hell's portal.

Thus we witness another break, another apparently incongruent shift from one expression of God's justice to another. Again the incongruence is resolved by the logic of actions and reactions, namely of the good deeds of the virtuous pagans, and God's response to those actions, whereby He "saves" in a way that to a certain degree is analogous to the salvation of His coming as Christ *Victor mortis*, by creating a luminous place in the darkness of Limbo and of Hell. It is especially significant—for the question of Virgil's salvation, as well as for our insight into Dante's dramaturgy— that the winning of God's grace bestowed on the virtuous pagans is attrib- uted by Virgil to their "honored fame" which "resounds" on earth. This obviously implies a dynamic, and *dramatic*, relationship between man and God, the living and the dead, and time and eternity, for if Virgil (and his companions) can help Dante win God's grace, so can Dante, or anyone who on earth honors Virgil, win God's grace for the pagan poet. In other words, in the spirit of a Christian humanism, Dante here suggests that to "honor science and art" has a power analogous to that of the prayer of those who—as we read in *Purgatorio* VI, 37–39—living in a state of grace, can speed the way to Heaven of the souls in Purgatory, without lowering "the summit" of God's justice. For such prayer is a "foco d'amor" ("fire of love") which *acts* upon God and with God, in perfect consonance with His will, "in un punto" ("in a moment")—the eternal now.

In the action of honoring the poets, we find that the wayfarer is now both a spectator and an actor. Having enunciated this action, Dante deftly transforms it into the living form of drama as he introduces the voice that intersects Virgil's words:

> Intanto voce fu per me udita:
> "Onorate l'altissimo poeta;
> l'ombra sua torna, ch'era dipartita."
> Poi che la voce fu restata e queta,
> vidi quattro grand'ombre a noi venire:
> sembianz' avevan né trista né lieta.
>
> (*Inf.* IV, 79–84)

Meanwhile I heard a voice which said, "Honor the great Poet! His shade, which had departed, now returns." After the voice had ceased and was still, I saw four great shades coming to us, in semblance neither sad nor joyful.

In this scene we easily recognize the deep interrelation of drama and ritual. There is first the single voice which, like a chorus, represents the community, with its values and aspirations—in a word, its *ethos*—and there are those members of the community who are called upon to interpret that *ethos*, to be the *dramatis personae* who can best give form to the main action upon which the very life of the community depends. And we should add that in this scene a dimension of the sacred is manifested by the procession of the four great shades led by Homer, "sovereign poet," who holds a sword in his hand, followed by Horace, Ovid, and Lucan. This ritual of honoring Virgil, the "great Poet" and therefore the persona that represents the "poet" in each of them, is then extended to the wayfarer *as poet*, so that his journey through Limbo and his imminent entrance into the luminous space of the noble castle takes on, through analogy and contiguity, a meaning similar to Virgil's return to the community of poets. For Dante the wayfarer this is a kind of ritual of initiation. Aided by his guide and sponsor, he is admitted to the privileged circle of the ancient poets. As they honored Virgil before, they now bestow honor on him, making him "sixth amid so much wisdom" (*Inf.* IV, 94–102).

The main action of moving towards the noble castle and, in the larger sense we have come to know in the preceding pages, of Dante's return to Eden, is then resumed:

> Così andammo infino a la lumera,
>   parlando cose che 'l tacere è bello,
>   sì com'era 'l parlar colà dov'era.
> Venimmo al piè d'un nobile castello,
>   sette volte cerchiato d'alte mura,
>   difeso intorno d'un bel fiumicello.
> Questo passammo come terra dura;
>   per sette porte intrai con questi savi:
>   giugnemmo in prato di fresca verdura.
> Genti v'eran con occhi tardi e gravi,
>   di grande autorità ne' lor sembianti:
>   parlavan rado, con voci soavi.
> Traemmoci così da l'un de' canti,
>   in loco aperto, luminoso e alto,
>   sì che veder si potien tutti quanti.

(Inf. IV, 103–117)

Thus we went onward to the light, talking of things it is well to pass in silence, even as it was well to speak of them there. We came to the foot of a noble castle, seven times encircled by lofty walls and defended round about by a fair stream. This we crossed, as on solid ground, and through seven gates I entered with these sages. We came to a meadow of fresh verdure, where there were people with grave and slow-moving eyes and looks of great authority; they spoke seldom and with gentle voice. Then we drew to one side, into an open place which was luminous and high, so that we could see all of them.

Once again we have before us the poetry of drama. To capture a measure of its force we must see the present scenes and actions against those that precede them. In other words, we must discover the rhythm created by the contiguity and contrast which at once links and separates, or unites by disjunction, one scene and another, one action and another. As we have observed throughout the preceding pages of this study, out of this tragic rhythm emerge unexpected meanings that, having escaped the grasp of our discursive reasoning, become integrally present, as life itself is present, to our "hystrionic sensibilities," to use Francis Fergusson's phrase, that is, present to our mimetic powers and the powers of our imagination. Dante the dramatist awakens these powers in us as he, by virtue of his creative intuition and his craft, produces scenes and actions whose meaning asserts itself through each scene individually as well as through their interrelationship or rhythm. Following the poet's invitation, we seek those meanings, first by direct reaction to, or to use a technical term, by a phenomenological reading of the scene of the noble castle and of the actions it contains, and then by a reading that will encompass, retrospectively, the turning point of the entire episode.

Our attention is struck by the presence of distinctive elements of the *topos* of the *locus amoenus*—the fair stream, the meadow of fresh verdure, and the open, luminous high place within the walls of the castle. They of course speak of the paradisal state, but also, because of the pre-eminence given here to the poets, of a kind of Parnassus. Equally striking is the presence of the city motif, as we have already noted with Bartlett Giamatti. The seven walls of the castle probably symbolize the social order achieved through the arts (*trivium* and *quadrivium*), or the moral and intellectual virtues to which, significantly, the poets lead, and of which they have a privileged view (they in fact occupy a high ground from which they survey all the noble souls who embody those virtues). This contiguity of the castle and the garden may represent humanity's attempt to reconcile the forces of nature and of art and thus to recapture the lost pristine order. For our Christian poet this would constitute a partial recovery of the original harmony existing between ourselves and nature, between work or art and the forces of nature, as we find expressed in Genesis 2:15–16: "Yahweh God took the man and settled him in the garden of Eden to cultivate and take care of it."

Another important feature draws our attention: the curious fact that the poets cross the stream surrounding the castle as if it were solid ground ("come terra dura"). This scene seems to echo the Israelites' crossing of the Red Sea: "The waters parted and the sons of Israel went on dry ground right into the sea" (Exodus 14:22). If we follow the full trajectory of the analogy linking the two scenes, we see (but only as "through a glass darkly") that the garden which Dante and the ancient poets are about to enter corresponds to some degree with the Israelites' promised land (a traditional figure of paradise). And we also see that the way to this garden or "paradise"—the extraordinary, "miraculous" crossing of the stream—is similar to the miraculous parting of the Red Sea, with the only difference that the former represents the "miracle" of poetry—with its power to imitate but also to transfigure nature—while the latter represents God's direct intervention. We should note, however, that the poets' "way" to the garden, if seemingly autonomous, is a constitutive part of Dante's journey to the Celestial Paradise, and it manifests, in the spirit of a Christian humanism, human cooperation with divine grace.

This is what the present scene suggests to me, "dramatistically" speaking. Doubtless, it primarily tells of the crossing of a stream that the poet intended to be mysterious, in a landscape that at once is reminiscent of the garden of the Adamic myth and is an incomplete or distorted version of it.[8] Conscious of the limits of the present reading and of the limits that the poet has built into his representation, we must now curb our *ingegno*, patiently awaiting flashes of insight that other scenes of the *Commedia* may later offer us.

Meanwhile, we must note that if there is an imbalance or disproportion between the city and the garden as represented in the scene of the noble castle—for the *locus amoenus*, with the pristine forces of nature it embodies, is contained within the fortress of human art—the entire scene nevertheless constitutes an important victory over the darkness and chaos of the "selva." This "selva," given the particular context in which we find the noble castle and its garden, belongs first to the "throng of spirits" through which the wayfarer and Virgil have come to the luminous place, and therefore those many undistinguished souls who live in darkness outside the noble castle; in a larger economy, it is also the "selva oscura" of the Prologue scene. We should again recall those seemingly obscure words uttered by the poet at the very beginning of *Inferno* about the good found in the "selva oscura": "Ma per trattar del ben ch'i' vi trovai" ("But, to treat of the good I found in it"). As we see these scenes side by side as it were, we recognize the main action of the wayfarer's movement away from the terrifying dark wood to the place of light, and we interpret it as an expression of his attempt to recapture the pristine innocence and bliss of Eden.

As he enters the noble castle, in the company of the ancient poets, Dante the wayfarer is experiencing, at least in part, a kind of return to Eden, a form of recapturing what had been denied him by the threatening presence of the three beasts in the Prologue scene and therefore by the reality of sin. What was essentially illusory there—as we have noted, a fraudulent flight of the mind towards Eden (or a Golden Age) which ignored the harsh path of virtue—is now real, authentic. For it takes the form of an encounter with those who have been truly *present* in history and indeed have made—and still make—history, in proportion to men's "honoring" their art and wisdom in this life's journey. And like all encounters, it is problematic. Its meaning is dependent on the rhythmic relationship of acts, agents, and scenes, as we find represented on the stage of history. In other words, in place of the idyllic mirage experienced in the Prologue scene, now the wayfarer, still moved of course, as everyone, by the nostalgia for Eden, recaptures in a certain measure a true Eden. This is the Eden that we, like the noble souls of Limbo, may reconstruct through the virtuous life and the toil of *poiein*.

As we direct our attention to the end of the episode, we read:

La sesta compagnia in due si scema:
   per altra via mi mena il savio duca,
   fuor de la queta, ne l'aura che trema.
E vegno in parte ove non è che luca.

(Inf. IV, 148–151)

The company of six diminishes to two; by another way my wise guide leads me, out of the quiet, into the trembling air; and I come to a part where there is naught that shines.

Meaning again comes to light intermittently, through disjunction, the moment a new action and a new scene come into view to increase and transform the preceding chain of scenes. Now that the journey continues "per altra via . . . ne l'aura che trema" ("by another way . . . into the trembling air"), the character of the privileged, luminous space of the noble castle gains greater relief by contrast. Significantly, the poet sets the new action and scene in the present, thus emphasizing the immediacy of the journey through the dark, trembling, and therefore terrifying air of Hell. The luminous oasis of Limbo is now perceived as remote. In the silence that at once separates and links the end of Canto IV and the beginning of Canto V, we may pause to cast a retrospective gaze upon the entire episode in order to extract deeper meanings. The first scene, we recall, is filled with the thunderclap that awakens the wayfarer. This turns out to be the "clamor of endless wailings" arising from the infernal abyss. It signals the presence of one of the central themes in *Inferno*: pain as suffering and as punishment. As we have already observed, it is connected with fear and of course with Divine Justice, or the justness of God's retribution. The fear experienced by the wayfarer is akin to the fear of death he experienced in the dark wood. One reason for this fear is that death is incomprehensible, is perceived as *totally other* and implies an irreparable separation. This is what the wayfarer had refused to face in the Prologue scene, preferring to it the illusion of an easy, almost instantaneous return to the innocence of Eden.

This fear is then partially transformed by the pity the wayfarer sees "painted" on Virgil's face, and finally by Virgil's recollection of the coming into Limbo of Christ *Victor mortis*. This event, we have already noted, stands in sharp contrast to God's inflexible law of punishment inscribed above Hell's portal. It is an irreconcilable opposition from the temporal perspective, of course; from the perspective of God—Who is eternal and yet enters history, Who is both judge and victim, Who allows evil to exist and freely suffers evil—that opposition is resolved. The human economy is at once absorbed and transcended by God's economy. As we face this mystery, we catch a glimpse of the underlying tragic vision and its creative force. And if, with Dante as actor and dramatist, we have not found the answer to the question of evil and the terror and pity that it engenders, we have nevertheless learned to face a measure of the irreducibility of evil and fear, transcending them through suffering and pity. But within Dante's journey and the particular economy we are exploring, this is only a temporary victory, for we are soon thrust—as "in the journey of our life"—back into scenes that elicit fear and trembling.

Notes

1. A. Bartlett Giamatti, *The Earthly Paradise and the Renaissance Epic* (Princeton, NJ: Princeton University Press, 1966), p. 95.

2. Ibid., pp. 95–96.

3. Paul Ricoeur, "Herméneutique des symboles," p. 68.

4. *Paradiso* XX, 106–117: "For the one came back to his bones from Hell, where none ever returns to right will; and this was the reward of living hope, that gave power to the prayers made to God to raise him up, that it might be possible for his will to be moved. The glorious soul I tell of, having returned to the flesh for a short time, believed in Him that was able to help him; and, worthy to come to this rejoicing." *Paradiso* XX, 118–124: "The other [Ripheus], through the grace that wells from a fountain so deep that never did creature thrust eye down to its wave, set all his love below on righteousness; wherefore, from grace to grace, God opened his eye to our future redemption."

5. The most recent, and most convincing study in support of Virgil's possible salvation is Mowbray Allan's "Does Dante Hope for Virgil's Salvation?" *MLN*

(Jan. 1989): 193–205. I read this article after completing the present work. I am happy to note that Professor Allan and I have independently followed a similar line of argument—although his analysis is more extensive—and have reached the same conclusion.

6. On p. 129 of Robert Hollander's *Il Virgilio dantesco: Tragedia nella "Commedia"* (Florence: Olschki, 1983) we read ". . . Catone, il pagano attivo, raggiunge la fede nella sua mistica adesione alla libertà, mentre Virgilio, per Dante personalmente il massimo pagano contemplativo, manca di fede. Quel che è peggio, Traiano, che ha vissuto un'intera vita da pagano, è fatto rivivere ed è tirato fuori dal Limbo dalle preghiere di papa Gregorio; richiamato in vita, egli ora abbraccia il cristianesimo, come sicuramente avrebbe fatto Virgilio, ed è salvato. Anche Virgilio è riportato dal Limbo sulla terra, ma solo per effettuare un servigio per il quale non riceve nessuna ricompensa (tranne una visione dell'Eden quale vera età dell'oro), prima di essere rimandato in inferno per l'eternità." Then on pp. 153–154 we find the following interpretation of Beatrice's praise of Virgil, which coincides with mine except in its conclusion: "La fama di Virgilio passerà così oltre il mondo mortale nell'immortale secolo ed egli conseguirà una forma d'immortalità più vera di quella a cui egli stesso aveva aspirato. Le ultime parole di Beatrice non possono essere viste semplicemente come un'altra *captatio*. Poichè, o esse sono lusinghe—una supposizione impensabile in questo contesto—oppure devono essere accettate letteralmente. . . . Nel contesto della *Commedia*, la promessa di Beatrice circa una lode reiterata dinanzi al Signore deve essere accettata come autorevole e come il presagio di un fatto futuro. Essa ci rammenta l'immensa importanza di Virgilio nella vita e nell'opera di Dante, come pure il desiderio di Dante di onorare Virgilio a prescindere dalle sue manchevolezze. Anche se il poeta latino deve essere giudicato alla fin fine come un fallimento, si tratta pur sempre per Dante di un fallimento straordinariamente commovente. . . . Nell'universo poetico di Dante, il tragico protagonista all'interno della sua stessa commedia è al tempo stesso dannato e lodato fino al cielo." I find it quite puzzling that the critic, having accepted Beatrice's promise to praise Virgil before God as "autorevole" and as "il presagio di un fatto futuro," concludes that in the end, this praise has no other end than itself. Thus Virgil's "reward" for having contributed to the salvation of Dante (not to mention Statius and all the unknown others, including perhaps many readers of the *Aeneid* and/or the *Commedia*) is reduced to a fame that has passed from the mortal to the immortal century.

7. Kenelm Foster, O.P., *The Two Dantes and Other Studies* (Berkeley and Los Angeles: University of California Press, 1977). On p. 245 we read: "An ethic of the active life or of life in time no longer, of course, applies in Limbo; except in so far as the adults there are still 'honored' by the afterglow of the virtues they acquired on earth (*Inferno* IV, 67–68). But, surviving bodiless in this 'honor,' there is nothing left for them to *do*. One is tempted to say that the only 'life' left for them is that of the hopeless desire of which Virgil pathetically speaks (ibid., 42). Yet this desire itself must presuppose some knowledge, and appreciation, of God; *at least* as much as—according to *Convivio* III, xv, 6—is attainable by unaided reason on earth. And on this kind of God-knowledge would be based the 'piety' of Virgil and his companions. There is no hint, of course, of any rebellion on their part, since their arrival

in Limbo." We can further "tip the scale" in favor of Virgil (and his companions in Limbo) by stating that, indeed, Virgil *does* something, when, in response to God's command and grace, as manifested to him through Beatrice, he becomes Dante's first guide in his journey to the Celestial City. As the author himself notes, on p. 247, "the moral nobility of Virgil as a visible *persona* in the Poem is intact"; and "Virgil prepares Dante, his 'son,' for grace; as in a different way, he had prepared another 'son' of his, Statius, for grace." Finally, on p. 253, after the critic has pointed out that Dante allowed a "bare possibility" of the "contact between human nature [as embodied in Virgil and the other virtuous pagans] and divine grace," "for *all* adult human beings," he affirms that there remains an "important defect" in Dante: "an over-readiness to conceive of moral virtue in isolation from Charity." "Christianity," he concludes (with the obvious implication that Dante's Virgil is cut off from it), "requires that the moral virtues themselves be offered to God as a way— as *the* way—of cooperating with his grace." Surprisingly, the author fails to recognize that in the *Divine Comedy* Virgil, as the embodiment of the moral virtues, is indeed protrayed as the *way* of cooperating with divine grace, for he is ultimately *moved* (through Beatrice) by God and His grace to guide Dante from the "selva oscura" to the "selva antica" of the Earthly Paradise. How can we, then, reduce Virgil's role to what Fr. Foster calls (p. 247) a "transient contact with Christian things"? And again, how can we ignore the possibility of salvation foreshadowed by Beatrice's promise to Virgil to praise him before God?

8. Cf. Giamatti, p. 116: "All the landscapes of Hell and Purgatory are either defective or incomplete versions of the terrestrial paradise."

III. The Paradise of Paolo and Francesca and the Negation of the Tragic

The principal objective of this chapter is to show that the "first root" of Paolo's and Francesca's sin may be interpreted as the desire to create their own paradise, their own myth of a "second innocence." What decisively characterizes their love story as an illusory and ultimately destructive attempt to recapture the innocence of the garden is their negation of the tragic that informs the original myth of Eden. As we have noted previously, this is a negation of the irreducibility of evil, of evil as a condition or ground for the Fall, and of evil that, like the serpent in the garden, *is already there*. The lovers' nostalgia for a garden-without-the-serpent is thus an evasion from the conflict between good and evil and from the *history* of this conflict, which begins in the garden. And as Paolo and Francesca attempt to live outside this history, they suppress ethos and fear. As Renato Poggioli has demonstrated, they are governed only by pathos and pity and are therefore eminently romantic rather than tragic figures.[1] More important, by negating the tragic, Paolo and Francesca fail to experience the transfiguring, redeeming power of tragic vision.

Along with Dante the protagonist, we may attain tragic vision, but only if, as Irma Brandeis has observed, "we do not block our ears and eyes": "[Paolo and Francesca] are sorry for themselves. They are shut up in their sorrow, unable to escape it by turning their attention to those others whom they involved in blood and grief. . . . We on our part pity them through our human identification with their love-longing. But if we do not block our ears and eyes we shudder simultaneously, for we hear the inevitable storm headed our way. So the poem plunges us into the tragic emotion: pity and terror aroused together by a twin insight into a single situation."[2]

The new scene within which we now move with Dante the wayfarer— "into the trembling air . . . where there is naught that shines" (*Inf.* IV, 150–

151)—stands in opposition to the one that we have just left behind, the garden (and city) fashioned by the great men of antiquity, especially the poets. The shift is from the luminous space of human reason and wisdom to the dark space of a passion that has been allowed to obliterate reason and its light:

Io venni in loco d'ogne luce muto,
    che mugghia come fa mar per tempesta,
    se da contrari venti è combattuto.
La bufera infernal, che mai non resta,
    mena li spirti con la sua rapina;
    voltando e percotendo li molesta.
Quando giungon davanti a la ruina,
    quivi le strida, il compianto, il lamento;
    bestemmian quivi la virtù divina.

(*Inf.* V, 28–36)

I came into a place mute of all light, which bellows like the sea in tempest when it is assailed by warring winds. The hellish hurricane, never resting, sweeps along the spirits with its rapine; whirling and smiting, it torments them. When they arrive before the ruin, there the shrieks, the moans, the lamentations; there they curse the divine power.

Our first response to this scene is to ask, in the words of Charles Singleton, "Why is there a 'ruin' in this circle? And why should the lamentation of the damned souls be louder here as they pass before the ruin?"[3] And with the same critic we may remark that we must defer understanding until the moment when the poem will throw light on this passage, adding that "meanwhile a sense of mystery prevails."[4] Doubtless this sense of mystery is intended by the poet.

The economy of the present study forces us to do violence to Dante's intentions, however, by anachronistically turning to *Inferno* XII, where we find Virgil's explanation of the cause of the "ruina":

Ma certo poco pria, se ben discerno,
    che venisse colui che la gran preda
    levò a Dite del cerchio superno,
da tutte parti l'alta valle feda
    tremò sì, ch'i' pensai che l'universo

sentisse amor, per lo qual è chi creda
più volte il mondo in caòsso converso;
   e in quel punto questa vecchia roccia,
   qui e altrove, tal fece riverso.

(Inf. XII, 37–45)

But certainly, if I reckon rightly, it was a little before He came who took
from Dis the great spoil of the uppermost circle, that the deep foul valley
trembled so on all sides that I thought the universe felt love, whereby, as
some believe, the world has many times been turned to chaos; and at that
moment this ancient rock, here and elsewhere, made such downfall.

In the light of these words we can see more clearly what earlier we perhaps
perceived obscurely (if we recall that in Limbo Virgil had told Dante of
Christ's Harrowing of Hell): that as the damned souls of the lustful curse
the divine power, when they reach the "ruina" they curse the life-giving,
redemptive power of love they negated by remaining obdurate in their
inordinate passion—that love whose highest expression is Christ's death
on the cross. Significantly, Virgil's allusion to Empedocles' theory of love
as the force that returns the world to the primal chaos—when it joins the
elements of the universe in perfect harmony—underscores, by implicit
analogy, the apparently destructive and yet creative power of divine love
revealed by Christ's death. The "ruina" is in fact a breakdown of the rocky
structure of Hell and a "way" or "passage" which makes Dante's journey
possible, as we learn at the beginning of the canto (Inf. XII, 1–30). Here
we find another illuminating commentary on the curse of the "ruina" by
the lustful in the figure of the Minotaur—the offspring of the lustful Pa-
siphaë, "who bestialized herself in the beast-shaped planks" (Purg. XXVI,
87)—who, significantly, guards the "ruina" and thus, like the lustful, represents a force that opposes or negates love's "way."⁵ In the course of our
analysis of Inferno V, we shall understand more deeply the reason of the
lustful spirits' curse of the "ruina," and we shall see that, in the end, their
sin is indissolubly bound to their negation of the tragic.

   Let us now turn our attention to the following simile, the first of a series
of three that have in common the bird motif:

E come li stornei ne portan l'ali
   nel freddo tempo, a schiera larga e piena,
   così quel fiato li spiriti mali
di qua, di là, di giù, di sù li mena;

nulla speranza li conforta mai,
non che di posa, ma di minor pena.

(Inf. V, 40–45)

And as their wings bear the starlings along in the cold season, in wide,
dense flocks, so does that blast the sinful spirits; hither, thither, downward, upward, it drives them. No hope of less pain, not to say of rest,
ever comforts them.

The scene is still that of the "hellish hurricane." Yet it is now likened to an
autumn scene animated by the flight of starlings. Moreover, the violent
wind that hurls the sinners is represented as a breath, a "fiato." Thus there
is a subtle but significant shift of perspective, which calls attention to the
sinners' "flight." Equally significant is the change in the scene-agent ratio:
the emphasis is now placed on the agents—the starlings (or the spirits-as-
starlings)—so that the action is principally identified with them. Yet a certain passivity that at first defined the agents' state of being, as they were
pushed on by the hurricane, is still preserved to a certain degree. Renato
Poggioli has written a penetrating commentary on this passivity of the
souls and of the starlings:

> Since the sinners do not move on their own power, but are pushed and pulled by
> the wind, so likewise, the movement of the starlings is seen as caused not by their
> will, but by the automatic action of their wings, which are treated as organs differ-
> ent from and independent of the birds themselves. Yet this willful and arbitrary
> equivalence is deliberately misleading, since it distracts our attention from the dev-
> astating power of the hurricane, thus attenuating the impression of its irresistible
> force.[6]

But why should the poet deliberately mislead us? Or, put in another way,
what is the poet, or the poet as dramatist, creating here? What scene is he
constructing for us and for the wayfarer? Again, we can answer by simply
being attentive to the movement, the rhythm produced by the shift from
one scene to another. We are now invited, with the wayfarer, to witness a
transformation of the scene we have first encountered. The very break or
caesura that at once separates and links the two scenes provokes the following reflections.

The scene of the starlings *acts* upon us in such a way that we cannot
identify the lustful passion exclusively with the hurricane or the restless,
unbridled natural force it symbolizes. As we have hinted above, this would

reduce the sin of the spirits of the second circle to a total passivity with regard to the hurricane and therefore to their passion. But is there really such a total passivity? Is there not at the root of this an act of will that surrenders to this passivity and in a sense *seeks* it? In the crucial moment of decision, is there not a kind of active passivity before passion takes the form of an overpowering force that obliterates will and intellect? Is this act not present in the definition of these sinners' state that Virgil first offered to the wayfarer—that they are "the carnal sinners, who subject reason to desire"? (*Inf.* V, 38–39). What motivation triggers this act of allowing passion to overrun reason? In other words, how is reason led to its subjugation? Again, we are asking the most difficult question concerning the nature of evil (in the measure that Dante attributes it to the lustful of *Inferno* V) and, by extension, of the human condition—the ground shared by all sinners. There is, of course, no definitive answer. But there is, as the poet shows us, the direct experience of the sequence of scenes and actions, and hence the vision that a story or drama engenders.

In this drama we may witness the emerging of meaning, if only temporarily and partially—a meaning that is soon followed by its absence, vision being followed by blindness, indeed vision being the ground for such blindness, the latter becoming in turn the ground (and motivation) for vision, and so on, *ad infinitum* we might say. The meaning we seek is therefore bound to or dependent upon the dramatic form we are learning to find embedded in the text, and proportionately, in our very act of reading. And so we attempt to answer such questions with the only material that we have before us, which implies a kind of leap, a transference (and therefore a mimetic act by analogy) into the scene and perspective of the wayfarer. As we shall soon see more clearly, this is essentially what Dante the poet is producing on the page we have before us. Indeed there is at first a similarity between the scene of the sinners carried off by the hellish hurricane and the scene of the starlings carried by their wings in the "cold season." But the transition from a more destructive and—for the observer (the wayfarer and the reader)—more terrifying to a less destructive and less terrifying scene is possible, as we have seen on other occasions, because of the ambiguity that marks each of these scenes.

The spirits tossed and pushed on by the hurricane are in a certain sense "in flight." This flight asserts itself as such the moment we begin to isolate it from the force that is actually producing it. And as flight it can exercise over the observer a certain fascination. We may note that the tempest itself, again if seen in isolation (that is, if we do not think of its potential destructiveness), with its display of force, and power, elicits a kind of awe or fascination. This marks the awakening of a "passion" that places one outside the sphere of ethos, in other words, in the sphere of pathos, which, we could add, is attenuated by a kind of aesthetic detachment. But of course the scene of the tempest cannot be completely obliterated. Its presence still lingers, though it is gradually receding from the wayfarer's attention. The flight of the sinners, analogous to the flight of birds, is suddenly transformed not into one that is part of an entirely pleasing, attractive scene, but into the dark, "heavy" flight of starlings that "in wide, dense flocks" seem to fill the autumn sky. This transformation, with the fascination that accompanies it, is still bound to a negative scene, for if the image of the spirits' flight produced by the hurricane has been replaced by the less destructive and terrifying flight of the starlings, this is still not the pleasing, joyful scene of birds flying in spring—the natural, and in a literary sense, conventional season of love, in which, of course, starlings would be quite out of place.

Before we turn our attention to the second bird simile, we should add that the attenuation of the devastating force of the infernal storm also marks the emergence of pathos and pity and, correspondingly, of the clearer opposition and tensions between terror and pity and between ethos and pathos. We identify ethos with the sin and retribution represented by the hellish hurricane and therefore with the expression of God's justice (and of course with human justice, in the measure that it conforms to or interprets divine justice). With fear we identify the reaction of the wayfarer (and of the poet and reader) as he beholds both the power and the mystery of this manifestation of God's justice. And we should add that this fear is also the reaction to the power and mystery of the very passion that the hurricane also symbolizes. This is a God-given passion, we should not forget, just like all other passions with which He has endowed His creatures. For this very reason it exhibits a measure of the power and mystery of the Creator. But of course, as will become increasingly clear in the later scenes of Dante's dramatization of the nature and roots of the sin and punishment of the carnal lovers, it is not passion that is condemned in Hell's second circle but its adulteration, or the inordinate way in which the lustful have let it become an all-powerful, unbridled force that has blinded them to all other forces and other goods, by obfuscating the light of their intellect.

The attenuation of ethos and fear, which in the first bird simile is inversely proportional to the emphasis given to pathos and pity, is significantly intensified in the second simile:

E come i gru van cantando lor lai,
    faccendo in aere di sé lunga riga,
    così vid'io venir, traendo guai,
ombre portate da la detta briga . . . .

(Inf. V, 46–49)

And as the cranes go chanting their lays, making a long line of themselves in the air, so I saw shades come, uttering wails, borne by that strife . . . .

Here we may recall Renato Poggioli's keen observations:

Since Dante's sensitive attention is now attuned to the lamenting voices of the tormented, the detail standing out from this second simile concerns the singing of those birds, and the sadness of their song. Such is the suggestion contained in the words *lai*, "lays," which Dante uses both in the general sense of complaint, and in the more special and technical meaning, designating a particular kind of medieval poetry, which in Provençal verse takes the form of the lyrical and melancholic re-evocation of an adventure of love. This all too significant allusion is but the first among the frequent literary references of the Canto: and like almost all of them it reiterates the underlying pathos of the story. So the poet checks again the natural tendency of both the simile and the literary reference to idealize the situation: and achieves such a controlling effect by introducing a qualifying parallel between the singing of the cranes and the lamenting of the sinners, by degrading the "lays" of the former to the level of the latter's *guai* or "wails." Despite the shift to a lower key, even in this case the comparison obtains an absolute equivalence between the referential tenor and the emblematic vehicle.[7]

While essentially agreeing with these remarks, I would like to offer a reading that to an important degree departs from them. Whereas Poggioli sees a "parallel" and an "absolute equivalence" between tenor and vehicle, between the "guai" of the sinners and the "lai" of the cranes, I instead see a correspondence that is symmetrical only at first glance, and that upon closer scrutiny proves to be asymmetrical, with greater emphasis placed on the "emblematic vehicle," and therefore on its literary dimension, as well as on the intrinsic nature of the cranes' "lai," which, as Poggioli has aptly observed, stress the "underlying pathos of the story." More specifically, I detect an imbalance in favor of pathos and pity. Another significant shift in the direction of pathos and pity may be discerned in the transformation of "spiriti mali" ("sinful spirits"; V, 42) into "ombre" ("shades"; V, 49), which is similar to the transformation of the "bufera infernal" ("infernal hurricane") into a "fiato" ("breath").

There is no doubt that the poet is consciously constructing these scenes, with the shifts and breaks that characterize their succession, as an interpretation of the wayfarer's gradual fascination with and attraction to the inordinate passion of lust. And if there is still the presence of ethos and fear, it is slowly diminishing as that fascination and that attraction prevail. We should also note that in the second simile the emphasis is given to the active, autonomous force of the cranes' flight—clearly expressed by their "making a long line of themselves in the air"—in contrast with the obviously passive "flight" of the sinners who are "borne by the strife." Both the natural and the literary dimensions of the cranes' flight and melancholy song, which the wayfarer "reads" into the state of the sinful spirits, reveal a significant departure from the ethos and fear of the contemplation of lust's mysterious power and, correspondingly, of God's justice. They are an affirmation of the pathos and pity inherent in the sinners' misdirected love. Of course, as we have already remarked with Poggioli, there is a certain balance between tenor and vehicle, between object and trope, so that the object also appears attenuated. But in a subtle way this reveals the power of transformation that pathos and pity exercise over ethos and fear inherent in the sinners' state.

Dante gives further expression to this process of transformation of fear into pity and of ethos into pathos, experienced by the wayfarer, through Virgil's identification of those "whom love had parted from life," from Semiramis to Cleopatra, from Paris to Tristan (V, 52–69). The poet sharply contrasts Virgil's identification of the "more than a thousand shades" of the lustful (V, 67–68) with the wayfarer's reception of his guide's words. Again, the distinction is sharply defined in terms of the opposition of ethos and pathos, fear and pity. Almost with each figure named by Virgil, lust is defined not merely intrinsically but, with evident emphasis, in relation to the world of ethos, namely, the *civitas* and its laws. Beginning with Semiramis, of whom Virgil says that "she was so given to lechery that she made lust licit in her law, to take away the blame she had incurred" (V, 55–57), lust, like any other sin—though to a different degree of course—is seen by Dante not in isolation, but as a sin that severs one's relation to the community, a severance that also corresponds to a separation from the true self and from God. The destructiveness brought upon the city by this sin, which more than any other the conventional wisdom holds to be confined to the individual sphere, is brought into sharper focus in Virgil's identification of Helen of Troy:

"Elena vedi, per cui tanto reo
   tempo si volse. . . ."

(*Inf.* V, 64–65)

"See Helen, for whom so many years of ill revolved. . . ."

And when Virgil finishes pointing out and naming the carnal lovers, the wayfarer's reaction is exclusively one of pity, which almost overwhelms him:

Poscia ch'io ebbi 'l mio dottore udito
   nomar le donne antiche e ' cavalieri,
   pietà mi giunse, e fui quasi smarrito.

(*Inf.* V, 70–72)

When I heard my teacher name the ladies and knights of old, pity over-came me and I was as one bewildered.

   The transition from Virgil's perspective of ethos to the wayfarer's per-spective of pathos is underscored by the shift from the verb "vedi" ("see") uttered twice by Virgil ("Elena vedi . . . vedi Paris, Tristano"; V, 64, 67) to "udito nomar" ("heard name"). The opposition is evident. As Virgil invites his disciple to see directly, pointing to and naming the objective reality of the sinners' state, the latter's attention is directed not so much to that re-ality but to the words with which his guide evokes it. It is these words that constitute the ground, the precondition of the pity that overcomes the wayfarer. Dante does not say, "When I *saw* those sinners I was overcome by pity." These words would have revealed an awareness of the world of ethos which we have identified earlier. Meaning, once again, emerges dra-matistically, by the contiguity and opposition of the different modes of seeing and representing reality. Dante the wayfarer breaks the correspon-dence or proportion between events and words constituting Virgil's per-spective, and gives himself to the allure, the fascination of words alone. The "sinful spirits" of Hell's second circle are now transformed into "the ladies and knights of old." As we read these words, we recognize the formula with which Dante the poet defines at once the wayfarer's view-point—as we have remarked, the fascination that the very *names* of those lovers of old exercise over him—and the poet's own, at least "suggested" viewpoint. The poet, in fact, does not distance himself from the perspective of the world he is representing, as we have seen him do earlier, and as we shall see him continue to do later on in the episode of *Inferno* V. Here, for a moment at least, we have the impression that even he has transformed the sinners into the "ladies and knights of old." And of course this view which now he seems to share with the wayfarer, by the force of its presence and closeness to us his readers, induces us to accept this further transformation of the sinners into the "ladies and knights of old."

As we pronounce these words, and as they resonate within us, we find ourselves transformed from detached spectators, whose perspective was governed by ethos (or by ethos and pathos), to active spectators whose perspective is—at least temporarily—exclusively that of pathos, of pity. This pity is closely dependent on the new perception of the shades: as soon as they are seen as "ladies and knights," as worthy, noble people, their present suffering can only be seen as disproportionate, even unjust, and therefore pitiable. Significantly, the poet obliterates those distinctions between ethos and pathos, fear and pity, with which he had so carefully constructed the scene of the wayfarer's entrance into the world of the lustful, by abolishing the distinction between words and events, indeed by giving to words the power to transform events. It is words and their power to create illusion that now seem to overtake the reality of the "bufera infernal" and its effect. Perhaps it is not fortuitous that the wayfarer calls Virgil "poeta" ("poet") and not "maestro" or "dottore" ("master," "teacher") when he expresses his wish to speak to the two shades who have attracted his attention:

> I' cominciai: "Poeta, volontieri
>   parlerei a que' due che 'nsieme vanno,
>   e paion sì al vento esser leggieri."

> *(Inf.* V, 73–75)

"Poet," I began, "willingly would I speak with those two that go together and seem to be so light upon the wind."

It should strike us as especially significant that, as he expresses his desire to speak to the two lovers, the wayfarer sees them "so light upon the wind," in marked contrast, therefore, to the first perception he had had of the "sinful spirits" smitten by the "hellish hurricane." Charles Singleton's commentary of this line reads: "This suggests that these two spirits are more violently tossed by the wind than the others are. According to the principle of just punishment, the heightened violence of the wind signifies that the love, which led them in life and leads them now, was, and is, most passionate."⁸ This reading is correct only within the field of vision of the allegorist. As it correlates the power of the wind with the exceptional violence of Paolo's and Francesca's passion, it fails to capture an important facet of that passion, namely the illusory sense of lightness—the lightness of *flight*. This is an essential component of their inordinate love, one that Dante the dramatist does not want us to ignore as he develops a scene in which the wayfarer's response helps reveal the ambiguities of a love that destroys. If the wayfarer (and the reader) saw only the wind as passion—as the allegorist in us and among us is inclined to see—he would have the clear, detached view of the moralist and judge, which is only one facet of Dante's representation. And if he did not feel the lightness of flight inherent in lust, if he were not *seduced* by it, he would never experience the illusions and ambiguities brought about by the adulteration of love. He would never truly *know* this love.

Here we may ask: is it the lightness of the two shades—as well as the fact that they are the only pair of lovers among all those named who are seen together—that moves the wayfarer to speak to them, or is it his desire to speak, and hence his fascination with words and their power to transform what he sees into an attractive fiction that "causes" him to see the two lovers "so light upon the wind"? The rationalist in us, or among us, will not rest until he identifies the "authentic" cause, and therefore the correct "sequence," the linear logic of cause and effect. The dramatist in us, however, whom Dante is here inviting us to become, sees the two as contiguous and dialectically related. The wayfarer's desire to speak is connected mimetically to the words just uttered by Virgil—words with which he has identified the "ladies and knights of old."

The tercet we have just reproduced must also be read in connection with what follows, where the poet creates a further attenuation of ethos in favor of pathos and of fear in favor of pity. To the wayfarer's request to speak to the two lovers who are coming near, Virgil responds:

> . . . "Vedrai quando saranno
> più presso a noi; e tu allor li priega
> per quello amor che i mena, ed ei verranno."
>
> (*Inf.* V, 76–78)

. . . "You shall see when they are nearer to us; and do you entreat them then by that love which leads them, and they will come."

What does Virgil mean by "love"? Does he identify it with the "hellish hurricane" and therefore with the power that, analogous to the unbridled, inordinate passion of the lustful, now torments them, and is at once an expression of their sin and their punishment, a punishment willed by God? In other words, does he relate it to the sphere of ethos and fear or to the sphere of pathos and pity, thus adhering to the idea of love that the lustful have fashioned? And since this word is addressed to Dante the wayfarer, should we not say that for him it contains both these meanings? But why the ambiguity? What is its function in terms of the main action of the way-farer's journey, of his drama of acquiring knowledge through experience? How does this ambiguity inherent in the word "love" pronounced by Virgil constitute the creative ground for the successive scenes in which we see the wayfarer move?

Once again, our answers will take shape as we read dramatistically and follow the tragic rhythm created by the very sequence of scenes and actions we see before us, and as we detect the essentially mimetic transformation that accompanies this rhythm. The wayfarer's response to his guide's words elicits such a reading:

> Sì tosto come il vento a noi li piega,
>   mossi la voce: "O anime affannate,
>   venite a noi parlar, s'altri nol niega!"
>
> (*Inf.* V, 79–81)

As soon as the wind bends them to us, I raised my voice, "O wearied souls come speak with us, if Another forbid it not."

The wayfarer interprets and enacts Virgil's suggestion to entreat the two lovers in the name of love by implicitly equating love with "affanno" ("suf-fering"), and hence with passion, and by expressing pity for this suffering. Significantly, the wayfarer qualifies his request with the words "if Another forbid it not," therefore, revealing—if only momentarily—his awareness of an absolute horizon—the presence and power of God and His justice. Once again, pathos and pity are defined only temporarily in isolation, and in opposition to ethos and fear. This opposition suggests that, as now for the living wayfarer so for those like Paolo and Francesca in Hell, the rejec-tion of true love is always carried out in the presence of the Creator, and that ultimately evil "rests on a relation, is the subversion of a relation."[9] Thus in this scene the contiguity and opposition of ethos and pathos creates a dramatic tension and a tragic rhythm whereby the wayfarer experiences alternately pathos and pity and ethos and fear without being able to reconcile them. This is especially evident in the moment when his adherence to the world (and the world view) of Paolo and Francesca—and therefore to their language and code—reaches one of the highest degrees of intensity in the entire episode, in the crucial moment when the two lovers, moved by the wayfarer's voice, draw near:

> Quali colombe dal disio chiamate
>   con l'ali alzate e ferme al dolce nido
>   vegnon per l'aere, dal voler portate;
> cotali uscir de la schiera ov'è Dido,
>   a noi venendo per l'aere maligno,
>   sì forte fu l'affettüoso grido.

(*Inf.* V, 82–87)

As doves called by desire, with wings raised and steady, come through the air, borne by their will to their sweet nest, so did these issue from the troop where Dido is, coming to us through the malignant air, such force had my compassionate cry.

In the scenes created by these words the wayfarer plays the role of prime mover. This is a role that he has been gradually fashioning and performing in the preceding scenes. The most recent of these is the one in which he sees the two lovers as figures "who seem so light upon the wind." To see them a moment later as doves that glide toward their nest seems to grow quite naturally from his previous vision, just as this in turn "developed" from the images of the flight of starlings and cranes—all, of course, as we have observed, stemming from the first scene in which the lustful souls appear and by which they are defined: that of the "hellish hurricane." But how far we are now from the terrifying scene of the hurricane and the gloomy scenes of the starlings and cranes in flight! True, the poet does speak of the "malignant air," thus injecting a measure of ethos in what otherwise would be a scene governed only by pathos. But the emphasis seems to fall mostly on the delicate image of the doves.

In contrast to the scenes evoked earlier in the episode by the similes of the starlings and cranes, this scene is animated by a pair of doves, birds traditionally identified with love and peace, although they are at times also associated with lechery.[10] The season, we can surmise, is not, as before, that of the "freddo tempo" ("cold season") of late fall, but its opposite, spring, the season of love. As the reference to the nest clearly suggests, this love is a positive, creative force. Significantly, the doves are not seen as being only drawn to one another, or as lovers carried by unbridled passion (a "tempest"), but as drawn by desire which is activated by its object, the "sweet nest," which obviously represents the fruitfulness of love. An important feature emerges as we compare this image with the other two bird similes: if at first glance the doves seem to exhibit the same passivity noted earlier in the flight of the starlings "borne by their wings," on closer examination we see that instead they are called "by desire" and are "borne by their will," that is, the force that moves them involves an interaction and an equilibrium between subject and object. In fact, as we have seen, the desire kindled by the nest is met with an equal and opposite response of the will.[11] We might also say that passion and will are in harmony. The mechanism of desire, which reflects natural necessity—the instinct to love and to build a nest for the offspring—, is counterbalanced by the act of will that responds to that desire. We should add that, as a scene of natural innocence and bliss, this also speaks of the garden and hence of the paradisal state. As Glauco Cambon has noted, "the doves are the birds of love, and here they introduce a ray of Paradise, but only as a foil to the lovers' distress; there will be no sweet nest for the latter!"[12]

In the other half of the dove simile—the tenor, which speaks of the present experience of Dante the wayfarer—there is a shift in perspective. The very direction of the main movement is now reversed: if the doves are said to be gliding towards their "sweet nest," the two shades are seen to emerge from "the troop where Dido is"—a notation that, however briefly, brings into view the world of sin and punishment. Even more striking is the image of "l' aere maligno" ("the malignant air") which contrasts sharply with what we can easily construe as spring air through which we have just seen glide the two doves. Another important shift is produced by the poet's interpretation of the wayfarer's words addressed to the two spirits as an "affettüoso grido" ("compassionate cry" or, as Mandelbaum more accurately translates, "loving cry"),[13] whose very intensity ("sì forte") makes the two spirits draw near the wayfarer and his guide. This seems to correspond to the force of the nest that, in the vehicle of the simile "calls" the doves to itself. Doubtless this constitutes a significant transformation and disjunction that bring to light the emphasis given to pathos and pity and the abandonment of ethos and fear. We thus witness a departure from the balanced twin perspectives of pathos and ethos, of pity and fear that, as we have noted, were clearly present in the wayfarer's words—respectively in "O anime affannate" and in "s'altri nol niega!" In other words, here Dante represents a reduction to pathos and pity of what is essentially a conflictual condition, one in which human passion and pity are set against the fear associated with God and His judgment.

What is the meaning of these transformations, these disjunctions, and what scenes, with their respective actions and motivations, do they help create? What movement of the wayfarer's soul is expressed through them? In the light of what we have so far observed, we can attempt the following somewhat schematic reading. Departing from Virgil's counsel, to "entreat them . . . by that love which leads them," Dante the wayfarer calls the two spirits not in the name of love, by appealing to a force or an authority that lies outside and above the two lovers. He instead calls them with words that appeal to their self-pity, by addressing them as "wearied souls," while, as we have observed, he qualifies those words with the phrase "if Another forbid it not." This pity then acquires greater relief with the poet's further definition of the wayfarer's apostrophe as a cry, which was uttered with such intensity, such passion, that it alone—overshadowing words, and the world of both pathos and ethos, and pity and fear—stood out as the sole force that drew the two spirits near, that *moved* them. As it has been recently observed, "The pilgrim's compassion Dante stages reflects the passion Francesca narrates. It is framed compassion. The *compassio* of the pilgrim is not the 'spiritual disposition' *misericordia*, but a (false) passion. . . . The pilgrim's compassionate cry, that calls the couple by the 'love which leads them,' corresponds to their passion."[14]

But how were the pilgrim's words transformed and reduced, if not through what we can only call the wayfarer's "performance"? Indeed, as Renato Poggioli notes, they may have been "accompanied by an unmistakeable beckoning gesture."[15] This transformation has also been "produced"—in cooperation we might say, with the two spirits who have interpreted the wayfarer's apostrophe mainly as a cry—as an expression of pathos and pity. In other words, this transformation, and therefore the movement and action that it engenders, takes place and asserts itself as meaningful not in a discursive manner, that is, following a continuous line of causality, but essentially through the dramatic structure of action and reaction, of assertion and counter-assertion. Virgil's words "You entreat them then by that love which leads them, and they will come" provoke the wayfarer's mimetic response. This, by the way, is also coupled with a similar response to the figures of the approaching lovers—figures already "constructed," "derived" through the previous associations with starlings and cranes in flight, that is, through other interpretations grounded in mimesis.

Before we continue with the summation of our reading of the scenes conjured up by the dove simile, we must pause a moment to comment on the validity or creativity of the "logic" inherent in the sequence of actions and scenes we have just enumerated. As we note that the wayfarer departs from his teacher's counsel, we cannot fail to see that this very departure reveals a mimetic power that enables him to reach beneath Virgil's words (to speak in the name of love) and to interpret them in such a way that by essentially expressing with a cry the identity of love with passion and pity, he achieves the desired effect of attracting the two spirits. Paradoxically, by not doing exactly as Virgil enjoins him to do, he does what Virgil, at a deeper level we might say, indeed wants him to do, namely to speak the only language that the two lovers know and to which they necessarily will be drawn—the language of pathos and pity. And now we may add—returning to the simile of the doves—that by virtue of this same "logic" the wayfarer interprets and transforms the coming of Paolo and Francesca into the loving, blissful, and innocent scene of the pair of doves which, in spring, glide toward their "sweet nest." Our analysis must take into account the fact that as we speak of one scene, its action, and so on, we are actually speaking of essentially two scenes and actions which coexist in creative opposition to one another. These are respectively inscribed in the tenor and the vehicle of the doves simile.

Turning our attention to the "scene" of the tenor, we wonder how it can be seen or interpreted by the wayfarer as similar to that of a pair of doves approaching their nest, and furthermore, how the "malignant air" through which the two lovers move, earlier implicitly likened to the air of the "cold season," can be associated with the (implied) spring air through which the two doves glide. We may find an answer the moment we recognize, as we have done earlier in this study, the motivational force of the scene of the two lovers that calls forth the scene of the doves, or in other words, how it constitutes the "ground" for the other scene.

The very fact that it is an infernal scene, whose character bears some proportion with the nature of both the sin and the punishment of the two lovers, calls into being its opposite, a paradisal scene, or its equivalent. It is too simplistic to say that the pilgrim idealizes the two lovers and their love, seeing them increasingly as attractive, sympathetic figures. It is more accurate to speak of a mimetic response to them and to their setting or scene, whereby he gradually moves into their world, analogously experiencing what they have experienced and now continue to experience: a love whose power and whose form proved and now proves to be a false, destructive imitation of the recovery of the paradisal, edenic state and, correspondingly, an adulteration of *caritas*. In other words, in Paolo's and Francesca's inordinate love there is an ambivalence which makes it appear as true love, directed to the ultimate good. As we have remarked earlier, the very force of their love, which the poet has first represented as a hurricane, simultaneously produces and "imitates" flight. This is at first experienced by the wayfarer and represented by the poet as something as terrifying and dark as the hellish hurricane or the flight of the flock of starlings in the "cold season," but also as pleasing and alluring as the gliding of the doves (which, as noted previously, also contains the secret suggestion of its opposite, the dark side of love). If the terrifying, dark flight of the two lovers were not also perceived and experienced as the light, blissful gliding of two doves, how could he (and the reader) come to know the nature of the lovers' sin and punishment and therefore their deepest motivation? As we are beginning to understand, did they not long to recapture, in their own fashion, the edenic state of innocence and bliss? Since they obviously failed, was it not because there was some fundamental disproportion between what we may call their "myth of Eden," and the authentic myth of Eden? And is this not the disproportion that Dante as dramatist represents through the simile of the doves, so that the infernal scene lives side by side with the paradisal scene in irreconcilable opposition?

The story of Paolo and Francesca contains both a confirmation and an expansion of what we have now glimpsed:

"O animal grazïoso e benigno
   che visitando vai per l'aere perso
   noi che tignemmo il mondo di sanguigno,
se fosse amico il re de l'universo,
   noi pregheremmo lui de la tua pace,
   poi c'hai pietà del nostro mal perverso.
Di quel che udire e che parlar vi piace,
   noi udiremo e parleremo a voi,
   mentre che 'l vento, come fa, ci tace."

(*Inf.* V, 88–96)

"O living creature, gracious and benign, that go through the black air visiting us who stained the world with blood, if the King of the universe were friendly to us, we would pray Him for your peace, since you have pity on our perverse ill. Of that which it pleases you to hear and to speak, we will hear and speak with you, while the wind, as now, is silent for us."

Francesca constructs a world that is at once innocent and sinful, benevolent and harsh, light and somber, and one which is essentially animated by sentiment, by pathos and pity, so much so that it annuls ethos and fear, or it transforms them into pathos and pity. As we pause a moment, turning our attention to Francesca's first words, "O animal grazïoso e benigno," we see with her not Dante the wayfarer, and therefore, we could add, a sinner among sinners, but an innocent, primordial man, who is endowed with graciousness (and grace?) and benevolence, or goodness, by virtue of being a "living creature," one who shares the status of all other creatures. And here we must note what we have already perceived in a flash: the striking similarity between this characterization of the wayfarer and his earlier association of Paolo and Francesca with the two doves, "living creatures" who could equally be characterized as "gracious" and "benign." In other words, both Dante the wayfarer and Francesca see each other in a state of innocence that harks back to and in a sense re-enacts the edenic state. This paradisal innocence is evoked, or nostalgically relived in an infernal scene. As Roger Dragonetti has aptly stated, "In the moral and religious perspective of the *Divine Comedy*, evil, in its roots, goes back to the origin of creation, such as the story of *Genesis* relates it to us."[16]

But is the paradisal state that Francesca momentarily sees represented in the wayfarer a correct, authentic "recovery" or interpretation of the story of Eden, or more precisely of the original myth of Eden? At first glance we are inclined to answer affirmatively. As we look closely and more deeply into the text, however, we discover subtle yet significant divergences that reveal a distortion, an adulteration of the myth which is deeply related to the lovers' sin and damnation. We begin to understand that the paradisal scene, the garden Francesca is fashioning here, is essentially illusory and false, for the power that gives impetus to this "creation" is exclusively pathos or sentiment, while ethos, as we shall soon observe, is present only as a semblance or shadow. This is evident—as we have already noted in passing—in her reduction of the wayfarer's figure to that of a mere "living creature," a reduction that does not speak of fallen man, nor does it recognize him as a person, with his individual drama of sin and salvation—

his journey to God. Significantly, she interprets the journey as a "visit" to herself and Paolo alone. By calling the infernal air "aere perso" ("black air"), she appeals more to the senses and pathos than to ethos; the poet had represented the latter in the wayfarer's scene (in which both perspectives of pathos and ethos were expressed) by calling the air malignant. And when she uses the metaphor of the world stained with blood to refer to Paolo's and her death, the power of pathos (self-pity) reaches such an intensity that it momentarily obliterates any preoccupation with life's moral and spiritual dimensions. Hence it destroys any semblance of the tragic vision that this metaphor may have at first suggested, because the terror and fear accompanying ethos have been overrun by the pity, or the self-pity to which pathos, once it becomes dissociated from ethos, is necessarily reduced. Commenting on Francesca's extravagant metaphor Renato Poggioli writes:

The metaphor of the world painted red by human blood appears also in Shakespeare's Macbeth. There the image always fulfills a tragic function, since it recurs in the protagonist's mind as the most obsessive detail of the murder he once committed, which he continuously rehearses in his memory, and relives in his remorse. But in Dante the same image produces a pathetic effect: the blood of which Francesca says that it stained, not only the sea, but the whole world, was shed by no others than Paolo and herself. . . . In Aristotelian terms, one could say that in the Shakespeare version of the same trope terror overwhelms pity, while in Dante's variant the self-pity of the heroine and the poet's compassion triumph over terror itself.[17]

To these penetrating remarks I must add the elucidation of an important detail. When the critic mentions the "poet's compassion" he is referring to the poet as protagonist, who temporarily shares Francesca's perspective, and not to Dante as author and narrator of the *Commedia*, who, in the words of the same critic, "is a moral realist, always subordinating pathos to ethos."[18]

There is a tenuous yet significant representation of ethos in Francesca's words "se fosse amico il re de l'universo." This paraphrastic reference to God injects in a scene dominated by pathos a measure of the moral and spiritual dimension characterizing ethos. She seems to be aware of being separated from God, yet she expresses this in such a way that the accent does not fall on the real cause of this separation—her sin and God's just punishment, and therefore on ethos. "By describing God as the supreme sovereign," Poggioli notes, "she reveals . . . her aristocratic bent, her feudal frame of mind. By the very clause *se fosse amico*, 'if He were our friend,'

Francesca indicates that she conceives of God's blessing or God's curse in terms of courtly grace or disgrace, as honors or privileges which a crowned head may bestow on his subjects, or withdraw from them."[19] Another tenuous presence of ethos is of course manifested in Francesca's unfulfilled wish to pray for the wayfarer's peace. For a moment we see her abandon the narrow circle of self-absorption, of self-pity, turning this into compassion as her attention centers on the other. Yet she is still primarily moved by sentiment, by pathos and its many nuances. And when she expresses her willingness (also in the name of Paolo) to hear and speak according to Dante's (and perhaps Virgil's) wish, this also soon proves to be only a momentary sign of benevolence, only a fragile presence of the perspective of ethos, for, without waiting for a response from either the wayfarer or Virgil, she begins to speak:

> "Siede la terra dove nata fui
>   su la marina dove 'l Po discende
>   per aver pace co' seguaci sui.
> Amor, ch'al cor gentil ratto s'apprende,
>   prese costui de la bella persona
>   che mi fu tolta; e 'l modo ancor m'offende.
> Amor, ch'a nullo amato amar perdona,
>   mi prese del costui piacer sì forte,
>   che, come vedi, ancor non m'abbandona.
> Amor condusse noi ad una morte."
>
> (*Inf.* V, 97–106)

"The city where I was born lies on that shore where the Po descends to be at peace with its followers. Love, which is quickly kindled in a gentle heart, seized this one for the fair form that was taken from me—and the way of it afflicts me still. Love, which absolves no loved one from loving, seized me so strongly with delight in him, that, as you see, it does not leave me even now. Love brought us to one death."

The peaceful landscape of Francesca's birthplace stands in sharp contrast to the story of her turbulent, destructive love that immediately (and abruptly) follows. This dramatic opposition calls to mind similar oppositions we have encountered in *Inferno* V, the most recent being the one between the pair of doves gliding toward their "sweet nest" and the two lovers coming towards Virgil and Dante through Hell's "malignant air."

More important, perhaps, is the reaffirmation of the opposition between what we have already identified as a paradisal scene of innocence and bliss and an infernal scene of lost innocence and death. Roger Dragonetti, studying the Paolo and Francesca episode in a critical perspective entirely different from mine, proposes a similar interpretation when he writes: "The three tercets [beginning with the word "Amor"] stand out against the background of remembrance of the native land which is the very image of the lost paradise."[20]

What kind of "Eden" does Francesca construct here, as she evokes the landscape, the setting of her birthplace, and how does she "lose" this Eden? In other words, what correlation is there between the myth of Eden and her sin and consequent state of damnation? In a sense, this is the question that, in dramatic form, Dante the wayfarer asked as he moved through the scenes we have just studied, when he saw the "hellish hurricane" of the lustful and thought of the flight of birds in the "cold season," and when Paolo and Francesca drew near through Hell's "malignant air," he saw them as a pair of doves gliding toward their nest, unable to dissociate an infernal from a paradisal scene. In the same sense, the scenes and actions which we are now beginning to examine, as we hear Francesca's words, constitute an "answer" to that question.

The specific nature of the paradisal scene fashioned by Francesca is first expressed by the generic terms with which she characterizes her city, as she depicts its natural setting or landscape. Clearly, the emphasis falls on the natural forces and on the principle of order that governs them, organizing them in such a way that as they interact they move together towards their final goal, the sea. The image of the Po that "descends to be at peace with its followers," calls to mind this passage from St. Augustine's *Confessions* (XIII. 9, 10):

In thy gift we rest; then we enjoy thee. Our rest is thy gift, our life's place. Love lifts us up thither, and thy good spirit advances our lowliness from the gates of death. In thy good pleasure lies our peace. Our body with its lumpishness strives towards its own place. Weight makes not downward only, but to its own place also. The fire mounts upward, a stone sinks downward. All things pressed by their own weight go towards their proper places. . . . They are driven by their own weights to seek their own places. Things a little out of their places become unquiet; put them in their order again, and they are quieted. My weight is my love: by that am I carried whithersoever I be carried."[21]

Francesca's landscape embodies the ordering of love toward its proper end. This is the natural love by which all "living creatures" are moved. And does the sea not symbolize God, toward Whom mankind journeys, being restless until resting in Him? Moreover, as the image of the Po joining its tributaries in the sea suggests, to rest in Him necessarily implies a communion with others, for the very nature of Divine Love is to gather all loves in its infinity.

With the irruption of the word "Amor," this landscape and the paradisal scene that it conjures up prove to be very fragile, just a fleeting recollection of a lost order and harmony. Significantly, this landscape speaks not only of innocence and peace, but also of a journey, and therefore, though implicitly, of struggle, conflict, and drama. This is what Paolo and Francesca have negated, and, correspondingly, in their apparent imitation of it have falsified the original myth of the Earthly Paradise. The latter in its integrity and the fullness of mystery, cannot be identified exclusively with the innocence and bliss preceding the Fall, but must also be identified with the Fall, and finally with redemption through time and history.

As we witness the sudden shift from a scene that tells of a drama and a mode of being in the world that through suffering finds peace to a scene that tells of a drama and of suffering that ends in misery and death, we want to understand how Paolo and Francesca could have rejected one for the other. Our text does not provide an explicit answer. It merely juxtaposes two scenes. At first glance we notice only the opposition between them. Yet if we look closely we discover significant similarities that suggest that one has been transformed into the other. The love of which Francesca speaks is a force not unlike the one that moves the Po—towards its "death" we might say. This death, however, unlike that of Paolo and Francesca, coincides with peace—the peace of communion with others and with God. Paolo's and Francesca's love, whose power is analogous to that of the Po's love, is directed away from the community and God. True love, Dante suggests here, is *social*. This idea will be given full expression in the heaven of Venus (*Par.* VIII–IX), where Dante meets first Charles Martel, the good friend and good prince, and then Cunizza, the passionate woman who has been conquered by the light of Venus and whose main concern, in contrast with Francesca, is the corrupt state of her land and Italy, and therefore with man's tragic condition. Here the predomindant note is the love of *civitas*, and the confluence of *eros* and *caritas*, pathos and ethos.[22]

The lovers' natural longing to be, like the Po, united with others within that which transcends them, cannot be fulfilled as long as it is directed to an inappropriate object, a false image of good. Their torment and their hell is in the disproportion between the naturally expansive love that can find peace only in Infinite Love—as love of the Infinite—and their search for the Infinite or Eternal in a fleeting image, like that of Francesca's "bella persona," or as we shall soon see, in the fictional paradise of a "moment" appropriated from the world of literature.

Meanwhile, the crucial question still remains: how did Paolo and Francesca turn away from an ordinate to an inordinate love, or as we said earlier, from the life that Francesca's landscape evokes, to the death of which her "love story" speaks? Of course once again we are confronting the fundamental problem of the nature of sin, and therefore of the reality of evil. How does it come into being? What is the crucial point at which one moves from a virtuous to a sinful life? These are essentially the questions that Dante as dramatist formulates in the contrasting scenes we have just analyzed. As we ask these questions, another immediately forces itself upon us: can we ever define that *point*, that instant in which, or through which, there is a sudden shift of perspective, an abandonment of the orientation of one's being towards the good that by necessity it desires? This is the necessity that drives the soul to seek its good and, in absolute terms, God, just as it drives the Po to seek the natural peace in communion with its tributaries and the sea.

The wayfarer ponders the same questions, and seeks the answers that we are seeking:

> Quand'io intesi quell'anime offense,
>   china' il viso, e tanto il tenni basso,
>   fin che 'l poeta mi disse: "Che pense?"
> Quando rispuosi, cominciai: "Oh lasso,
>   quanti dolci pensier, quanto disio
>   menò costoro al doloroso passo!"
>
> (*Inf.* V, 109–114)

And when I heard those afflicted souls I bowed my head and held it bowed until the poet said to me, "What are you thinking of?" When I answered, I began, "Alas! How many sweet thoughts, what great desire, brought them to the woeful pass!"

The words "afflicted souls" echo Francesca's "e 'l modo ancor m'offende" ("and the way of it afflicts me still"). By adopting her language and her perspective, and by imitating them, he creates a space which is shared not only by the wayfarer and Francesca, but also by the reader. At least momentarily, we are invited to see Paolo and Francesca as souls who have been wronged, and therefore as victims of a power that is external and ineluctable, much like, as we have already observed, the power of the hellish hurricane that smites them without rest. Like the wayfarer, we react with compassion and pity to the lovers' affliction. We see them as tragic figures, especially if we think that this affliction marks not only the suffering brought upon Francesca's "fair form" by Gianciotto's murderous hand, but also the suffering that divine punishment inflicts on her and Paolo.

Once again, it is the world of pathos and pity, which at least temporarily seems to obliterate that of ethos and fear. But is there another way to "know" Paolo's and Francesca's state and the nature of their sin? Simply to discourse upon it in the light of ethos and fear would amount to condemning it without true understanding. Only a leap of the soul into the world of the two lovers, and therefore an act of sympathy and imitation, can come close to this understanding.

This movement of the soul is expressed by the wayfarer's inward gaze as he, with his bowed head, ponders the words he has just heard from Francesca. We may wonder if his reaction to what those words evoke is somewhat similar to ours, and if there is some proportion between his and our view. How does his first declared response to Francesca's speech reveal what those words have meant to him? Since he wonders about the "many sweet thoughts" and "the great desire" that "brought" Paolo and Francesca to "the woeful pass," is this not fundamentally an attempt to formulate the problem both of the origin of the lovers' sin and of their passage from a state of innocence and bliss to one of woe and despair, not unlike the one we found formulated in the opposition between the harmonious, peaceful landscape of Francesca's origins and the world of her passion?

The pilgrim does not define the problem of good and evil—or of the fall from a state of innocence into one of sin—in the light of reason and according to its logic, but rather in the light of emotion, of sentiment and desire, and according to their logic. As he exclaims, "How many sweet thoughts, what great desire, brought them to the woeful pass!" the wayfarer is saying in essence: what a pity that those thoughts and such desire, the lovers' natural longing for happiness and peace, should have led them to the "woeful pass." But he is also asking: how could these thoughts and desire bring them to that pass? How could sweet thoughts and desire, things that can only be defined as intrinsically good, lead not only to physical but also to spiritual death? Significantly, like Francesca, he does not speak of the will and discrete moments in which, cutting through the necessitarian world of natural forces, this will transcends them. He speaks instead of sweet thoughts and of desire, and therefore of sentiment and passion. Moreover, as he focuses his attention on the quantity of those thoughts and on the intensity of that desire, he sees them in isolation, as autonomous forces that in a sense have no object, or are not clearly directed towards a goal. With wonderment and awe, he directs his attention to the magnitude and intensity of the lovers' sweet thoughts and desire and to their effect—the "doloroso passo." Thus, what he utters does not constitute a "thought," and therefore an appropriate reply to Virgil's question, "Che pense?" The wayfarer's exclamation reflects an aporia, an insoluble conflict between what is intrinsically good—the lovers' sweet thoughts and great desire—and the "doloroso passo," the death that *somehow* that good has caused.

This "somehow" implicit in the wayfarer's words expresses the gap that separates the two areas (good and evil). Its special function is to prepare the ground for a further formulation of the problem of the lovers' loss of their original state of innocence and happiness, the loss of their "garden." Perhaps we should now speak of a "fall," thus adopting the language that pertains to the myth of Eden, because the text we are studying dictates it in a way that is becoming increasingly evident as the scenes to which we will now turn clearly attest. After revealing to Virgil his "thoughts," which are expressed as sentiment, the wayfarer turns to Paolo and Francesca, but in reality speaking to Francesca alone:

Poi mi rivolsi a loro e parla' io,
    e cominciai: "Francesca, i tuoi martìri
    a lagrimar mi fanno tristo e pio.
Ma dimmi: al tempo d'i dolci sospiri,
    a che e come concedette amore
    che conosceste i dubbiosi disiri?"

(*Inf.* V, 115–120)

Then I turned again to them, and I began, "Francesca, your torments make me weep for grief and pity; but tell me, in the time of the sweet sighs, by what and how did Love grant you to know the dubious desires?"

As the new scene enters our field of vision, we refocus our lens, experiencing at once a break and a sense of progression and transformation. This comes about as we share to some degree the pilgrim's experience of turning his gaze to the actions and agents that constitute Francesca's love story, especially to its beginning, after having reflected on the power of sweet thoughts and desire to lead to the "doloroso passo," but as we have noted, without discerning why or how this should be so. That Dante is still in search of a causal link is confirmed by the way he reformulates the problem when, in his question to Francesca, he introduces love as the new agent, or the persona who has "granted" the two lovers knowledge of the "dubious desires." We also observe that the "sweet sighs" and the "dubious desires" at once echo and depart from the "sweet thoughts" and the "great desire" of which he had spoken earlier to Virgil. What does this new formulation mean? What is its function in the economy of the wayfarer's search for understanding the nature of Paolo's and Francesca's sinful love, and, of course, ultimately, for understanding and accepting the justice of God's punishment of these two lovers? Why does he not ask Francesca: by what and how did her and Paolo's sweet thoughts and great desire bring them to the woeful pass? We can begin to answer with Singleton's commentary: "The questioner Dante has entered into the spirit of Francesca's words and joins her in speaking the language of courtly love. It was Love, as she had said, that brought the lovers to 'one death'; and it is Love again, he therefore assumes, who allows the lovers to manifest their desire."[23]

This "answer" sheds some light on that mimetic process of which we spoke earlier whereby the wayfarer "enters" Francesca's world and interacts with her sympathetically (as when he "moved" the two lovers with his "affettüoso grido," for example), thus provoking a mutual specularity, with one seeing mirrored in the other an image of the self, characterized essentially by pathos and pity. But this specularity would not be creative or bring about any change in the wayfarer (and in us) if it were perfectly parallel. If it did not contain and reveal some discrete differentiating element that would break the "perfect" symmetry of the subject reflecting itself fully into the object, or rather into its image, it would produce a death like that of Narcissus. In other words, if by adopting Francesca's language Dante were to enact a perfect mimesis that would enable him to see himself absolutely contained within the image of Francesca, concurrently seeing flawlessly represented in her idea or philosophy of love his own idea and philosophy of love, he would incur a "death" not dissimilar to that of Paolo and Francesca, which, as I have suggested, is similar to Narcissus' death.

In order for it to be creative, mimesis has to be partial and imperfect; in other words, it has to reveal the difference within a continuum. A moment's closer inspection of the text will show that this risk of death—of thought and of action—is avoided by affirming instead, in an established or positive continuity, a break, a differentiating space, or its equivalent. When we speak of a given continuum and of a discrete, differentiating break or shift, we necessarily also speak of an opposition or a conflict. Returning to the text, we observe that there is already a significant though subtle opposition between Virgil's question "What are you thinking of?" and the wayfarer's response—which, significantly, comes after a pause and therefore a "space" or *caesura*—"Alas! How many sweet thoughts . . ." This reply asserts itself on another plane, different from and in a sense opposite to that of the question. We then find that this opposition between thought and emotion, mind and heart, characterizes the wayfarer's exclamatory phrase in which "thoughts" and "desire" are both contiguous and opposite to one another. In a sense, the "seed" of this opposition or its creative ground is already constituted by the contiguity-opposition of the adjective "sweet" and the noun "thoughts." In other words, as we have observed several times throughout this study, movement and transformation occur because of the creativity inherent in ambiguity, that is, in the admixture or contiguity of two different areas or categories of being, or two different modes of apprehending reality. As he speaks of "sweet thoughts," he at once brings together and separates the heart and intellect—feeling and seeing—thus creating the ground or the matrix of the new term "desire" which at once is related and stands in opposition to the very thing that has engendered it.

At first, if we may attempt to briefly define this process, we can only think of desire as it inheres in "sweet thoughts," because of the obvious "nearness" of thinking and feeling in the inner world of the I. This is a kind of "first love" of both the idea of the object and the feeling that accompanies that idea. Then we think of the desire turning to the object itself—the *other*—the not-I that originally set in motion or gave rise to that idea (or image) and that feeling. But now a conflict ensues: between the first and second desire, between the desire of the image, of the idea, and the desire of the object itself. Or we might say it is a dialectic between what one *thinks* he sees and desires and what one *sees* and desires, in other words, between the "narrow economy" of the thinking and imagining of the object, and the "large economy" of the I being present to the not-I, that is, being open to its many manifestations, to the epiphanies of the Other. This obviously incomplete, schematic discourse helps us to catch a glimpse of the alternating movement, the tragic rhythm we are learning to discover and define as we participate in Dante's journey.

The wayfarer's words addressed to Francesca are another example and another stage of this process of transformation. Within the general economy of these words, the wayfarer, on one hand, defines his experience of sorrow and pity—one sentiment turned inward (suffering, pathos), the other turned outward and directed at the lovers (compassion, pity)—and on the other, he enunciates his question in the light not of pathos and pity but of knowledge and ethos. In this economy we observe the cooperative dialectic of suffering and knowledge, of *pathema* and *mathema*—for the eternal, tragic human condition of experiencing suffering and pain, inevitably provokes questions. Why is there suffering? And more pointedly, why do *I* suffer, and who or what causes it? This first attempt is one of transforming tragic *condition* into tragic *vision*; and when this does not produce an answer, one rephrases and reformulates the question, asking: how and when does suffering come about, and within this perspective who or what causes it? But more significantly for our investigation, when we ask, as Dante does in our text, "how does love grant two lovers to know the dubious desires that lead to death?", we delineate a space, a scene that only as dramatists or as actors we may occupy. This, incidentally, is the "mask" or the "persona" that we as readers are usually inclined to wear occasionally—in some discrete, "privileged moment"—leaping out of it to find ourselves wearing the mask now of the dramatist himself, now of his characters and creations, in proportion to our mimetic powers, to our capacity or gift to transfer ourselves, through make-believe, into their space and their world.

This is the world that the wayfarer wants to know, by hearing it and seeing it represented by Francesca. In fact he does not simply ask about the nature of Paolo's and Francesca's desires, and what makes them dubious, and therefore unclear to the mind, but also dangerous, destructive. He also asks how the "time of the sweet sighs" could have been transformed into a time of sin and misery. Thus he asks for a *story* and therefore a narration of a sequence of events having a beginning, a middle, and an end. But for this to have creative resonance, crossing the limits of what could only be defined as episodic and a mere personal confession devoid of any paradigmatic force for an audience or a community, it would have to reveal a certain correlation or analogy between the individual myth (and mythology, as we shall soon see) and the myth (and mythology) of that community.

As Dante the wayfarer speaks of the "time of the sweet sighs," of the time preceding the lovers' "doloroso passo," is he not in fact speaking of a paradisal *illud tempus* of innocence and bliss, not unlike the one collectively recalled and relived as the myth of Eden? What is the meaning and function of the wayfarer's introduction of Love in the otherwise "Manichaean" opposition of good and evil, of "sweet thoughts" and "great desire" on one hand and the "woeful pass" on the other? And how does it assert itself in the "edenic" scene of which we just spoke? In the light of what we have already observed concerning the creative break or difference between Francesca's and the wayfarer's perspectives, another important question to ask is: how does Dante the wayfarer's "love"—the "persona" he fashions in his question—differ from the love of which Francesca had spoken earlier?

One significant difference is manifested by the opposition of a love (Francesca's) that acts upon the lovers with an ineluctable necessity (that of an axiom or a law) to a love (the wayfarer's) that "grants" the lovers the knowledge of "dubious desires" and allows a certain autonomous "space" or "scene" within which the lovers may exercise certain freedoms, such as that of knowing or recognizing the "dubious desires." The wayfarer's question contains a creative ambiguity that Francesca's characterization of love does not possess. His words speak at once of the paramount power and authority of love, and of its ability to grant a certain autonomy—that of knowing—and therefore of not being totally passive before such power. Another important and equally creative ambiguity is present in the adjective "dubbiosi." Singleton offers the following commentary: "Given the context of the two perspectives, human and divine, this adjective, like 'offends' in vs. 109, is rich in ambiguity. *Dubbioso* referring to the desire of lovers, can mean 'hesitant,' 'not yet manifested,' i.e., desire of which neither lover is wholly conscious. . . . But *dubbioso* can also mean 'dangerous,' 'that which is to be feared'. . . ."[24]

These observations help us to define more sharply the opposition between the human world of sentiment and pathos, and the divine world of fear and ethos. We can more clearly understand what we have glimpsed earlier concerning the creativity of the wayfarer's "imperfect" mimesis of Francesca's language and of the perspective this language reflects. By virtue of the first meaning of "dubbiosi," he can engage Francesca through a kind of natural, sympathetic solidarity that binds like to like; at the same time, by the force of the second meaning, he can distance himself from her world. As we have seen throughout the entire episode, he never totally abandons the perspective of ethos and fear (in whose center is that ever-present interlocutor, that most fear-inspiring Other, God). Rather, he alternates from one perspective (pathos and pity) to another (ethos and fear) or, as in the present scene, he experiences them as contiguously present. This enables him to move within Francesca's world, eliciting from her a full, coherent response, a *definition*, such as only the "strict economy" dictated by love-as-passion can produce. At the same time he introduces in the scene the expansive perspective or economy in which humans live and act in the presence of the Absolute, for his own (though somewhat "delayed") benefit—as we shall see—and for the benefit of the reader-spectator.

We should add—thus elaborating what we sketched earlier—that "love" is another key word which, introduced in the scene by the wayfarer, expresses a creative ambiguity, a dual perspective. As the wayfarer utters the word "love," he delineates two perspectives within which love represents, both the force or the "agent" that Francesca identified earlier—what she in a sense fashioned out of the courtly love tradition and the poetry of the Dolce Stil Nuovo—and the force or the "agent" that for the Christian is God Himself (*Deus caritas est*). We must note in passing that this dual perspective was already present in Francesca's declaration, "Love, which absolves no loved one from loving." "Francesca's second law of love," writes Charles Singleton, "echoes a dictum which the cult of courtly love characteristically had taken over from Christian doctrine. See I Ioan. Apos. 4:19: 'Nos ergo diligamus Deum, quoniam Deus prior dilexit nos' ('Let us therefore love, because God first loved us')."[25] The essential difference, of course, between Francesca's and the wayfarer's use of the word "love" is one between the "restricted economy" of a false love that asserts itself as a substitute for the "general economy" of true love, and an economy in which those two loves coexist, in creative opposition, such as we have observed in the wayfarer's question addressed to Francesca.

This difference in perspectives makes us pause for deeper reflection. As we sharpen our focus, we see that here lies the fundamental rupture between the "hell" of Francesca and the "temporary" and therefore creative "hell" of Dante the wayfarer. The "hell" of the former is manifested by what we may call the single or fixed vision that excludes or suppresses multiple vision. More specifically, it is the world of desire that asserts itself as autonomous and self-sufficient in its "perfect" identification with a formula, such as the one that Franscesa fashions out of the courtly convention or law (not without distortions or misinterpretations, as we shall later see), and thus proves to be an illusion. "Illusion," notes Northrop Frye, "is whatever is fixed or definable and reality is best understood as its negation, whatever reality is, it's not that."[26] Significantly, to the seemingly coherent, self-enclosed universe of Francesca where love reigns unchallenged, the wayfarer opposes a universe where conflict reigns, the conflict (never resolved) between love as understood and lived by Francesca, and analogously experienced by himself, and love as *totally other*, as being always *not* what any formula, code or convention may claim to define perfectly.

If there were no ambiguity present in the word *love*, what could the wayfarer (and the reader) hope to learn from Francesca's story? If, as we have at first remarked with Singleton, he used the word "love" exactly as Francesca has used it, mimetically defining it and understanding it as she defines and understands it, all he could expect to hear is a more detailed narration of how love acted upon Paolo and Francesca, finally bringing them to "one death." In other words, given the strict determinism at work in such a "story," the wayfarer would never find any meaning and justification in the way this story ended. The state of damnation of these lovers would appear totally unjust. Therefore, the opposition between the human *idea* of love and God's *reality* of love, between the lovers' personal economy and God's economy, would prove to be irreconcilable, with no possible proportion linking them.

When Dante the wayfarer asks Francesca: "By what and how did love grant you to know the dubious desires?" he is implicitly asking: how did God grant you to choose the false desires instead of the true ones? As we utter these words, we cannot avoid seeing them also addressed in this fashion: how did love (God) grant Adam and Eve to know their "dubious desires"? In other words, we can, with the wayfarer, direct the same question to Paolo and Francesca and, analogously, to Adam and Eve, and hence to both the "myth of Eden" of Paolo and Francesca and the original myth of Eden. This question (like all important questions) is of course addressed ultimately to God. We must not fail to perceive at once Francesca's perspective (which is partly, temporarily, shared by the wayfarer) and the new perspective that the wayfarer has introduced, though obliquely. In this perspective, love is not merely a personification or a fictional rendition of human passion and desire that have become inordinate and therefore tyrannical, but the Infinite source and goal of the human desire and love.

We can find answers to our questions by turning once again to the text, and specifically to Francesca's reply to the wayfarer's question:

E quella a me: "Nessun maggior dolore
   che ricordarsi del tempo felice
   ne la miseria; e ciò sa 'l tuo dottore.
Ma s'a conoscer la prima radice
   del nostro amor tu hai cotanto affetto,
   dirò come colui che piange e dice.

(Inf. V, 121–126)

And she to me, "There is no greater sorrow than to recall, in wretchedness, the happy time; and this your teacher knows. But if you have such great desire to know the first root of our love, I will tell as one who weeps and tells."

Again, but only with greater relief, the myth of Eden shows through the words of Francesca. Roger Dragonetti notes: "Francesca . . . begins her narration by associating to the suffering for the lost paradise Virgil himself, the *dottore* whose reason, deprived of God, reveals its exemplary function by showing to the disciple the sense of that privation."[27] Having recognized the presence of the myth of Eden as a significant component of Francesca's love story, not satisfied by the mere identification of this presence, we ask: what is the creative force of this presence? In other words how does it help, or indeed how is it essential to the definition of the sin of Paolo and Francesca and of their damnation? Or, putting the question in yet another form: what is the sense of the privation of paradise of which Dragonetti speaks? What does it really mean to be excluded from paradise and therefore from the original innocence and bliss that, like all human beings, Paolo and Francesca sought to attain? We thus find ourselves asking the very questions that the wayfarer has asked: how could the original "sweet thoughts" and the "great desire" have brought them instead to the "woeful pass"?

Our answers, though as always temporary and tentative, depend once again upon our perception of the difference, of that narrow but creative space, that Dante as dramatist produces by juxtaposing the individual myth of Eden of Paolo and Francesca and the original and collective myth of Eden. When Francesca sharply contrasts the "happy time" preceding her fall into sin with the present state of "wretchedness," she already reveals, unwittingly of course, the deepest root of that fall, the *real* first root, which as we shall soon see differs substantially from the "first root" of which Francesca speaks. What strikes me as particularly significant in Francesca's statement that "there is no greater sorrow than to recall, in wretchedness, the happy time" is that it tells of a vision according to which happiness and misery are irreconcilable and cannot be thought of as coexistent or contiguous. In this perspective, the myth of innocence is seen in opposition to the history of sin. This is the "dream of the second innocence" which we encountered at the very beginning of our study in the Prologue scene— that second innocence that the wayfarer had "dreamt" *before* discovering the Other (Virgil). Here, in the presence of Francesca, he in a sense relives that dream, but with the difference that now he moves in the privileged space that allows him to be both actor and spectator and hence to see objectified in her what earlier he had experienced only subjectively.

As for us readers, we have *our* privileged space, *our* scene, within which we can alternately see or mimetically experience now Francesca's single view and perspective and now the wayfarer's double perspective. We can see and experience the juxtaposition of a false myth which denies the presence of evil in the garden and the true myth which comes into being as the re-enactment of the *original* myth, which always exposes the "rupture of the origins."

In the light of these observations we can better understand Francesca's declaration that "there is no greater sorrow than to recall, in wretchedness, the happy time." Francesca cannot accept the contiguity of the happy time and the time of misery, and consequently the separation or the rupture which is a constitutive part of that contiguity. Correspondingly, her infernal punishment is to experience the dialectic of innocence and guilt, of good and evil, and of happiness and misery, but in such a way that this dialectic can never be resolved and thus assert itself as the creative suffering of the tragic drama of sin and expiation.

This (and more) is present in Francesca's words about her greatest of sorrows. Further elucidation of what we have so far seen and deeper meanings are to be sought in Francesca's narration of the first manifestation of her love, that is, in her dramatization of what constitutes the "first root" of this love. This is a "discourse on the origins" *sui generis* and therefore a specific, individual myth that, as we have already observed (and as it will soon become clearer), is really an anti-myth of paradise, the story of a false garden which is also a false *story* of the garden, for to live and to narrate, to be and to act are one on the stage that Dante has constructed at the end of

Inferno V. Francesca fashions her story—in opposition, we might say, to her first enunciation of the ineluctable power of love that, according to its fixed, necessary law, took hold of her and Paolo and brought them to one death—by constructing it in a form that, as we shall soon see, clearly echoes the mythic form. Thus, she makes intelligible to the wayfarer and the reader a portion of her story of the "first root" of her sin: something no discourse could do as creatively or as fully. So it becomes possible for the wayfarer (implicitly) and for the reader (somewhat explicitly) to compare her "myth" with the original myth. In fact, there is an ultimate leap of creativity in the juxtaposition which, unwittingly produced by the character Francesca, is intended by Dante as dramatist, for it forces us to re-examine both *our* tentative and false myth of Eden (the anti-myth that to some measure individually and collectively we think and live) and the original myth of Eden. In other words, we are compelled to measure more accurately and to see more keenly the narrow space separating the restricted economy of the myth we fashion and the unrestricted or general economy of the original myth which by its very nature is, and will always be, inaccessible because *totally other*, and therefore belonging to the sphere of the sacred. We may say again with Paul Ricoeur, "Myth cannot exercise its symbolic function except by the specific means of the narrative or narration: what it wants to say is already drama."[28] In addition, such a function is necessarily dependent on the authenticity or "truth" of the narration, and that to fail in the narration is to falsify the myth and misrepresent its drama.

It is this kind of misrepresentation that I find in Francesca's narration of her love story and the underlying myth of the Earthly Paradise:

> "Noi leggiavamo un giorno per diletto
>   di Lancialotto come amor lo strinse;
>   soli eravamo e sanza alcun sospetto.
> Per più fïate li occhi ci sospinse
>   quella lettura, e scolorocci il viso;
>   ma solo un punto fu quel che ci vinse.
> quando leggemmo il disïato riso
>   esser basciato da cotanto amante,
>   questi, che mai da me non fia diviso,
> la bocca mi basciò tutto tremante.
>   Galeotto fu 'l libro e chi lo scrisse:
>   quel giorno più non vi leggemmo avante."

(Inf. V, 127–138)

"One day, for pastime, we read of Lancelot, how love constrained him; we were alone, suspecting nothing. Several times that reading urged our eyes to meet and took the color from our faces, but one moment alone it was that overcame us. When we read how the longed-for smile was kissed by so great a lover, this one, who never shall be parted from me, kissed my mouth all trembling. A Gallehault was the book and he who wrote it; that day we read no farther in it."

The indistinct, generic "one day" already evokes a remote beginning that seems to lie outside history. The fact that Paolo and Francesca were reading "per diletto" ("for mere pleasure") further suggests a scene of original innocence and happiness, reinforced by the declaration that they were alone, suspecting nothing. At first glance, we share Francesca's view in identifying this scene with innocence and happiness. But if we pause to reflect on the "passage" ("doloroso passo") from this scene to the scene of sin and misery, we are compelled to ask again: how is this possible? As we do not or cannot find an answer, we shift focus and ask other questions. Is the first scene really one of innocence and happiness? Are Paolo and Francesca really alone? And what does it really mean to "suspect nothing"—to be without fear? We can answer that Paolo and Francesca were innocent and alone (and without suspicion or fear) only in the fictional, illusory world they created for themselves—a fiction, an illusion whose form they appropriated from a literary text. In other words, we can see them as innocent only if we isolate the space, the scene within which the two lovers experienced such innocence, that is, if we isolate it from other scenes, those which as they succeed one another form a history and a drama, a history and a drama that cannot exclude the very *first* scene of which the original myth of paradise speaks, where innocence and evil were contiguous.

The moment we see the lovers' paradisal scene against the backdrop of that original scene (of Adam and Eve), we cannot fail to notice the similarities as well as the differences that correspondingly reveal them as related by continuity and by discontinuity. Thus we apprehend alternately the narrow closure and fixity of one and the "ruptured" expansive space of the other—the false and the true garden: one excludes history and drama and the other, with the Fall, opens into history and marks its beginning. In Burke's dramatistic terms, Paolo and Francesca ignored the inherent power of the scene, its "motivational force,"[29] namely the fundamental condition or ground of human life of which evil is a constitutive part, substituting for it a scene of their own making. Hence they subverted the creative conflict between act and scene, between the self and the other, that is to say, the very life of drama.

We can better understand this negation of drama if we see its deep connection with the desire to create one's own innocence. "The malice of sin," writes Renato Poggioli, "threatens and ruins our souls when they yield to self-oblivion, when they abandon themselves, deceitfully, to their own innocence."[30] This could also be said of the original myth, of the first scene, in which Adam and Eve desired a "second innocence"—one of their own making, one which they felt was not given to them but was instead the fruit of their own "creation." Similarly, being "alone and suspecting nothing" may be said of Paolo and Francesca as well as of Adam and Eve, for they share essentially the same perception of what, with Kenneth Burke, we earlier in this study called the "scenic" dimension of reality. To say that one is alone is to say that one moves and acts in a scene in which the objective, or "scenic" dimension of reality—what is *outside*—is strictly and absolutely commensurate to the subject, and in a sense solipsistically receives its reality from it. This scene, not "disturbed" by the presence of the Other, alluringly appears—to the mind of course—peaceful and blissful, a paradise. In other words, the unrestricted economy of the scene seems to be contained perfectly within the restricted economy of the thinking self. Speaking in absolute terms, in both scenes the phrase "being alone and suspecting nothing" implies a denial of the presence of God (the Infinite Other).

We may more keenly understand this denial if we turn for a moment to the *Epistle to Cangrande* (*Epist.* XIII, 62–63), where we find this commentary on the first verse of *Paradiso*, which begins with the words "La gloria" (of God):

The Holy Spirit says by Jeremiah [23:24], "Do I not fill heaven and earth?" and in the Psalm [138 (139):7–9], "Whither shall I go from Thy spirit, and whither shall I flee from Thy presence? If I ascend into heaven Thou art there; if I descend into hell Thou art present. If I take my wings," and the rest. And *Wisdom* [1:7] says that "the spirit of the Lord filled the whole world," and *Ecclesiasticus* in the forty-second [42:16], "His work is full of the glory of the Lord." Whereto the scripture of the pagans bears co-witness, for Lucan in the ninth [*Phars.* IX, 580], "Iuppiter est quodcumque vides quocumque moveris." ("Whatsoever thou seest, wheresoever thou goest, is Jupiter.")[31]

To ignore this presence, to suppress it, is to abandon the creative differentiation by contiguity whereby man interacts with God, and it is also to remove from one's scene the dimension of ethos and fear. In this scene the presence of the tempter or false mediator is also ignored; it is not seen as a menace, as the "other" to be feared (but in this case a fear of the *negative* in opposition to the positive fear that man experiences when confronting the absolute good, the *Summum Bonum*). Once again this is true of Adam and Eve and of Paolo and Francesca, who respectively do not perceive as other or as the enemy the serpent and the book of Lancelot. In both scenes heteronomy and tension are suppressed. And significantly, it is in the name of—or because of the allure of—an *identification*, that in each scene a disastrous rupture is brought about.

In Eden's temptation scene the serpent (who, obviously, appears to be harmless, undifferentiated, and therefore as we mentioned earlier inspiring no fear) promises Adam and Eve an identification with God (*eritis sicut Deus*) through the knowledge of good and evil. It is a treacherous, fraudulent promise because they *were* already like God, having been created in His image and sharing with Him (of course as a creature may share with his Creator) an existential knowledge of good and a knowledge of evil "by inference," as Thomas Merton has observed in a passage we will soon quote. The serpent promised, in fact, an impossible identification of man with God by suggesting that this could be achieved by an "existential knowledge" of evil, namely by *experiencing* it. Attempting to define Adam's sin, Thomas Merton offers the following interpretation of the temptation scene:

What was this sin? It was first of all an attitude of mind. No doubt there was some overt act which reached forth to eat the fruit of the "forbidden tree." But before the act was done, the attitude was there. It was a way of looking at reality that condemned man, by its very nature, to become unreal. What was the attitude? It was simply this: that Adam, who possessed an existential, an experimental knowledge of all that was good and all that was real, and who was mystically united with God, the infinite source of all actual and possible reality, wanted to improve on this by knowing something else, which, he thought, would be something more. In desiring to eat of the fruit of the tree of the knowledge of good and evil, he wanted, in fact, to add to the knowledge of good, which he already had, the knowledge of evil [Cf. St. Bernard, *De Duodecim Gradibus Superbiae*, c. 10]. To be more precise he wanted to have an experience, an existential knowledge of evil. He wanted not only to know evil by theoretical inference from good (which he could well have done without sin) but he wanted to know evil in a way in which it was not even known to God: that is to say, by *experience*.[32]

In the light of these observations we can say that Paolo and Francesca desired to "add to the knowledge of good" the knowledge of evil, under the guise (the fiction) of recapturing or "fashioning" a *second* paradise of innocence and bliss. For if at first they enjoyed a state of innocence and happiness—of course relatively speaking, and therefore to the degree that humans, weakened by the sin of Adam after the Fall, can be said to experience a kind of paradise before sinning—why would they wish to change such a state, if not because they thought that they could add something to it?

Lest we make our analysis too abstract, let us return to Dante's dramatization of the lovers' "fall." As we read Francesca's words, we notice that when she speaks of that which moved her and Paolo to know and to experience the "dubious desires," she does not say it was "love," but their reading of an episode of the love story of Lancelot and Guinevere, most crucially, the point when they read of these lovers' first kiss. Obviously this "cause," this "prime mover," is neither the love of which Francesca had spoken earlier (echoing in an ambiguous light the love of the *dolce stil nuovo*), nor the love to which the wayfarer had referred (and whose creative ambivalence we have discussed), for Francesca now identifies it with the moment in which the fictional scene of the kiss merges with the existential scene of her being kissed by Paolo. This is a drastic reduction, and indeed an adulteration of the ever-expanding, truly creative and undefinable power of love, which, if considered within the economy of the Absolute, is one with God and hence is infinite. And even if this power is considered within the narrower economy of the courtly love tradition, it is still as undefinable, almost equally resisting definition, as the centuries-old critical interpretations of that tradition clearly attest.

Another sign of this adulteration is in how Paolo and Francesca read the fictional kiss of Lancelot and Guinevere, which Francesca identifies as the *point* that conquered her and Paolo, that is, the "first root" of their love. To fathom the deep significance of this crucial moment, we may begin by focusing on the image of the "desired smile." Roger Dragonetti has interpreted this smile as the sign of beatitude—and therefore of paradise—in light of a passage of Dante's *Convivio*. "Dante states in the *Convivio* that the smile is a sign of beatitude. What binds Paolo and Francesca is an image of paradise. Their passion reveals itself under the bewitching action of a poetic fiction, on which the gesture of their desire is modeled."[33] This reading corroborates what we have shown throughout this chapter, that Paolo and

Francesca's story presents striking resemblances to the myth of Eden.[34] What we are particularly interested in exploring are the profound and far-reaching implications of this resemblance.

The figure of Francesca is not a perfect *imitatio* of Eve (nor, as we shall soon see, of Guinevere), for her story is both a kind of re-enactment of the myth of Eden and a falsification of it. As a dream of a "second innocence," it negates the irreducible fact of evil and therefore the consequences of the Fall, that is, the fall into history as a form of expiation and redemption and finally as the manifestation or actualization of God's *oikonomia*. An important component of the sin of Paolo and Francesca and its "first root" is how they model their desire upon a poetic fiction. Theirs is a "mimetic desire,"[35] a desire that has no true, real object. This desire is not creative but destructive, not merely because it stems from fiction—that which the lovers have created within themselves—but because this fiction does not point to the vastness beyond it, to the *totally other* of the transcendent, and it is considered instead identical to it. In other words Paolo and Francesca, like Adam and Eve at the moment of their sin, destroy all heteronomy, all differentiation between illusion and reality, between fictional and actual, between created beings' "restricted economy" and God's "unrestricted economy."

Before the Fall, man and God existed in creative opposition to one another, the former standing in a never-ending, dynamic and truly creative relation of analogy with the Other: the finite and the Infinite, or the fiction of the finite grounded in the reality of the Infinite. For how else can the created being subsist, move, act, and know if not through fiction, through *poiein* (Adam's work in the garden), that at its best will always be inadequate to "contain" and "represent" the Infinite? By destroying this difference, this heteronomy, Paolo and Francesca, again like Adam and Eve, have destroyed both the natural, creative power of the fictional (and hence the power of limit) and the power of the relation to the real, and hence to God. One significant facet of the lovers' sin (and of all sins in general) is its obliteration of the distance, the space—indeed the void or nothingness—the *caesura* of which we spoke earlier in this study, which at once separates and links the fictional and the real, the finite and the Infinite. This obliteration is brought about by identifying experience with an image or an idea, in other words by linking the potentially vast, inexhaustible universe of action (in which being and existing interact) with the narrow, easily exhausted product of the mind.

This destructive elimination of the differentiating space is emphatically revealed by what we may call the destruction of the *point*. To begin to understand the special function of this image in the story of Paolo and Francesca, and specifically, in what they have destroyed, we must recall that it has a long history, both within and outside the *Divine Comedy*. Its meanings range, to mention only a few examples, from the undefinable, opaque moment of *Inferno* I, 11 which marked the pilgrim's straying from the right path—"Tant'era pien di sonno a quel punto . . ." ("I was so full of sleep at the moment . . .")—to the point signifying God—"il punto / a cui tutti li tempi son presenti," "the point to which all times are present"; *Par.* XVII, 17–18 .

As I have argued elsewhere,[36] the point of which Francesca speaks cannot be interpreted merely as a thematic moment, that of the kiss of Lancelot and Guinevere inscribed in the book that our two lovers were reading. The "first root" of the destructive passion of Paolo and Francesca would thus coincide with that moment of the narration which more than any other before it had a powerful effect on them. But to say, as Francesca does, that it was this moment in the narrative or this scene that overcame them, is to imply that there was no free choice, which pivots, so to speak, on an instant or a point. It has been aptly observed that "all that counts in the moral world of sin, of conversion, of decision, belongs to the order of the instantaneous."[37]

We can catch a glimpse of the real root of Paolo's and Francesca's sin if we observe that the thematic point must somehow be related to a *punctum temporis*, an indivisible instant in which the problematic relationship between time and eternity comes into play: if we attempt to explain what really happened in that point when the two lovers' fate has been decided— a point that must necessarily mark the crucial passage (the "doloroso passo") not only from the reading of the fictional kiss to the actual kiss of Paolo and Francesca, but from a state of innocence to one of damnation, from life to death. It is indeed this point, this instant, in which literature and life seem to flow together, and in which it is not clear if it is literature that exclusively acts upon life (as Francesca wants us to believe) or if it is life that influences literature and modifies it, that has escaped the attention of the two lovers. And it is this point that Dante the character, and with him the reader, is invited to discern.

The reading I propose is an attempt not to define this point, for its very character and function is to resist definition, but to apprehend some proportion, some ratio between this image and the experience of which it speaks. It must obviously be excluded that the kiss of our lovers was simultaneous to the reading of the kiss of Lancelot and Guinevere. The point of this kiss must therefore have coincided either with the point that, for the two readers, *immediately preceded*, or with the one that *immediately followed* the thematic point of the kiss inscribed in the page of the Arthurian romance. Yet Francesca speaks of a moment in which both the thematic and the temporal point coincided. If it is impossible that the two points *actually* coincided, it is however possible, explainable, that the first was imagined, or rather that it was *experienced* as being one with the other. Significantly, an important, and indeed crucial sign of this identity of the fictional with the actual, of literature with life, is the fact that Francesca "remembers" having read that it was Lancelot who first kissed Guinevere, and not, as we read in the *Lancelot of the Lake*, that true to the courtly love convention it was the queen who took the initiative. It is not difficult to imagine that in the course of their reading, as Paolo and Francesca identified more and more with the fictional lovers and were thus moved by "mimetic desire," when they came upon the moment in which Lancelot either *was about* to obtain or *had just obtained* Guinevere's kiss, they stopped reading. In this very moment their passion erupted and they kissed. But it was not this that led them to their spiritual death.[38] It was rather that in this same instant their consciousness was obfuscated, or to put it in other terms, it was fixed upon one single image. Hence, they effaced all distinctions, all differentiation between the fictional lovers and themselves. The thematic point and the existential point were artificially made to coincide perfectly. But this was obtained by doing violence to the text, by superimposing on the figure of Lancelot the figure of Paolo. In this point the very perfection of mimesis brought about not growth and transcendence but sterility and death, because the aesthetic distance was obliterated, and *imitatio*, with its potential creativity, was adulterated. In other words, Paolo and Francesca destroyed that creative space that allows a dynamic exchange, a constructive mimesis with its ever-changing, inexhaustible interaction of actors who never become perfect doubles. For Francesca, Lancelot has become the perfect double of Paolo.[39]

The very image of the point was emptied of its inherent creative force when it was "filled" by one single image, not even the thematic kiss of Lancelot and Guinevere, but the *image* created by Paolo and Francesca.

Thus, the undefinable has been "artificially" defined. This is hell. Moreover this obliteration of difference, which only a break or a *caesura* can produce and maintain, corresponds to the obliteration of conflict and finally of the tragic. For to fix one's whole being on one image, on one point, is to refuse the eternal conflict between the vastness of experience and the narrowness of one's definition and one's fiction.

Significantly, as Paolo and Francesca destroyed the creative space of their drama by surrendering to a false point, they also destroyed the creative space of the fictional drama they were reading. They were equally destructive as lovers and as readers. As they began reading "per diletto " ("for pastime") thus revealing their desire to construct a "second innocence," they were not predisposed to find exemplified in the love story of Lancelot and Guinevere the drama of sin and expiation, that is, the story of a conflict finally resolved. Conquered by a single point in their reading, they were unable to discover the evolution of the story and its "happy ending"—the conversion of Lancelot and Guinevere to religious life, as Dante relates in the *Convivio*.[40] Their reduction of the book and its fictional story to only a point coincides with the reduction of their life and their story to a single point, in which they thought they could find a substitute for the absolute, infinite love in which the blessed participate. This is the fallacy of romantic love. "Romantic love," writes Jean Pucelle, "believes that the absolute is attained in the instant, and that there is nothing else to expect from the future."[41]

Another proof of the suppression of the creative space, of difference and conflict, is the merging of Paolo's identity with Francesca's. Her words "this one, who never shall be parted from me, kissed my mouth all trembling" (*Inf.* V, 135–136) express both the moment when the two lovers kissed and their eternal union. But that this is not a true union in love, or a communion, becomes evident as soon as we pause to note that both Paolo's silence throughout the episode and his inseparability from Francesca speak of a total suppression of their reciprocal and always problematic "otherness" analogous to their suppression of Lancelot and Guinevere and their whole drama. Creative love, like creative reading, implies a paradoxical union in difference, and a mimesis that does not destroy that difference and the conflictual relation, the tragic rhythm that at once binds and separates the I and the Not-I, the individual and the collective (or "original") myth of paradise. Creative love, therefore, accepts and indeed asserts the reality of the tragic.

This effacement of the true self and of its natural expansiveness and dynamism is given final expression in the closing scene of *Inferno* V:

Mentre che l'uno spirto questo disse,
   l'altro piangea; sì che di pietade
   io venni men così com'io morisse.
E caddi come corpo morto cade.

(*Inf.* V, 139–142)

While the one spirit said this, the other wept, so that for pity I swooned, as if in death, and fell as a dead body falls.

We now realize that Paolo has been weeping the entire time of Francesca's narration. More important, we discover that when she had said to Dante "I will tell as one who weeps and tells" (*Inf.* V, 126), she was in fact speaking also of Paolo, but in such a way that each of them was a part of one person. There have been several other instances of this earlier in the episode. But now for the first time Paolo communicates to the wayfarer and the reader his own role, or his own presence as an integral component of a single persona, of which until now Francesca had been the sole representative. Renato Poggioli, commenting on a statement of Francesco de Sanctis in which Paolo is characterized as "the mute expression of Francesca; the string trembling at what she says, the gesture accompanying her voice," writes: "This statement, a perfect aesthetic justification of Dante's conception, implies that the main character of the episode absorbs the lesser one; that its protagonist is this couple of lovers, even more than Francesca herself; that the two lovers form a single personality though such a personality is shaped by its feminine component, rather than by its masculine one."[42]

The moment the wayfarer witnesses the end of Francesca's speech, when her presence is no longer active and prominent, he becomes aware of Paolo's silent weeping and of the fact that because of this weeping he cuts such a tenuous figure. This weeping, which in a sense recalls the wayfarer's own weeping upon his hearing of Francesca's suffering ("Francesca, your torments make me weep for grief and pity"; *Inf.* V, 116–117), must be interpreted in such a way by the wayfarer that he is moved to pity so vehemently that he swoons ("as if in death"; *Inf.* V, 141). This is obviously a mimetic response—the conclusive one of the episode, and one of several similar responses we have already recognized and discussed in the present chapter. Renato Poggioli has observed: "For a while, at the close of the canto,

Dante the character becomes . . . the equal of Paolo, and even of Lancelot, who for a while seems to swoon himself, while talking to the Queen of his still unrewarded love. In this brief moment, Dante himself is but a creature of pathos, a victim of pity and self-pity, like Paolo and Lancelot."[43] While essentially concurring with this reading, I must sharpen the discourse by calling attention to the nature and creative function of the wayfarer's mimesis. If we state with Poggioli that Dante the wayfarer is for a moment "the equal of Paolo, and even of Lancelot" and understand this to mean a "perfect" imitation of Paolo by wayfarer, then we can only conclude that Dante the wayfarer acts upon Paolo much like Paolo had in turn acted upon the figure of Lancelot, by appropriating his image, and therefore by merging with it, at once reducing and fixing his own form and the form of the other. This would mean the negation of transformation and transcendence. Yet the wayfarer does achieve some degree of transformation and transcendence, as we read of the "return" of his mind "which had closed itself before the piteousness of the two kinsfolk" (*Inf.* VI, 1–2).

But what could account for such a transformation or catharsis through the mimetic experience of pity? We may answer that this transformation is possible only if the mimetic relation is imperfect, in other words, if there is a certain "space," a certain difference or rupture in the mimetic mechanism that would at once permit the "temporary" specularity or coincidence and a departure from it. Dante the wayfarer gradually moves into the universe of Paolo and Francesca, adopting their language, sharing their single vision of pathos and pity, and experiencing a kind of "return to Eden"; yet in varying measure, he also does not completely abandon the vision of ethos and fear and hence tragic vision. But does he suddenly abandon this vision at the moment of his swooning? Or does he not instead experience it—though dimly and unconsciously—along with pity? Is there not a point of intersection between pity and fear and between pathos and ethos? As he sees Paolo weeping, does he not "read" in this not only sentiment, pathos, and pity, but also a measure of fear and its correlative, ethos? In other words, does he not experience, though partially, what in Joyce's *A Portrait of the Artist as a Young Man*, the character Stephen Dedalus identifies as the double vision of the "tragic emotion"? "Aristotle has not defined pity and terror. I have. . . . Pity is the feeling which arrests the mind in the presence of whatsoever is grave and constant in human sufferings and unites it with the human sufferer. Terror is the feeling which arrests the mind in the presence of whatsoever is grave and constant in human sufferings and unites it with the secret cause."[44] "Tragedy, then," notes Louis L.

Martz, "seems to demand both the human sufferer and the secret cause: that is to say, the doubt, the pain, the pity of the human sufferer; and the affirmation, the awe, the terror of the secret cause. It is an affirmation even though the cause is destructive in its immediate effects: for this cause seems to affirm the existence of some universal order of things."[45] (This brings to mind the image of the "ruina" created by Christ's Passion and manifesting God's love—the "secret cause"—which is cursed by Paolo and Francesca and the other spirits of the Second Circle.)

We now see more sharply what we have been tentatively formulating throughout this chapter: that there is an essential correlation between the sin and state of damnation of Paolo and Francesca and their nostalgia for a garden-without-the-serpent, their longing for a "second innocence," which transforms them into figures who, governed exclusively by pathos and pity, ignore ethos and fear, and therefore the "double vision of tragedy." This is the vision which Dante the wayfarer (and the reader) learns to acquire as his mind is united both "with the human sufferer" and with "the secret cause."

Notes

1. Renato Poggioli, "Tragedy or Romance? A Reading of the Paolo and Francesca Episode in Dante's *Inferno*," *PMLA* 72, 3 (1957): 313–358. For a recent survey of the exegetical tradition of *Inferno* V, see Dante Della Terza, "*Inferno* V: Tradition and Exegesis," *Dante Studies* XCIX (1981): 49–66. A portion of the present chapter has appeared under the title of "The Paradise of Paolo and Francesca and the Negation of the Tragic: A Dramatistic Reading of *Inferno* V (97–138)," in *Italiana*, ed. Albert N. Mancini, Paolo Giordano, and Pier Raimondo Baldini (River Forest, IL: Rosary College, 1987), pp. 87–96.

2. Irma Brandeis, *The Ladder of Vision* (Garden City, NY: Doubleday and Co., 1960), p. 32.

3. Singleton, *Commentary* 1, n. 34, p. 76.

4. Ibid.

5. I should note that, surprisingly, in his commentary ad loc., Singleton does not explain how what we learn about the "ruina" in *Inferno* XII sheds light, as a retrospective gloss, on the curse by the lustful souls of the "ruina" of *Inferno* V.

6. Poggioli, "Tragedy or Romance?" p. 317.

7. Ibid., p. 318.

8. Singleton, *Commentary* 1, p. 82.

9. Paul Ricoeur, "Herméneutique des symboles," p. 64.

10. Cf. Lawrence V. Ryan, "*Stornei, Gru, Colombe*: The Bird Images in *Inferno* V," *Dante Studies* XCIV (1976): 36: "In classical times, while the turtle-dove (*turtur*) was considered an example of chastity, ordinary doves, or pigeons (*columbae*), were associated with lechery. 'Quas antiqui,' notes Isidore [*Etymologiarum . . . libri*

XX, XII. vii. 61] 'Venerias noncupabant, eo quod nidas frequentant, et osculo amorem concipiant' ['Which the ancients called *Venerias*, in that they nest frequently, and incite love by kissing'].''

11. Cf. Mark Musa, *Advent at the Gates* (Bloomington: Indiana University Press, 1974), p. 17: "If one thinks of the type of movement on the spiritual plane to which the flight of doves to their nest could be best compared, surely it would be the spiritually instinctive ascent of the soul to God whence it came and where it must return. (Cf. *Psalms* LIV, 6: 'Et dixit: Quis dabit mihi pennas sicut columbae, et volabe, et requiescam?') And the suggestion in our passage of the harmony of desire ('. . . dal disio chiamate') and will ('. . . dal voler portate') could surely corroborate such an association. It is with a reference to that same harmony that the *Divine Comedy* will end: 'ma già volgeva *il mio disio e 'l velle* (sì come rota ch'igualmente è mossa / l'Amor che move il sole e l'altre stelle)'." While I agree with this reading, I do not share Professor Musa's interpretation of the function of the doves simile within the economy of Dante the wayfarer's experience of lust exemplified by Paolo and Francesca: "Yet the Pilgrim applies this image to two unrepentant sinners in Hell. . . . Why did the poet allow the Pilgrim to apply this 'Christian metaphor' to these lovers condemned by God? Was it to suggest a contrast between the sublime connotations of which this image was capable, and the trivial use which the Pilgrim made of it, being at this stage unaware of such connotations, unaccustomed to thinking in terms of the soul's ascent toward God?" My reading is much closer to the one offered by Lawrence V. Ryan in the already cited "*Stornei, Gru, Colombe*: The Bird Images in *Inferno* V," which recognizes the ambivalence of the image of the doves: "The dove is the most attractive and yet the most ambivalent of the three images, a symbol at once of the Christian soul's natural aspiration toward God and of the lechery which countervails that ascent." (p. 41) As I shall soon argue, it is this ambivalence which, on the one hand makes lust attractive, giving it the semblance of true love and of the ascent to paradise and to God, and on the other, if experienced dramatically (that is, as conflict)—as the pilgrim and the reader experience it—may cause a transformation in vision.

12. Glauco Cambon, "Francesca and the Tactics of Language," in his *Dante's Craft: Studies in Language and Style* (Minneapolis: University of Minnesota Press, 1969), p. 64.

13. Mandelbaum, *Inferno*, p. 45.

14. Barbara Vinken, "*Encore*: Francesca da Rimini: Rhetoric of Seduction-Seduction of Rhetoric," *Deutsche Vierteljahrsschrift für Literaturwissenschaft und Geistesgeschichte* 62 (1988): 409.

15. Poggioli, "Tragedy or Romance? " p. 324.

16. Roger Dragonetti, "L'épisode de Francesca dans le cadre de la convention courtoise," in his *Aux frontières du langage poétique: Etudes sur Dante, Mallarmé, Valéry* (Gand: Romanica Gandensia, 1961), p. 94. (Translation mine)

17. Poggioli, "Tragedy or Romance? " p. 327.

18. Ibid., p. 356.

19. Ibid., p. 328.

20. Dragonetti, "L'épisode de Francesca," p. 101.

21. Saint Augustine, *Confessions*, vol. II, trans. William Watts, Loeb Classical Library (1631; London: W. Heinemann, 1912), p. 391.

22. See Franco Masciandaro, "L'amor torto' di Francesca e il 'diritto amore' di Cunizza," *Pacific Northwest Council on Foreign Languages, Proceedings*, XXIX (1978): 91–94.

23. Singleton, *Commentary* 1, n. 119, p. 92.

24. Ibid., n. 120, pp. 92–93.

25. Ibid., n. 103, p. 90.

26. Northrop Frye, *Anatomy of Criticism* (Princeton, NJ: Princeton University Press, 1957), pp. 169–170.

27. Dragonetti, "L'épisode de Francesca," p. 112.

28. Ricoeur, "Herméneutique des symboles," p. 56. (Translation mine)

29. Burke, *A Grammar of Motives*, p. xx.

30. Poggioli, "Tragedy or Romance?" p. 336.

31. Cited in Singleton, *Commentary* 3, n. 1, p. 4.

32. Thomas Merton, *The New Man* (Toronto: Bantam Books, 1961), pp. 61–62.

33. Dragonetti, "L'épisode de Francesca," p. 112.

34. In her discussion of *Paradiso* XVI, 13–15—

onde Beatrice, ch'era un poco scevra,
ridendo, parve quella che tossio
al primo fallo scritto di Ginevra.

at which Beatrice, who was a little withdrawn, smiled and seemed like her who coughed at the first fault that is written of Guinevere.—

which alludes to the scene of Lancelot's and Guinevere's kiss, Barbara Vinken (*"Encore*: Francesca da Rimini," p. 405) has arrived at the same conclusion, seeing Francesca—like Guinevere—as a *figura Evae*: "Dante underlines Guinevere's responsibility for the 'primo fallo' and puts her with these words in a typological relation with the seductress Eve: it was by the first fault that man fell. From the perspective of paradise, Dante disavows Francesca's narration explicitly and ranks her among the *figurae Evae*." The typological relation of Francesca's "prima radice" to Guinevere's "primo fallo" and to Eve's first fall now appears to be quite striking.

35. See René Girard, "The Mimetic desire of Paolo and Francesca," in his *"To double business bound," Essays on Literature, Mimesis, Anthropology* (Baltimore, MD and London: Johns Hopkins University Press, 1978), pp. 1–8.

36. Franco Masciandaro, "Notes on the Image of the Point in the *Divine Comedy*," *Italica* LIV, 2 (1977): 215–226.

37. Jean Pucelle, *Le Temps* (Paris: Presses Universitaires, 1972), p. 59. (Translation mine)

38. Cf. Maria Simonelli, "Bonaggiunta Orbicciani e la problematica dello stil nuovo (*Purg.* XXIV)," *Dante Studies* LXXXVI (1968): 80: "Per Dante non si tratta di distinguere tra *amore spirituale* e *amore carnale* (ed è questo un travisamento critico dovuto in gran parte alla tradizione neoplatonica tardo-quattrocentesca), ma piuttosto tra passione e virtù."

39. Vinken ("*Encore*: Francesca da Rimini," p. 405) argues that, in light of her *imitatio* of Guinevere, it must have been Francesca who kissed Paolo: "If it was *imitatio*, as Francesca suggests, then Francesca must have kissed Paolo and is trying, through false citation, to obliterate her initiative. In declaring this initiative an imitation, she distorts her part in the story, that—worse than *imitatio*—consisted in seducing. She is the seductress and not the seduced. Francesca denies her fault and repeats Eve's primordial speech act in Paradise: 'The serpent tricked me, and I ate' (Gen. 3:13). Mutatis mutandis, the book seduced me and that's why I did it.' Francesca twists this into an outright lie; she blames it all on the book she has to distort in order to exculpate herself." I find this interpretation as cogent as my own but not as convincing in regard to Francesca's "lie." That Francesca would lie about who took the initiative, in the presence of Paolo (and, in the presence of Dante, about Lancelot's initiative), thus accusing her lover for his role in a seduction for which the book they were reading was the prime mover, seems a little strained. It can be argued that Paolo's initiative does not exclude or lessen Francesca's (perhaps more subtle) initiative as a seductress. I would speak, instead, of a reciprocal seduction, with Francesca (along with the lovers' *reading* of the Arthurian romance) playing the predominant role, as she does in her relation to Dante the pilgrim, whom, along with the (male) reader—as Professor Vinken has observed—Francesca also tries to seduce. See also Anna Hatcher and Mark Musa, "The Kiss: *Inferno* V and the Old French Prose Lancelot," *Comparative Literature* 20 (1968): 97–109; and Susan Noakes, "The Double Misreading of Paolo and Francesca," *Philological Quarterly* 62 (Spring 1983): 221–239.

40. Cf. Dante's *Convivio* (IV. xxviii, 60–65), trans. William Walrond Jackson (Oxford: The Clarendon Press, 1909), pp. 292–293: "Truly the knight Lancelot, and our noblest of Latins, Guido da Montefeltro, did not wish to enter port with sail full set. These noble men indeed shortened the sail of their worldly occupations, for in their extreme age they surrendered themselves to religion, laying aside all worldly delights and pursuits."

41. Pucelle, *Le Temps*, p. 102.

42. Poggioli, "Tragedy or Romance? " p. 354.

43. Ibid., p. 355.

44. James Joyce, *A Portrait of the Artist as a Young Man* (New York: Viking Press, 1964), p. 204.

45. Louis L. Martz, "The Saint as Tragic Hero. *Saint Joan* and *Murder in the Cathedral*," in *Tragic Themes in Western Literature*, ed. Cleanth Brooks (New Haven, CT: Yale University Press, 1955), p. 153.

IV. The Recovery of the Way to Eden: Rites of Expulsion and Reconciliation in *Purgatorio* I

In *Purgatorio* the drama of the return to the Earthly Paradise is given new expression in the forms that are connatural to it, those of ritual. If in *Inferno*, with the exception of the garden in Limbo's "noble castle," the wayfarer has encountered various forms and degrees of negation or adulteration of the myth of the Earthly Paradise, and in a sense, as we have seen in the episode of Paolo and Francesca, he has returned to a false Eden, in *Purgatorio* he learns to recover the way to the true Eden. Correspondingly, he gradually discovers the deep meaning of the original myth of the Earthly Paradise. More important, he now awakens, as spectator and actor, to a new life, the life of ritual and hence of the sacred. To a certain degree this is true of the reader as well. There is a solidarity between us and the wayfarer, between our drama and his drama, which stems from a common ground, an "original scene" of our deepest and most secret aspirations and fears that the myth of the Earthly Paradise both expresses and hides from the light of discursive reason. It *hides* them in the measure and form in which we are either blind to this myth, or are presumptuous in our attempt to define it in *our* terms, refusing to meet it on its own terms, namely those that have been entrusted to the Scriptures—as a *story*, a *drama*, and not as a *system*. On the other hand, the myth *reveals* those aspirations and fears, in the measure and form in which we, individually and collectively, in isolation from and in the presence of the community, attempt to "remember" the myth of Eden through interpretation and performance.

To reiterate the generally accepted notion that ritual, myth, and drama are intimately connected is only to describe them from "outside" and to separate them. What should be stressed instead is that the very life of drama, and hence the creative force of its inner form, is closely dependent upon the dynamic relation between ritual and myth, that is, the never-to-be-realized, inexhaustible attempts of ritual to "contain" or "embody" myth. Our task, as we examine the opening scenes of *Purgatorio*, is to bring to life the creative force of this process whereby ritual, as it interacts with myth—as it interprets and performs the action of the myth—develops into drama, and therefore renders *actual*, in the space or scene it creates, what the actors and the spectators (or readers) share: the longing to enter the Earthly Paradise, to recapture what is felt as a lost harmonious relation with the world and its Creator (or with the world as sacred, as a manifestation of the divine).

Our special concern is to discover in Dante's dramaturgy at once the inner forms of drama and their salvific function. In other words, as we encounter and analyze scenes, actions, agents, and purpose, with the varying ratios that bind them, and therefore the tragic rhythm that their interrelation produces, we shall be asking, at least implicitly: how do they constitute a strategy, a method of conversion, and therefore of transformation and transcendence?

Having announced the new theme and action of his poetry—the purification of the human spirit—Dante gives form to the first scene of *Purgatorio*:

Dolce color d'orïental zaffiro,
   che s'accoglieva nel sereno aspetto
   del mezzo, puro infino al primo giro,
a li occhi miei ricominciò diletto,
   tosto ch'io usci' fuor de l'aura morta
   che m'avea contristati li occhi e 'l petto.

(*Purg.* I, 13–18)

Sweet hue of oriental sapphire which was gathering in the serene face of the sky, pure even to the first circle, to my eyes restored delight, as soon as I issued forth from the dead air that had afflicted my eyes and breast.

The restoration of delight at the sight of the beauty of the morning sky clearly speaks of a paradisal state. "Diletto" is a key-word in our "grammar" of the return to Eden.[1] We recall that in the story of Paolo and Francesca, the goal of their reading ("Noi leggiavano un giorno per *diletto*") coincided with a false paradise; and we also recall the essentially illusory paradise of the "mountain of delight," the "*dilettoso* monte" of the Prologue scene. That the present scene is one of a merely temporary and partial recovery of the edenic state is elucidated by the scenes that follow. We can thus summarize them. The pilgrim sees the planet Venus, that "made the whole east smile"; then, turning his gaze to the South Pole he sees the "four stars never seen before save by the first people," that is, Adam and Eve. As the poet recalls the scene in which "the heavens seemed to rejoice in their flames," he exclaims:

> oh settentrïonal vedovo sito,
> poi che privato se' di mirar quelle!
>
> (*Purg.* I, 26–27)

O northern widowed clime, that are deprived of beholding them!

But this sense of loss and the accompanying nostalgia for Eden, as well as the knowledge that the four stars are those that only Adam and Eve saw before the Fall, belong only to the poet, who writes in the here and now of this life's journey.[2] Dante the pilgrim, at least in this scene, does not seem to share this lament for the lost paradise, nor the knowledge of the four stars' identity. Indeed, he now seems to continue to experience the delight felt when he first emerged from the "dead air" of Hell, a delight that springs from a kind of elementary or primordial awareness of being part of a natural order and hence from a natural sympathy with the beauty of creation.

The text shows us a pilgrim who now essentially sees but without understanding. And, significantly, much as in the early scenes of the Prologue, here Dante the pilgrim seems to experience things in isolation. There is no explicit or implied reference to Virgil. This reinforces the impression created by the first scenes of *Purgatorio*, that Dante the character re-enacts or recollects (the kind of *anamnesis* that we all experience when, in certain timeless moments, we feel at one with nature) a primordial state of innocence and of harmony with the world. These scenes are analogous to those of the Prologue where the pilgrim found himself to be part of the first scene of creation, "the beginning of the morning" when "Divine Love first set those beautiful things in motion" (*Inf.* I, 37–40). But as in that scene, so now this recapturing of the edenic state, or rather this interpretation of that state, proves to be insufficient, if not false. We discover these insufficiencies only when we follow the dramatic shift from one scene to another, when, reading dramatistically, we detect the ruptures separating and yet joining dialectically the different scenes. But, as we have noted many times in the course of this study, in that very moment of rupture, we experience at once the "death" of the earlier scene and the "birth" of a new scene.

The creative rupture we announced above comes with the sudden appearance of an old man (later to be identified as Cato):

> Com'io dal loro sguardo fui partito,
>   un poco me volgendo a l'altro polo,
>   là onde 'l Carro già era sparito,
> vidi presso di me un veglio solo,
>   degno di tanta reverenza in vista,
>   che più non dee a padre alcun figliuolo.
> Lunga la barba e di pel bianco mista
>   portava, a' suoi capelli simigliante,
>   de' quai cadeva al petto doppia lista.
> Li raggi de le quattro luci sante
>   fregiavan sì la sua faccia di lume,
>   ch'i' 'l vedea come 'l sol fosse davante.
>
> (*Purg.* I, 28–39)

When I had withdrawn my gaze from them, turning a little to the other pole, there whence the Wain had already disappeared, I saw close to me an old man alone, worthy in his looks of so great reverence that no son owes more to his father. His beard was long and streaked with white, like his locks of which a double tress fell on his breast. The rays of the four holy lights so adorned his face with brightness that I saw him as if the sun were before him.

As in the Prologue scene at the moment of Virgil's appearance, so now the pilgrim discovers the presence of the Other, the one who will break the solipsistic relation of the subject to the object, of the I to the Not-I, creating a new and problematic relation of intersubjectivity that will dispel the danger of the subject mistaking his perception of the object for the object itself, and, in our scene, of thinking that the luminous beauty of the sky, of Venus, and of the four stars signal the presence of the paradisal state rather than merely a foretaste of it.

As the rays of the four stars illuminate the patriarch's face, they constitute an essential component of the manifestation of his presence. Significantly, now the poet calls the four stars "sante" ("holy"), thus conferring to the figure of the "veglio" the character of the sacred, which was already announced by his sudden, mysterious appearance. Equally significant is the fact that Dante likens the illuminating power of the four stars to that of the sun, an obvious symbol of God. And as we recall that the venerable looks of the "veglio" inspired in the pilgrim the reverence of a son for his father, we can only conclude that here Dante is representing a hierophany. Like Virgil in the Prologue scene whom the wayfarer had addressed with the words of the Psalmist, "*Miserere* di me," Cato appears as a "mask" of God.[3]

There is a well-known passage in the *Convivio* (IV. xxviii, 13–15) that foreshadows this scene. Speaking of Marcia's return to her first husband Cato after the death of Hortensius, to whom Cato himself had given her, Dante says that her return symbolizes the noble soul returning to God at the beginning of old age, and that no man is more worthy than Cato to symbolize God. If, in the light of this text and our preceding analysis, we can identify the main action of *Purgatorio* I as the return of the pilgrim's soul to God, we should direct our attention to Dante's dramatization of this return, lest we miss essential meanings of both its nature and validity. How does the very representation of the pilgrim's return to God constitute an authentic strategy of conversion? We may begin to answer that Dante is constructing this return as a re-enactment of the original myth of the Earthly Paradise, in order to recover its deepest structure, its inner form. But this is possible and authentic only if it does not exclude the deficient or false journey back to the Earthly Paradise, in other words, if it lives side by side, dialectically, with the false attempts to represent the original Adamic myth.

If we glance back at the first scenes of *Purgatorio* I, we can already detect a significant measure of this creative dialectic inherent in Dante's representation. The pilgrim first experiences delight at the sight of the beauty of creation. For a moment at least, he seems to experience something analogous to what Adam must have experienced at his first awakening to the world around him. Then he discovers the presence of the four stars, which he has never seen before, and which only Adam and Eve ("the first people") have seen. As I have already observed, there is a significant, creative distance between what the pilgrim sees and what the poet sees, as he narrates and constructs his scenes. The first, unlike the second, does not know the identity of these stars or that they are "holy." At least he does not know it in the same way the poet knows it. He cannot name them, yet he knows them and their holiness intuitively we might say, both directly by experiencing their luminous presence and indirectly through the delight that they provoke in him. Of course, this is the delight that the poet experiences by analogy as he creates the words and images through which he "remembers" what he has seen. Needless to say, if we did not accept this "play," this make-believe within which we imagine the pilgrim experiencing directly— "actually"—what the poet creates, everything would collapse, as any play would the moment we refused to accept its rules. The pilgrim continues to experience a kind of "second innocence" still in terms of delight and pleasure, thus ignoring the Fall and the world of toil and strife that followed from it. This is reinforced by the correspondent delight he sees manifested in the sky, in virtue of an instinctive sympathy with nature ("the heavens seemed to rejoice in their flames"). But at this point the poet expresses his lament for the lost vision of the four stars caused by the Fall. In doing so, he interprets what the pilgrim (and the reader) must have felt obscurely: the sense of "loss," for these stars are not seen in the northern hemisphere. More important, here the poet is expressing the contiguity of two experiences or of two perspectives: delight at the sight of these stars, and sadness for their loss; in other words, of innocence and bliss possessed and soon lost.

And is this not the very form, and indeed the very substance of the original myth of Eden—that it was (and as we shall see, that it can be) only briefly possessed? Is this not what the pilgrim (and the reader) is gradually discovering as the true myth and therefore as the authentic model to imitate and re-enact in his life's journey? With these rhetorical questions we are attempting to formulate a working hypothesis whose validity awaits further evidence—something that other scenes of *Purgatorio* I and II will give us.

Let us turn to Cato's first words addressed to Dante and Virgil:

> "Chi siete voi che contro al cieco fiume
>   fuggita avete la pregione etterna?"
>   diss' el, movendo quelle oneste piume.
> "Chi v'ha guidati, o che vi fu lucerna,
>   uscendo fuor de la profonda notte
>   che sempre nera fa la valle inferna?
> Son le leggi d'abisso così rotte?
>   o è mutato in ciel novo consiglio,
>   che, dannati, venite a le mie grotte?"

(Purg. I, 40–48)

"Who are you that, against the blind stream, have fled the eternal prison?" said he, moving those venerable plumes. "Who has guided you, or what was a lamp to you issuing forth from the deep night that ever makes the infernal valley black? Are the laws of the abyss thus broken? Or is some new counsel changed in Heaven that though damned you come to my rocks?"

What we have so far learned to identify as a "return to Eden and to the Father," or as a re-enactment of a pristine paradisal state in which man is in harmony both with the natural order and with the Creator, now takes on new meaning. We have already noted that the pilgrim's discovery of the Other in the "veglio" injects in the paradisal scene of delight a new dimension, which is essential to refashion an otherwise false Eden, or false return to Eden. This becomes increasingly clear as we, with the wayfarer, discover more facets of the Other.

The venerable figure of the "veglio"—the "mask" of the Father—at first constitutes for the pilgrim a reassuring presence, as it must have been for Adam before the Fall. But then, unexpectedly, his harsh words transform him into a new figure, indeed into an obstacle and a threat to the pilgrim's climb up the mountain and to the journey as he envisages it. If we look closely at these words, we discover that the "veglio" appears as an obstacle because of his adherence to a law. In this he resembles the figure of God Who says to man "thou shall not . . . ," as we read in Genesis 2:16–17, where we find God admonishing Adam not to eat of the tree of Knowledge of good and evil. Here, as in the original myth, we can catch glimpses of the conflict, and therefore of the essentially dramatic relation between the created being and God. What concerns us most here, as we identify the two "antagonists" and their respective "grounds" and motivations, is to discover in the manifestation of the conflict, in the play of action and reaction, the point of resolution in which there occurs a creative exchange whereby both agents and their initial positions are transformed and transcended.

What helps us define the figure of Dante as character, and in the present case as "antagonist," is first of all the main action in which he is engaged—his quest for Eden. As we have observed in the Prologue scene and in the episode of Paolo and Francesca, this action appears more like a flight than a quest, for the pilgrim mistakes his true object and goal for a deficient or false image of it. This deficiency or falseness is revealed through conflict, especially when his action, with the correlative motivation that propels him forward, is interrupted by an obstacle. In the Prologue, we recall, it was first the leopard, then the lion, and finally the she-wolf that barred his way to the summit of the sunlit hill and therefore to the paradisal state that he secretly longed to attain. Yet as we have seen, this obstacle or interdiction to what otherwise would have been, in the words of Virgil, a "corto andar," a "short journey," proved to be beneficial and salutary, for it forced the pilgrim to face his failure and to recognize the limits of his fallen nature. And significantly, it was in this moment of failure that he opened himself to what can only be defined as Other with relation to his previous attempt, his previous action. As we have already noted, this obstacle constituted a break or *caesura*, that narrow space which is highly creative because, paradoxically, *nothing* happens in it, and there is no representation—and therefore no danger—to fix the action of the quest within the confines of a given image, scene, word, or other context. This is the creative space that prepares the ground for the following action and scene. It coincides with the blind moment of innermost vision or intuition equivalent to an act of faith, that is, a total openness to what is Other.

Our task, once again, is to construct the kind of discourse, to find the appropriate words that will take us—in the company of our poet and protagonist Dante—to the threshold of such moments. As we return to the scene of the "veglio," we recognize another creative obstacle. What gives special force and significance to this obstacle is that he is a *figura Dei*, a "mask" of God, as we have said earlier. Therefore the conflict we are witnessing in *Purgatorio* I is essentially between Dante the pilgrim and God, both God as Judge and God as represented by Cato. Cato constitutes an obstacle for the pilgrim and Virgil as long as their presence remains unexplained in the light of his unbending adherence to law, that is, as long as he sees them as damned figures who somehow either have been able to break the laws of Inferno or have been granted access to Purgatorio because of "some new council changed in Heaven." Either violation would be an act of violence against divine law: in the first it would be human violence, while in the second it would be God's violence. Both alternatives, of course, appear impossible to the eyes of Cato. And as long as this view persists, he will represent a hindrance and a threat to the journey of Virgil and Dante to Eden.

The edenic delight at first experienced by Dante is suddenly destroyed by the irruption of the wrathful figure of Cato. In this aporia lies the most crucial moment of the drama we have before us. Here Dante invites us to ask how this aporia can be resolved, and therefore, how the drama of the pilgrim's return to Eden can keep on unfolding, asserting its creative function as it interprets and represents the human struggle with the Absolute?

The answers to these questions are given to us in eminently dramatic forms in the scenes that follow Cato's address to Virgil and Dante, which we can thus summarize. Virgil, playing the role of mediator, enjoins Dante to kneel before Cato. This is an act of reverence, and therefore of submission to one who represents a higher order or a higher authority than one's own. It is an expression of humility. It can also be seen as an act intended to appease the wrath of Cato and therefore to deflect or annul the violence connected to that wrath, which for our two pilgrims would take the form of expulsion from Cato's realm. This act of submission sums up all that Virgil says in defense of the legitimacy of his and Dante's presence in Purgatorio, through which he hopes to win Cato's approval for their journey to continue. Giving fuller expression to the humility implicit in the kneeling figure of the pilgrim, Virgil states that he did not come of himself but by the power of the prayers of a lady who "descended from Heaven" (*Purg.* I, 52–54). Then he mentions that Dante was near death when he came to his aid. As a remedy to this quasi-death, Virgil continues, he has shown him "all the guilty" people of Hell, that is, the roots of evil and the state of death. In other words, as Dante the pilgrim remains prostrate before Cato, Virgil recollects the salutary, beneficial death (and, therefore, violence) that the journey through Hell has essentially represented. Having spoken of this paradoxical liberation from death through death—a death by analogy, by partial contamination and dramatic interaction—Virgil addresses Cato with this peroration:

> "Or ti piaccia gradir la sua venuta:
>   libertà va cercando, ch'è sì cara,
>   come sa chi per lei vita rifiuta.
> Tu 'l sai, ché non ti fu per lei amara
>   in Utica la morte, ove lasciasti
>   la vesta ch'al gran dì sarà sì chiara.

(*Purg.* I, 70–75)

Now may it please you to approve his coming. He goes seeking freedom, which is so precious, as he knows who renounces life for it; you know it, for death for its sake was not bitter to you in Utica, where you did leave the raiment which on the great day will be so bright.

It is important to note that Cato's identity is now revealed by his death in Utica. This is the most significant trait of this *figura Dei* or mask of God. It is equally important to apprehend the correlation (established by Virgil, and constituting a kind of argument—a defense and a plea) between the liberating "death" that Dante the wayfarer has experienced in his journey through Hell and Cato's own death. And as Virgil states that Dante is seeking that same freedom for which Cato had renounced his life, he clearly establishes a parallel or a correspondence whose creative force lies in the fact that, as it recollects those two "deaths" and makes them present in *this* scene, it reasserts them for the future, in other words, it reactivates and reproposes the liberating, though mysterious, power of death, the death in humility, and the death of the self that surrenders to a higher power and order. This involves Dante the pilgrim and Cato—the two "antagonists" in this drama—equally. The two are in a sense each the "double" of the other. Undoubtedly, Dante the pilgrim occupies an inferior position, as his prostration obviously expresses; he is the initiate who must imitate his model, Cato (who, let us not forget, is a mask of God). Yet the pilgrim also constitutes a kind of reflection and even a "model" for Cato. In other words, Virgil essentially invites Cato to recognize in the figure of the humble Dante a paradigm and an echo at once of his "old" and of his true self, of what he has been on earth and of what he is now. There must therefore be a certain reciprocity between Cato and Dante, not only perceived but made actual, having consequently the vital power to transform.

The mirror-like correspondence between Dante the pilgrim and Cato is emphasized by Virgil's definition of Cato's death as "bitter," which clearly harks back to the Prologue (*Inf.* I, 7) where the dark wood is said to be "so bitter that death is only a little less so." Once again as we turn our attention to Virgil's "defense," especially its conclusion, we discover other areas of creative exchange and of transformation provoked by an alternation of opposition and similarity:

> "Non son li editti etterni per noi guasti,
>   ché questi vive e Minòs me non lega;
>   ma son del cerchio ove son li occhi casti
> di Marzia tua, che 'n vista ancor ti priega,
>   o santo petto, che per tua la tegni;
>   per lo suo amore adunque a noi ti piega.
> Lasciane andar per li tuoi sette regni;

grazie riporterò di te a lei,
se d'esser mentovato là giù degni."

(Purg. I, 76–84)

"The eternal edicts are not violated by us, for this one is alive and Minos does not bind me; but I am of the circle where are the chaste eyes of your Marcia, who in her look still prays you, O holy breast, that you hold her for your own. For love of her, then, incline yourself to us: let us go on through your seven realms. I will report to her your kindness, if you deign to be mentioned there below."

As we read Virgil's assertion that he and Dante have not violated God's eternal edicts, for they are not damned—Dante is alive and he dwells in Limbo—at first glance we take this to be merely another way to establish a correspondence and reveal a kinship with Cato's adherence to God's law. But upon closer scrutiny, we observe that Virgil's assertion of the legitimacy of his and Dante's coming to the shores of Purgatory is rather superficial, and in a sense merely "technical," posing more questions than it answers. For the fact that Dante is alive is more problematic, more a sign that the "eternal edicts" have been broken, than if he were dead. We recall the poet's words in the Prologue about the extraordinary event of the wayfarer's escape from the "selva oscura," of his crossing "the pass that never left anyone alive." Yet the assertion of the legitimacy of Virgil's and Dante's journey is apparently given as the "correct" answer to Cato's first inquiry "are the laws of Hell broken?" It is therefore expected to be a sufficient reason for Cato to admit them in his realm. Why, then, does Virgil beseech Cato for permission to enter with Dante Cato's "seven realms" for his love of Marcia? What is the special function of introducing this figure in the economy of Virgil's and Dante's encounter with Cato?

We can answer that, by appealing to Cato's love of Marcia, Virgil produces a significant shift in his "defense" of Dante the pilgrim, for it departs from the perspective of law and judgment which was first shared, as we have seen, by the two pilgrims and by Cato. The success of this defense now depends not on a strict interpretation and application of a law, but on a complex system of relationships between persons and therefore on a dramatic form through which such relationships are naturally manifested and actualized. The scene that Virgil constructs and evokes, as he mentions Marcia "who in her looks still prays" that Cato will "hold her" for his own, is clearly analogous to the scene of the kneeling Dante who also, by his prostration and through the intercession of his guide, prays that Cato, as a *figura Dei* (whom Virgil addresses with words that speak of divinity: "O holy breast"), will "hold him for his own."

As we look closely at the other components of the larger scene we have before us, we cannot fail to recognize the crucial action that in a sense Virgil "calls into being": the reconciliation of man with God as represented respectively by Dante the pilgrim and by Cato—a reconciliation that is closely dependent upon a reciprocal act of humility. It should not escape our attention that Virgil asks Cato that he and Dante be allowed to enter Purgatory with words that clearly suggest humility. They literally speak of a *bending*, not unlike that of the kneeling Dante: "a noi ti *piega*" ("*incline* yourself to us"). Thus Virgil is actually inviting Cato to be like the one who in turn is—or is becoming—like him, for in his descent to Hell the pilgrim has already experienced a kind of death and now in his state of prostration experiences something analogous to Cato's death. He too conforms his will to the will of another, to Cato's now, as, since his awakening in the Prologue scene, he has done not only directly in his relation with Virgil but also indirectly through Virgil—in his relation with Beatrice, Lucy, Mary, and ultimately God.

If Cato re-enacts or "makes new" in this scene what he once did in his life's journey—dying for freedom as he "died" for Marcia by doing her will—then a true creative exchange will take place between Virgil the mediator, Dante the petitioner, and Cato the guardian of Purgatory and mask of God. We can measure the creative force of Virgil's prayer—or more precisely of the scenes and actions through which he gives it form—by the effect it produces on Cato. As we turn our attention to Cato's response, our task is to identify, from this perspective, the "motivational force" of those scenes that Virgil has constructed, beginning when he enjoins Dante the pilgrim to kneel. In other words, we should attempt to define what really moves Cato and how the scene in which he interacts with Virgil and Dante constitutes the creative ground for his action, with which he decisively contributes to the solution of the conflict between himself and Dante the pilgrim (Virgil playing essentially the role of mediator).

> "Marzïa piacque tanto a li occhi miei
>   mentre ch'i' fu' di là," diss'elli allora,
>   "che quante grazie volse da me, fei.
> Or che di là dal mal fiume dimora,
>   più muover non mi può, per quella legge

che fatta fu quando me n'usci' fora.
Ma se donna del ciel ti move e regge,
   come tu di', non c'è mestier lusinghe:
   bastisi ben che per lei mi richegge."

(Purg. I, 85–93)

"Marcia so pleased my eyes while I was yonder," he then said, "that every kindness she wished of me I did. Now that she dwells beyond the evil stream no more may she move me, by the law which was made when I came forth from there. But if a lady of Heaven moves and directs you, as you say, there is no need of flattery: let it fully suffice that for her sake you ask me."

The creative force at work in the present scene is that of mimesis, of imitation of action. Hence this force is at once inherent in and manifested through the direct awareness of an experience or an event and therefore through the analogical relationship that such awareness calls forth. We might in fact speak of a sympathetic response on Cato's part to the scene of Marcia that Virgil has constructed. This response, by the very power of analogy that informs it, constitutes alternately a direct reflection of Virgil's "scene" and a departure from it. Cato first evokes and in a sense relives the scene of his past life in which for "love of her" he granted Marcia every kindness she wished of him.

As Cato recalls the past, we—like Virgil (and the pilgrim)—see him as a benevolent figure who contrasts with the stern figure of the early scenes in which we first saw him move and act. And as we see him in this new light, we are naturally inclined, again with the two pilgrims, to expect that for the love of Marcia he will now grant Virgil and Dante access to his realm. Instead, with the words that follow, Cato creates another, opposite "scene," that of Marcia who, because she "dwells beyond the evil stream" where she is bound by another law, can no longer move him. But immediately after, he constructs yet another scene which at once is analogous to and transcends the preceding scene, by introducing the figure of the "lady of Heaven" of whom Virgil had spoken at the very beginning of his address to Cato. What we witness here is a process of appropriation and transformation which is connatural to mimesis, and which is made manifest and can thus be apprehended as a sequence of actions characterized by the alternation of tragic rhythm. This eminently dramatic form, by asserting the vitality and creativity of mimesis and analogy, helps us to capture (with a directness that discursive reason or the reductive discourse of the allegorist can never attain) the "shifting life of the psyche"⁺ of the characters in whose presence we live and act, and through whom, mimetically, we are lifted out of our "old" conventional selves. In other words, by the power of Dante's dramaturgy, we see Cato as a persona who appears alternately as a stern, inflexible judge and as a benevolent figure, and who is seen to be moved first for the sake of his wife Marcia and then for a "donna del ciel."

This "donna del ciel" and her specific role as intercessor in the "conflict" between Dante the pilgrim (the postulant) and Cato (the stern judge) call to mind the analogous figure of Mary, another "donna del ciel," mentioned by Beatrice in the Prologue scene as the one who "broke" God's harsh judgment:

> "Donna è gentil nel ciel che si compiange
> di questo 'mpedimento ov'io ti mando,
> sì che duro giudicio là sù frange."
>
> (*Inf.* II, 94–96)

"In Heaven there is a gracious lady who has such pity of this impediment to which I send you that stern judgment is broken there above."

As we apprehend the significant analogies that link the two scenes, we again see Cato more clearly as a mask of God, and specifically as one whose "duro giudizio" is broken by the intercession of a "donna del ciel." We thus witness the paradoxical solution of conflict by virtue of a surrender to what can essentially be called violence—the violence that one will may suffer from another. In this context I must quote—though anachronistically, for it comes much later in Dante's journey to God—a strikingly illuminating passage from *Paradiso*:

> *Regnum celorum* vïolenza pate
> da caldo amore e da viva speranza,
> che vince la divina volontate:
> non a guisa che l'omo a l'om sobranza,
> ma vince lei perché vuole esser vinta,
> e, vinta, vince con sua beninanza.
>
> (*Par.* XX, 94–99)

Regnum celorum [the Kingdom of Heaven] suffers violence from fervent love and from living hope which vanquishes the Divine will: not as man overcomes man, but vanquishes it because it wills to be vanquished, and vanquished, vanquishes with its own benignity.

We now understand more deeply how Dante the dramatist has given life to the figure of Cato as a mask of God. A term that sums up what makes Cato a *figura Dei* is one we have already encountered in the course of this chapter: humility, whose highest expression is death. As we utter this word against the backdrop of the sequence of scenes we have just examined, we know that we have come full circle in our response to what Dante as dramatist has constructed for us. We now see in full light what we dimly glimpsed at the beginning of our episode. As we recall Virgil's words about Cato's death and freedom—"Tu 'l sai, ché non ti fu per lei amara / in Utica la morte"—we see in this death, in this act, the fullness and the mystery of this character, and we have a deeper sense of the creative, transfiguring force of his death and what makes it authentically tragic. We also see more sharply why he is the one of whom we can say, again with Dante's own words, "and what earthly man was more worthy of signifying God than Cato? Certainly, no one" (*Convivio* IV. xxviii, 15). More important, as we reflect on this death we perceive its vital, actual presence in a number of scenes where we have seen Cato move and live, such as the one of his surrender or "death" for the sake of Marcia, or the scene of his surrender or "death" for the sake of the "lady of Heaven," or, finally, that other undeclared but no less real surrender to Virgil and Dante, expressed by his "bending" toward them, as Virgil asked of him. What gains focus now is that this mask of God, this guardian of Purgatory (the realm which is "crowned" by the Garden of Eden) constitutes for Virgil and Dante a beneficent, providential obstacle by injecting conflict and drama into what at first appeared as a serene, blissful scene. This difficulty forces Virgil and Dante, but especially the latter, to find the true way to the Earthly Paradise.

In the scenes that immediately follow those we have just studied, we discover that, significantly, the solution to this conflict or drama of the pilgrims' admission into Cato's "seven realms" comes in the form of a shift, a departure from the perspective envisaged by Virgil and Dante (and, of course, shared by the reader). Having dismissed all but Virgil's mention of the guidance of a "donna del ciel" as inconsequential flattery, Cato moves Virgil to action, specifically that of ritual:

"Va dunque, e fa che tu costui ricinghe
    d'un giunco schietto e che li lavi 'l viso,
    sì ch'ogne sudiciume quindi stinghe;
ché non si converria, l'occhio sorpriso
    d'alcuna nebbia, andar dinanzi al primo
    ministro, ch'è di quei di paradiso.
Questa isoletta intorno ad imo ad imo,
    là giù colà dove la batte l'onda,
    porta di giunchi sovra 'l molle limo:
null'altra pianta che facesse fronda
    o indurasse, vi puote aver vita,
    però ch'a le percosse non seconda.
Poscia non sia di qua vostra reddita;
    lo sol vi mosterrà, che surge omai,
    prendere il monte a più lieve salita."

(*Purg.* I, 94–108)

"Go, then, and see that you gird him with a smooth rush, and that you
bathe his face so that you remove all defilement from it, for with eye
dimmed by any mist it would not be fitting to go before the first minister
of those of Paradise. This little island, round about its very base, down
there where the wave beats it, bears rushes on its soft mud. No other
plant which would put forth leaf or harden can live there, because it
yields not to the buffetings. Then let not your return be this way. The
sun, which is now rising, will show you where to take the mountain at an
easier ascent."

In the very moment when conflict appears to be resolved, with Virgil and
Dante granted access to Purgatory, this scene introduces another break in
the action. Cato's enjoining Virgil to take Dante the pilgrim down to the
shore of the island of Purgatory and not to return where they now are
suggests that their coming this way constituted a false attempt to enter
Purgatory and reach the Earthly Paradise. Like the failed conversion of the
Prologue scene, it can be seen as a transgression analogous to that of Adam
and Eve. In a sense, it is a re-enactment of their original transgression. And
as in the scene in Genesis, transgression provokes expulsion. Does Cato in
fact not expel Dante when he bids Virgil to take him down to the base of
Purgatory, as he "expelled" Marcia when he gave her to his friend Hortensius? And like God's expulsion of Adam and Eve from the Earthly Paradise,

is this expulsion not a beneficent, providential act necessary for the pilgrim's recovery of humility, without which he cannot enter Cato's "seven realms"?

We detect the presence of this pattern of transgression and expulsion that harks back to the beginning of the poem's action in the Prologue scene, just as it harks back by analogy to the beginning of a larger "poem," that of the race of Adam. At the same time we realize that once again Dante is representing the conflict between two modes of "returning" to Eden and therefore between two versions of the myth of the Earthly Paradise: one which we have called the myth of the "second innocence" which ignores conflict, violence, and speaks only of innocence and bliss; and the other, the "original myth" of the Earthly Paradise, speaks of conflict and violence as the foundation or ground of human existence. This conflict or violence, we remember, is something that is *already there*, as the serpent is *already there*, threatening Adam's and Eve's state of innocence and bliss and contributing to their fall into history and into culture.

By focusing on this conflict and making it in fact a fundamental and ever-recurring structure of this poem, Dante attempts to make present in a vital way a conundrum that we all live, collectively and individually (and whose outcome may determine whether a community or an individual will live or die). This conundrum is really our own. It is woven into the very fabric of our life. We ignore the dialectical relation between two opposed modes of being and ways of acting: one takes the form of violence, that of harsh judgment and of expulsion, and the other accepts violence; one manifests the Logos of Reason and of the ethics or justice of reciprocal violence, and the other manifests the Logos of Love, who breaks the false equilibrium of "just retribution" with its demands of endless exchange of violence, and who, to use Simone Weil's words, "changes violence into suffering."[5]

This is the conflict, the dialectic that Dante the pilgrim seemed to have forgotten in the first scene of his emergence into the light and order of nature: that his journey to the Earthly Paradise will constitute an act of transgression if he does not submit to the will of Cato and accept expulsion as salutary, and ultimately, if he does not directly suffer a death similar to the death that Cato had first suffered in Utica and that similarly he now suffers, as he yields to the "donna del ciel." Then, like Cato (and like God), he will "vanquish" by being "vanquished."

The pilgrim's acceptance of Cato's command that he be temporarily "expelled" from the Earthly Paradise is essentially a recovery and a reenactment of the expulsion narrated in the Adamic myth. But that expulsion is also the beginning of the process of reconciliation and of a "return" to Eden. We may gain a deeper understanding of this action as soon as we see it as the first of a series of rites of expulsion and reconciliation which mark crucial stages of Dante's purgatorial journey. Let us open a parenthesis and turn to *Purgatorio* IX. Here we find Dante the pilgrim before the gate of Purgatorio, which is guarded by an angel—one of "those of Paradise" of whom Cato had spoken. He is seated at the topmost of three steps, holding in his hand a "naked sword" with blinding rays. The harsh words which he first addresses to Virgil and Dante, and Virgil's reply, are strikingly reminiscent of Cato's and Virgil's exchange:

> "Dite costinci: che volete voi?"
>   cominciò elli a dire, "ov'è la scorta?
>   Guardate che 'l venir sù non vi nòi."
> "Donna del ciel, di queste cose accorta,"
>   rispuose 'l mio maestro a lui, "pur dianzi
>   ne disse: 'Andate là: quivi è la porta.' "
>
> (*Purg.* IX, 85–90)

"Say from there, what is it you seek?" he began to say; "Where is the escort? Take care lest the coming upward be to your hurt." "A heavenly lady who knows these things well," my master answered him, "said to us just now: 'Go that way, there is the gate.' "

As in the scene of *Purgatorio* I, Virgil's mention of a "donna del ciel" (Lucy this time) elicits here the angel's favorable response:

> "Ed ella i passi vostri in bene avanzi,"
>   ricominciò il cortese portinaio:
>   "Venite dunque a' nostri gradi innanzi."
>
> (*Purg.* IX, 91–93)

"And may she speed your steps to good!" began again the courteous doorkeeper; "Come forward, then, to our stairs."

Drawing on the *Pontificale Romanum*,[6] Dunstan Tucker has argued convincingly that Dante has modeled these scenes after the expulsion ceremonies of the medieval church, especially that of Ash Wednesday. Of special interest to us is the formula of expulsion pronounced by the bishop after placing ashes on the heads of the penitents, and after the latter, who were lying prostrate on the church floor, recited the penitential psalms with the clergy and the people.

The penitents then arose and the bishop delivered a discourse explaining that just as Adam, because of his sin, was expelled from Paradise, so they likewise were being expelled from the Church. Taking one of the penitents by the right hand, this one in like manner leading his neighbor so that they were linked together in a chain, he led them through the doors of the church into the open air, saying: "Behold—we expel you today from the portals of Holy Mother the Church, because of your sins, just as Adam, the first man, was expelled from Paradise because of his transgression." Finally ejected from the church and kneeling in front of the church doors, they were admonished by the bishop not to despair of God's mercy, but by fastings, prayers, pilgrimages, alms givings, and other good works so to conduct themselves that God might find them worthy of the grace of a true penance.[7]

We would fail to apprehend a great measure of the full meaning of this ceremony of expulsion if we did not continue to explore its deep, vital links with the myth of the Earthly Paradise and its relationship with the drama of salvation and tragic vision. The creative force inherent in the scene of expulsion of *Purgatorio* I is closely dependent on the correlation between ritual and myth and on the drama that is in a sense born "out of" the never-exhausted interplay and creative tension between them. Drama is itself at once ritual—a sacred act or actualization of the myth (the original narration or narration of the origins)—and myth as narration or representation of the here and now of our life. At the point where the two intersect, an original rite or a primordial sacred act is reactualized. We cannot insist enough on this correlation, on this exchange or reciprocity between ritual and myth, because if we fail to see it, there are two unfortunate consequences. On one hand, we may reduce ritual to a dry, empty shell—a relic without "memory"—and become incapable of being in touch with and *living* in the presence of the *totally other* of existence (and therefore of interrogating it despite the endless failings to receive definitive answers), and on the other, we may reduce myth to discourse, to "literature."[8]

The expulsion motif in the myth of Genesis is the focus of René Girard's illuminating discussion:

This text [of Adam and Eve's expulsion from Eden] appeals to some thinkers who believe that they can discover the Bible's essentially "repressive" character in it. For a number of centuries we have been treated to a flood of banal demystifications of this story. . . . All these demystifications fail to see that this text—just like the Prologue to the Gospel of John—establishes the relationship between God and humanity in terms of expulsion. The only difference is that *in the story of Adam and Eve, God manipulates and expels mankind* to secure the foundations of culture, whilst *in the Prologue to John it is mankind who expels God.*⁹

Another passage of his—an elucidation of John (1:4–5, 10–11)—is especially significant for our discussion:

The Johannine Logos is foreign to any kind of violence; it is therefore forever expelled, an absent Logos that never has had any direct, determining influence over human cultures. These cultures are based on the Heraclitean Logos, the Logos of expulsion, the Logos of violence, which, if it is not recognized can provide the foundation of a culture. The Johannine Logos discloses the truth of violence by having itself expelled. First and foremost, John's Prologue undoubtedly refers to the Passion. But in a more general way, the misrecognition of the Logos and mankind's expulsion of it disclose one of the fundamental principles of human society.¹⁰

In the light of these observations and of those cited from Dunstan Tucker's article, we can see more distinctly in the figure of Cato and in his scenes what earlier we perceived somewhat dimly. We now understand more deeply the nature and the rich implications of the main action that brings Dante the pilgrim and Cato together with the mediator Virgil. This action is *expulsion*. Its creative force and its efficacy are manifested and actualized when protagonists experience expulsion and accept it just as Christ, the Logos of Love, accepted it (and still accepts it), namely, when they are related to one another at once by what is in them and what transcends them. The crucial moment of resolution of the conflict or the drama we are studying coincides with the shift or difference between the action of harsh judgment and reproach (the menace of violence), which first defined Cato as the *figura* or mask of God the Father, and the action of surrender to another's will and hence of acceptance of what is beyond that judgment, which defines Cato anew as a *figura Christi*.¹¹ In this moment, to paraphrase Girard's words, the truth of the violence inherent in that judgment—a "generative," "founding" force of the Logos of violence—is revealed by the new, unexpected light of the Logos of Love. And now we see Cato's mysterious, unfathomable being (analogous to the Supreme Being of Whom he is a *figura*) manifested in some measure through *becoming*, that is through the shift or the "rupture" separating the two "masks," that of the judge (the Logos of violence) and that of the victim (the Logos of Love). Like God, Cato is "vanquished" by the "lady of Heaven" but at least in part also by Virgil and by the kneeling Dante, because his will, like the will of God "wills to be vanquished, and vanquished, vanquishes with its own benignity" (*Par.* XX, 98–99). We should add that Cato becomes truly effective and truly present to Dante the pilgrim when he reveals himself as a father and as a son, as one who commands and judges and one who is obedient, as both a *figura Patris* and a *figura Filii*, and therefore as one who expels and one who is expelled. Because of the confluence of these two "figures" in Cato, the pilgrim Dante can accept and be transformed by the "harsh judgment," the "expulsion," and therefore the "violence" coming from Cato as the "Father" as well as by the humility, the obedience of Cato as the "Son," as "Christ."

As we approach the highest point of tension in our discourse, when words are about to fail in the presence of this paradox and mystery, we must shift our attention away from words and their limits to the realm of experience, considering for a moment the historical Cato, and particularly his giving his wife to his friend Hortensius and later, after the death of the latter, taking her back once again "for his own." Do we not find here the double, apparently paradoxical action of expulsion on one hand and of acceptance and reconciliation on the other? For Cato does the will of Marcia, is "vanquished" by her, and as he "wills to be vanquished," he "vanquishes." And is this not the ground of what Dante as dramatist, constructs in *Purgatorio* I? If we think of Cato's death, of his suicide for the sake of liberty, we see that, paradoxically again, it is an act of transgression of moral and divine law, which on earth coincides with the expulsion from the community, the *civitas*. In the world beyond this transgression has provoked a similar expulsion from the City of God, for Cato is confined to the Anti-Purgatorio as its guardian until the Final Judgment, when his body—the "raiment he left in Utica"—will be "so bright" (a "resurrection" analogous to Christ's resurrection).

Once again we find ourselves in the presence of the paradoxically saving power of expulsion (like Adam's expulsion from Paradise) and of the transgression that provoked it, when, as a manifestation of the true God, it is freely accepted (loved) and is thus violence transformed into suffering. We have been led to these reflections or discourse on what we tentatively termed "experience," knowing quite well that discourse and thought cannot be ostracized or "expelled" from the so-called world of experience. They are bound to experience, but only as the Tree of Knowledge can be said to be "bound" to the Tree of Life, because their roots draw strength from a common secret source. In so doing, we have unwittingly reproduced and re-enacted the drama lived by the two interlocutors, Virgil and Cato, with Dante the pilgrim silently kneeling before Cato, constituting a kind of counterpoint to the ongoing dialogue. By turning to experience— to action—when words seem to have reached their limit or "death," we have done something analogous to what Cato does and to what he enjoins Virgil to do: to consider the preceding discourse, especially Virgil's *captatio benevolentiae*, as something ineffectual, as flattery that must be left behind and transcended, and to turn instead to action, the action of ritual (and therefore that special action through which the sacred is "remembered" and actualized). This is a movement from the word-as-discourse to the word-as-act, and, we should add, to the word-as-silence, which marks the moment when action itself reaches its limits, when it "dies" as it *must* if it is to assert the creative principle that brought it into being. This creative principle of "subordination" or "withdrawing" in the expectation of "something more" is the principle by which Cato has been moved and which has characterized him, and it is one that he has exchanged with Virgil and Dante.

Significantly, after instructing the two pilgrims to take the downward way to humility, telling them, "let not your return be this way," and after pointing to another "guide," the rising sun, he vanishes—"Così sparì" ("so he vanished"; *Purg*. I, 109–111)—"as suddenly and mysteriously as he appeared," notes Singleton.[12] This moment of withdrawal and becoming absent marks the fulfillment of all the previous words and actions of Cato. This is the culminating point of the discourse or the logic of surrender, the discourse or the logic of the Word—the Logos of Love.

We can easily detect the creativity of this absence when we look at the action that immediately follows, and which that absence dialectically calls forth:

Così sparì; e io sù mi levai
   sanza parlare, e tutto mi ritrassi
   al duca mio, e li occhi a lui drizzai.

(Purg. I, 109–111)

So he vanished; and I rose up, without speaking, and drew all close to my leader and turned my eyes to him.

The disjunctive structure of this scene is expressed by the shift from absence to presence. In strictly dramatistic terms, we see the figure of Dante the pilgrim "come into being," becoming present after a long "absence" from the scene in which Virgil and Cato were the protagonists, as soon as Cato vanishes. This sequence of absence-presence produces the effect of alternation and, in a sense, of substitution. The scene, until this moment filled by the presence of Cato—a presence that in the previous interaction with Virgil had already alternately been followed by absence—is now filled by the figure of the pilgrim and his action of rising. The very suddenness of this action, equal and opposite to the suddenness of Cato's disappearance, its piercing quality we might say, strikingly calls attention to the pilgrim's presence. Interestingly, as we reflect on this moment, we cannot help experiencing a kind of reawakening to or recollection of him. Now we realize with a fullness that eluded us earlier that during the entire dialogue between Virgil and Cato he had been kneeling in silence. In this moment of manifest, "dramatic" presence we are made aware—more keenly than before—of his "absence," his "withdrawing" or "surrendering" in the active presence of Cato and Virgil. In fact, in this very moment of action the pilgrim's silence is emphasized as the poet notes: "and I rose up, without speaking." In other words, now we are invited, by virtue of the inherent force of scene and action, to focus on the main action that earlier had constituted the very "theme" of the discourse of Virgil and Cato— death for the sake of freedom, self-surrender, accepting expulsion; in one word, humility. We now perceive the deeper implications of the first scene of the pilgrim kneeling before Cato, when we heard announced the main action and theme of the drama of *Purgatorio*.

In the last scenes of this drama lies a reaffirmation of the main action which has given life to the preceding scenes: the return to humility, or the rediscovery of the true road "back" to Eden, and therefore back to that state in which humanity lives in harmony with creation and with the Creator. In other words, this is a return to the world of the sacred. These last scenes of *Purgatorio* represent the creative power of the sacred; they speak of how it can, or rather *must*, be recaptured and made actual in the *hic et nunc* of the human journey, through gestures or rites whose very simplicity and *elemental* character mimetically reproduce the sacredness of primordial life and its mysterious emergence. But to return to the sacred is also to return to the world of conflict and of tragic rhythm, as we find expressed in the following tercet that inaugurates the sequence of scenes with which *Purgatorio* I comes to a close:

L'alba vinceva l'ora mattutina
   che fuggia innanzi, sì che di lontano
   conobbi il tremolar de la marina.

(Purg. I, 115–117)

The dawn was vanquishing the matin hour which fled before it, so that I
recognized from afar the trembling of the sea.

The first image clearly speaks of a conflict that echoes and re-enacts the
primordial conflict between light and darkness. Its resolution—light vanquishing darkness—is inherently creative, for it manifests and in a sense
brings to life the sea, and with it the mysterious force it symbolizes.

As in the scene of the pilgrim's first awakening in the dark wood which,
significantly, the poet likened to a stormy sea (Inf. I, 23–24), so now he
seems to awaken to the presence of this most powerful of natural forces,
whose symbolic function is universally known. "It is the principal function
of the symbolism of the waters," writes Paul Ricoeur, "to evoke the universal source of the virtualities from which existence emerges at once as
real and as intelligible."[13] Against this scene of emerging life which seems
to echo and reassert the creative fiat of Genesis, the poet delineates the
scene of his and Virgil's "return" to what he terms a "lost road"—the road
of humility:

Noi andavam per lo solingo piano
   com'om che torna a la perduta strada,
   che 'nfino ad essa li pare ire in vano.

(Purg. I, 118–120)

We were making our way across the solitary plain, like a man who returns
to the road he has lost and, till he comes to it, seems to go in vain.

The pilgrim's goal as he moves with Virgil across the "solitary plain" is a
"road" and therefore a journey. Thus we see this scene in sharp contrast to
the scene of the "desert strand" of the Prologue (Inf. I, 29), to which it
seems to correspond. There we witnessed the wayfarer's failure in his attempt to easily recapture the Earthly Paradise. We recall that only later, in
the scene of the "gran diserto" after he had addressed Virgil with the words
"Miserere di me" and thus recovered humility, did he learn that his real goal

was not a place, the *locus amoenus* of the Garden of Eden, but a journey, the "other journey" ("l'altro viaggio"; *Inf.* I, 91).

It is equally significant that here the poet speaks of the journey that precedes the rediscovery of the "lost road" as seeming to be vain. As we pause to reflect upon this perception which at first we readily, intuitively accepted as a commonplace experience we all share with a "man who returns to the road he has lost," we become aware of an important shift, and therefore of the creative space—the *caesura* that Dante as dramatist once again has introduced in the journey he represents. This *caesura* forces us, as it forces the pilgrim, to view the preceding scenes—from the most immediate (those of the encounter with Cato) to the most remote (those of the Prologue)—paradoxically we might say, as scenes *necessary* to his finding the "lost road" and yet *vain*. With the pilgrim we experience at once a sense of loss of what we thought we had just "possessed" in the presence of Cato (not to speak of all the other "possessions" we have gathered along the journey through Hell), and a sense that there is something greater—something *other*—that is soon to be gained. We again recognize the disjunctive form and therefore the tragic rhythm that characterizes Dante's art. Kenelm Foster has captured the essence of this tragic rhythm when he writes:

It is Dante's precision in grading spiritual experiences which enables him, at any stage of his way to God, at once to wring the last drop of meaning out of the actual situation and to suggest its falling short of a final and as yet unattained experience. In this way the natural order and all that it contains is both enhanced to the utmost and, at the same time, viewed as a sign of something infinitely greater.[14]

How does the "situation" or "scene" of the encounter with Cato (to mention only the most recent) fall short of the experience which the pilgrim is about to attain? In other words, how does his recovery of humility that we found represented in that encounter fall short of the "new" recovery he is about to experience? And what makes truly creative the scenes that follow those we have just studied? Finally, how do they constitute a measure of the "infinitely greater" and therefore of the transcendent, for which the preceding scenes—now appearing faint—were the ground? The answers to these questions are embedded in the following scenes:

Quando noi fummo là 've la rugiada
     pugna col sole, per essere in parte
     dove, ad orezza, poco si dirada,

ambo le mani in su l'erbetta sparte
  soavemente 'l mio maestro pose:
  ond' io, che fui accorto di sua arte,
porsi ver' lui le guance lagrimose;
  ivi mi fece tutto discoverto
  quel color che l'inferno mi nascose.

(Purg. I, 121–129)

When we came there where the dew strives with the sun, for being in a place where, in the breeze, it is little dispersed, my master gently laid both hands outspread on the grass. I therefore, aware of his purpose, reached toward him my tear-stained cheeks, and on them he wholly disclosed that color of mine which Hell had hidden.

What the poet had earlier defined as "the lost road"—the road of humility—he now represents as the scene of a ritual of purification. Like the scene of the dawn that "was vanquishing the matin hour," this is a scene marked by conflict, that of the dew with the sun. The ritual of cleansing and of recovery of the pilgrim's original identity occurs at this critical point where two opposing forces meet (or will soon meet when the sun is higher).

The paradisal scene of innocence that this *locus amoenus* tenuously evokes once again speaks to us of drama. Hence this is not the idyllic scene sanctioned by the traditional reading. And if we look closely at the constitutive elements of this dramatic scene—the gentle gesture of Virgil's laying "both hands out spread on the grass," that provokes *immediately*, without any intervening discourse, the pilgrim's response of offering his "tear-stained" cheeks—we discern once again the logic and the intrinsic creativity of *mimesis*. This is manifest in the mirror-like relation between Virgil's act, calling attention to the dew and its purifying power, and the pilgrim's immediate offering of his cheeks stained by what obviously resembles dew—"stained" because the tears in the journey through hell have mixed with smoke and grime, and now stained anew. In the obedient gesture of offering to his guide his tearful cheeks, and hence in the perfect harmony between his will and Virgil's will, we find at once repeated and transcended what the act of his kneeling in silence through Virgil's and Cato's dialogue had earlier represented. Meaning—or rather the "meaning of transformation" and the "transformation of meaning"—is now conveyed in silence, in the absence of discourse, by virtue of the simple yet mysterious power of action. In this action enveloped and "freed" by silence we also find again, but on a higher plane and in a single moment, what was represented by the preceding scenes—those of Dante's and Virgil's encounter with Cato—but also the scenes of their descent to Hell.

No sooner has this scene attained its fulfillment than it is in turn followed and transcended by yet another scene:

> Venimmo poi in sul lito diserto,
>   che mai non vide navicar sue acque
>   omo, che di tornar sia poscia esperto.
>
> (*Purg*. I, 130–132)

Then we came on to the desert shore, that never saw any man navigate its waters who afterwards had experience of return.

The shift from the scene of the dewy meadow to that of the "desert shore" echoes—distinctly this time (if we compare it to the scene of the "solitary plain")—the "desert strand" and the "vast desert" of the Prologue (*Inf.* I, 29, 64). This scene is obviously another expression of the "lost road" of humility that the pilgrim is now rediscovering. It reasserts the conflictual form we have underlined earlier, for "lito diserto" speaks of a peaceful, solitary shore, but it also evokes the danger inherent to the "piaggia diserta" such as Dante the wayfarer had experienced in the Prologue scene. This is also true of the "waters" which are at once serene as they glitter in dawn's light—and therefore speak of renewal, of the recovery of a pristine life and its beauty—and are treacherous, as the clear allusion to Ulysses' failed attempt to sail across them shows.

The reference to Ulysses contains deeper implications than Dante critics have so far brought to light.[15] We may begin our analysis with Singleton's commentary of line 132 of *Purgatorio* I, "omo, che di tornar sia poscia esperto":

We the readers know of no one except Ulysses who did attempt to sail these waters, and we are thus invited to realize, through transparent allusions, that the mountain which Ulysses finally saw loom in the distance "higher than any he had ever seen," and from which the whirlwind came to sink his ship, was precisely the mountain-island of Purgatory. This aspect of the meaning is glimpsed by Benvenuto, who comments: "Hoc dicit pro Ulyxe qui tentavit illuc accedere secundum fictionem poetae, sed cito ipsum poenituit." ("Here he means Ulysses, who according to the story of the poet sought to approach that place but soon regretted it.")[16]

What both these readings fail to see is that the mountain which Ulysses "saw looming in the distance" is not only the mountain of Purgatory, but is also the mountain of the Earthly Paradise. The moment we identify this essential dimension of the mountain, we discover many more significant correspondences between the journeys of Dante the wayfarer and Ulysses. Most important, we recognize that the deepest motivation of both journeys is the nostalgia for Eden. As we have previously noted, this nostalgia may prove to be a false return—an illusory recovery of a "second innocence"—and therefore a false "reading" of the original myth of the Earthly Paradise, or an authentic return to the Earthly Paradise and therefore a true "reading" of the myth.

What signs are there in the episode of Ulysses that speak of a destructive, false nostalgia for Eden? In other words, how does the poet, in his representation of Ulysses' journey, show the similarities to and departure from the original myth of the Earthly Paradise? In *Inferno* XXVI we read Ulysses' words:

> "né dolcezza di figlio, né la pieta,
>   del vecchio padre, né 'l debito amore
>   lo qual dovea Penelopè far lieta,
> vincer potero dentro a me l'ardore
>   ch'i' ebbi a divenir del mondo esperto
>   e de li vizi umani e del valore;
> ma misi me per l'alto mare aperto. . . ."

> (*Inf.* XXVI, 94–100)

"neither fondness for my son, nor reverence for my aged father, nor the due love which would have made Penelope glad, could conquer in me the longing that I had to gain experience of the world, and of human vice and worth. But I put forth on the deep open sea. . . ."

As we hear Ulysses tell of his longing "to gain experience of the world, and of human vice and worth," we cannot fail to note that his words resemble Adam's desire to know good and evil. And like Adam, Ulysses (fraudulently) hides under the "truth" of natural human desire to know good and evil and to acquire full experience of the world, the desire to assert his own will and autonomy against an order, with the limits that it sets, which he has not created. His error, Dante suggests, lies not in the desire to know but in the severance of a relation and of course, ultimately, in the act of pride that brings about such a severance. The natural and inherently good desire to know is thus transformed into a *vana curiositas*, into an evasion of the real world of the *civitas*—with its history and culture—the world that includes the fondness for his son, the reverence for his aged father, and the due love that would have made Penelope glad. In what appears to be a lofty, heroic quest for knowledge, Ulysses breaks the equally natural bonds between knowledge and virtue, that is, between knowing and acting within and for the *communitas*. These are the bonds that Dante the poet is careful not to sever, lest he also become a fraudulent counselor to his reader as he sets out to represent his encounter with Ulysses:

> Allor mi dolsi, e ora mi ridoglio
> quando drizzo la mente a ciò ch'io vidi,
> e più lo 'ngegno affreno ch'i' non soglio,
> perché non corra che virtù nol guidi;
> sì che, se stella bona o miglior cosa
> m'ha dato 'l ben, ch'io stessi nol m'invidi.
>
> (*Inf.* XXVI, 19–24)

I sorrowed then, and sorrow now again, when I turn my mind to what I saw; and I curb my genius more than I am wont, lest it run where virtue does not guide it; so that, if a kindly star or something better has granted me the good, I may not grudge myself that gift.

The hollow, treacherous beauty of Ulysses' words whereby he convinces himself and others of the worthiness of his quest is decisively expressed by his "orazion picciola" ("little speech") to his companions which made them "so keen for the voyage" (*Inf.* XXVI, 121–122):

> 'O frati,' dissi, 'che per cento milia
> perigli siete giunti a l'occidente,
> a questa tanto picciola vigilia
> d'i nostri sensi ch'è del rimanente
> non vogliate negar l'esperïenza,
> di retro al sol, del mondo sanza gente.
> Considerate la vostra semenza:
> fatti non foste a viver come bruti,
> ma per seguir virtute e canoscenza.'
>
> (*Inf.* XXVI, 112–120)

'O brothers,' I said, 'who through a hundred thousand dangers have reached the west, to this so brief vigil of our senses that remains to us, choose not to deny experience, following the sun, of the world that has no people. Consider your origin: you were not made to live as brutes, but to pursue virtue and knowledge.'

We can discern both the attractiveness and the destructiveness (the fraud) of Ulysses' promise to his men the moment we observe that it is meaningless to pursue virtue in "the world that has no people" (away from the *communitas*) and that only false, sterile knowledge can be pursued in such a world.[17] Ulysses' longing "to gain experience of the world" (XXVI, 97–99) and his reference to the Pillars of Hercules—

> quando venimmo a quella foce stretta
>   dov' Ercule segnò li suoi riguardi
>   acciò che l'uom più oltre non si metta . . .

(Inf. XXVI, 107–109)

when we came to that narrow outlet where Hercules set up his markers, that men should not pass beyond—

receive a significant gloss from the following explanation of the Fall that Adam in Paradise offers to Dante the pilgrim:

> "Or, figliuol mio, non il gustar del legno
>   fu per se la cagion di tanto essilio,
>   ma solamente il trapassar del segno."

(Par. XXVI, 115–117)

"Now know, my son, that the tasting of the tree was not in itself the cause of so long an exile, but solely the overpassing of the bound."

Another significant allusion to the myth of Eden is in the last scene of Ulysses' account of his journey:

> "Noi ci allegrammo, e tosto tornò in pianto;
>   ché de la nova terra un turbo nacque
>   e percosse del legno il primo canto."

(Inf. XXVI, 136–138)

"We rejoiced, but soon our joy was turned to grief, for from the new land a whirlwind rose and struck the forepart of the ship."

At the end of *Paradiso* XXVI there is another important "gloss" in Adam's words:

"Nel monte che si leva più da l'onda,
    fu'io, con vita pura e disonesta,
    da la prim'ora a quella che seconda,
come 'l sol muta quadra, l'ora sesta."

(*Par.* XXVI, 139–142)

"On the mountain which rises highest from the sea I lived pure, then guilty, from the first hour to that which follows, when the sun changes quadrant, next upon the sixth."

Analogous to Adam's short-lived paradise is the "paradise" that Ulysses thought he was about to possess. In both "stories" the "high mountain" with its promise of innocence and bliss is lost no sooner than it is possessed or, for Ulysses, is about to be possessed. Like Adam, Ulysses has transgressed an interdiction against going beyond human limits.

But if Ulysses' and Adam's stories are so similar, why is one condemned and the other saved? We can answer that this is so, and therefore that it is "just," as soon as we note that whereas Adam's fall is essentially a "fall into history" and, as we have remarked earlier in this study, the event that inaugurates culture and *civitas*, Ulysses' "fall" is a flight *away* from history, from *civitas* into the "world that has no people"—a "mad flight." Moreover while Adam's story speaks of the experience of both good and evil *in* the garden and hence the tragic dimension inherent in the human condition, Ulysses' story betrays a longing to create "another," "second innocence," an innocence of his own making that removes him from the real world of strife, from the drama of good and evil, and ultimately from God's *oikonomia*. In such a "flight" pathos is separated from ethos and fear is separated from "service and obedience," so that as Ulysses faces the dangers of crossing the waters—"l'alto passo" ("the passage of the deep"; *Inf.* XXVI, 132)—and as he experiences fear, this fear—to recall again Hegel's words—"remains formal and does not spread over the whole known reality of existence . . . ," and consciousness "without the initial state of absolute fear . . . has a merely vain and futile 'mind of its own'."[18] By contrast, Adam's experience of what Mircea Eliade has called the "terror of history"—the terror of a linear journey that ends in death—is accompanied by "service and obedience" as he accepts the life of toil and ultimately death.

We can more deeply understand this contrast between Ulysses' journey and Adam's as soon as we redirect our attention to Dante the pilgrim and his analogical relation to both Ulysses and Adam. We recall that in the Prologue Dante the wayfarer, much like Ulysses, attempted to reach the "delectable mountain" by the mere power of the "wings of the mind"[19] and hence by an act of evasion of history and its terror—a "corto andar" (*Inf.* II, 120). We also recall that for a brief moment, by virtue of the "motivational force" of the scene ("It was the beginning of the morning, and the sun was mounting with the stars that were with it when Divine Love first set those beautiful things in motion . . ."; *Inf.* I, 37–40), the wayfarer found himself in harmony with nature like Adam before the Fall, to the point of experiencing "good hope of that beast with the gay skin" (*Inf.* I, 41–42). In other words, he felt that he had suddenly recovered what the first man had lost, the original innocence of the garden which as we have seen is exactly what Ulysses had come within sight of and had hoped to possess (or "recover"). Like Adam and Ulysses, Dante the wayfarer soon experiences a "fall" from this "paradise" as the she-wolf thrusts him toward the dark wood. Adam's words, "Nel monte che si leva più da l'onda / fu' io, con vita pura e disonesta," as well as Ulysses' words, "Quando n'apparve una montagna . . . / Noi ci allegrammo, e tosto tornò in pianto," could also be said, by analogy, of this "fall."

That which finally distinguishes Dante's and Adam's journey from Ulysses' and therefore what justifies his and Adam's salvation and the condemnation of Ulysses, is—as Freccero has said of the journey of Ulysses and of Dante the pilgrim—"not in the objective, but rather in how the journey is accomplished. The difference is quite literally the journey through Hell, the descent *intra nos* which transforms philosophical presumption into a journey of the mind and heart to God."[20] In the light of what I have observed earlier (and throughout the preceding chapter) about the presence of the myth of the Earthly Paradise both in Ulysses' story and in the story of Dante the pilgrim, I must add that Dante's "journey of the mind and heart to God" is indissolubly connected with the power of mimesis, that is, with the imitation of action which is both the action of myth and of history—the myth and the history of sin and expiation. This mimesis is inseparable from tragic vision, whose ground is not flight from the reality of evil but recognition and acceptance of it. But this recognition and acceptance should not be mistaken for acquiescence or passive "coopera-tion" with evil but rather should be identified with the recognition and acceptance that coincides with the act of repudiation of evil (in oneself and in others). As it comes in contact with evil or with violence, this act of repudiation transforms it into suffering. In this lies the creative power of tragic vision.

Let us now turn to the last scene of *Purgatorio* I:

> Quivi mi cinse sì com'altrui piacque:
>> oh maraviglia! ché qual elli scelse
>> l'umile pianta, cotal si rinacque
> subitamente là onde l'avelse.

(*Purg.* I, 133–136)

There, even as pleased another, he girded me. O marvel! that such as he plucked the humble plant, even such did it instantly spring up again, there whence he had uprooted it.

This scene recalls by contrast that of the sinking of Ulysses' ship caused by the whirlwind that had risen from the mountain:

> Tre volte il fé girar con tutte l'acque;
>> a la quarta levar la poppa in suso
>> e la prora ire in giù, com' altrui piacque,
> infin che 'l mar fu sovra noi richiuso.

(*Inf.* XXVI, 139–142)

Three times it whirled her round with all the waters, and the fourth time it lifted the stern aloft and plunged the prow below, as pleased Another, till the sea closed over us.

In both scenes we see a man who confronts the mysterious power of the Other ("Altrui"), that is, God or one who is a *figura Dei* (as Cato is for the pilgrim Dante)—as this power manifests itself through a natural phenome-non. Hence in both cases man comes into contact with nature and the Creator, but with a fundamental difference. For Ulysses this contact or relation is brought on by defiance and is therefore a violation of the natural order willed by God. For Dante the pilgrim this contact is brought on by a voluntary submission to that order and hence by the recognition of personal limits in relation to it, in other words, by the virtue of humility.

It is important to note that on the shore of the mountain of Purgatory which is also the mountain of the Earthly Paradise, the human inclination to the good is—if only partially—restored and renewed through the power of ritual, that is, by that which by its very nature exists on this side or beyond discourse as *act*. By virtue of this act the pilgrim recovers a measure of the harmony with nature that Adam possessed before the Fall. He thus enters the creative realm or "scene" in which myth and history—the sacred and the profane—cross. But this scene of recovery through ritual has come into being against the background of scenes of "dangerous waters," disharmony, and chaos. In other words, it has asserted itself as something eminently dramatic. "The power of the sacred of nature," writes Paul Ricoeur, "is attested first of all in its menaced character. The sacred universe is a universe which emerges from chaos and which in every instant may return to it. The sky is not order and life is not benediction only because the depth of chaos has been and must unceasingly be vanquished. The sacred is dramatic."[21]

As we focus our attention on Virgil's act of plucking the "humble plant" and on the plant's "rebirth," we observe that the theme of the recovery of humility, which has been represented throughout the entire canto, is now manifest in a new synthesis and in a new relation of man and nature, which completes and transcends the earlier encounter with Cato, not to mention the preceding descent in humility, the "death" of the journey through Hell. Dante the pilgrim is as humble and obedient to his guide and to the Other that Virgil represents as the rush is to Virgil. As he is "vanquished"—like Cato (and God)—the pilgrim, like the rush, is reborn; they both "vanquish." And discourse similarly is "vanquished" by silence and reduced to gesture or act. It is renewed and "vanquishes." It is word reborn. The tongue of fire of Ulysses, with its treacherous power, like that of the "serpent" in Eden, is now—at least temporarily—transformed and transcended.

Notes

1. Cf. Ezio Raimondi, "Rito e storia nel I canto del *Purgatorio*," in his *Metafora e storia* (Turin: Einaudi, 1970), p. 70: "Il diletto a cui l'anima torna, così, ad aprirsi, non è però soltanto la gioia d'ogni uomo dinanzi alla luce di un nuovo giorno; ma è anche il primo annuncio di una gioia più durevole, che diverrà interamente chiara allorché, oramai al termine dell'ascesa, Matelda suggerirà, citando il salmo

Delectasti, che il suo emana dalla consapevolezza di una presenza divina, dalla gioia di contemplare le opere dell'Altissimo."

2. For the allegorical interpretation of these stars, see Charles S. Singleton, *Journey to Beatrice* (Baltimore: Johns Hopkins University Press, 1958), pp. 141–158.

3. See Raimondi's important discussion of Cato in "Rito e storia," pp. 75–89.

4. Fergusson, *The Idea of a Theater*, p. 240.

5. Simone Weil, *The Simone Weil Reader*, ed. George A. Panichas (New York: David McKay, 1977) p. 384: "The false God changes suffering into violence. The true God changes violence into suffering."

6. The Church Official compendium, containing ceremonies that reach back to the early days of the Church. Cf. the Gregorian *Liber Sacramentorum*, *Notae*, p. 439b, *Patrologia Latina*, vol. LXXVIII, ed. Hugo Ménard: "Et cum gemitu et crebris suspiriis eis denuntiet quod sicut Adam projectus est de Paradiso, ita et ipsi ab ecclesia pro peccatis abjiciantur. Post haec jubeat ministris ut reos extra janus ecclesiae expellant. Clerus vero prosequatur eos cum Responsorio *In sudore vultus tui vesceris pane tuo*." ["With groans and sighs (the priest) announces to them that as Adam was driven from Paradise, so they are to be expelled from the church for their sins. After this let him order the ministers to drive the sinners from the church doors. But let a cleric follow them singing the responsory *In sudore vultus tui vesceris pane tuo*."] Cited by O.B. Hardison, Jr., *Christian Rite and Christian Drama in the Middle Ages* (Baltimore: Johns Hopkins University Press, 1969), p. 99.

7. Dunstan Tucker, O.S.B., "Dante's Reconciliation in the *Purgatorio*," *American Benedictine Review* XX (1969), 78.

8. Cf. Paul Ricoeur, "Manifestation et Proclamation," in *Il sacro*, Archivio di Filosofia, ed. E. Castelli (Padua: Cedam, 1974), p. 60: "The function of myth is to fix the paradigms of rites which sacralize the action. Today we read myths, transforming them into literature. But we have previously extracted them from the act of recital which linked them to the ritual action." (Translation mine)

9. René Girard, *Things Hidden since the Foundation of the World*, trans. Stephen Bann and Michael Metteer (Stanford, CA: Stanford University Press, 1987), p. 275.

10. Ibid., p. 271.

11. Cf. Giuseppe Mazzotta, *Dante Poet of the Desert*, p. 49: "In the *effictio* of the old man Dante describes his face adorned with light. The description (ll. 34–39) faintly recalls the appearance of the exalted Christ in the Book of Revelation (1:12–16): 'his head and his hair were white as white wool . . . and his face was like the sun shining in full strength.' " For a discussion of the correspondence between Cato's and Christ's sacrificial death, see pp. 60–62.

12. Singleton, *Commentary* 2, n. 109, p. 20.

13. Ricoeur, "Manifestation et proclamation," p. 61.

14. Kenelm Foster, O.P., *God's Tree* (London: Blackfriars Publications, 1957), p. 10.

15. Given the immense bibliography on the episode of Ulysses, suffice it here to mention Anthony K. Cassell, "Ulisseana: A Bibliography of Dante's Ulysses," *Italian Culture* III (1981), 23–45; and of those whose interpretation is closest to my own, Bruno Nardi, "La tragedia di Ulisse," in his *Dante e la cultura medievale* (Bari: Laterza, 1949), pp. 153–165; Rocco Montano, "Il folle volo di Ulisse," *Delta*, n.s., II

(1952), 10–32; and Amilcare A. Iannucci, "Ulysses' 'folle volo': The Burden of History," *Medioevo romanzo,* III (1976), 410–445. Other important studies with which I essentially concur, but whose focus differs from the one I am presenting here, are Giorgio Padoan, *Il pio Enea e l'empio Ulisse: Tradizione classica e intendimento medievale in Dante* (Ravenna: Longo, 1977); John A. Scott, *Dante magnanimo: Studi sulla "Commedia"* (Florence: Olschki, 1977); and more recently, Anthony K. Cassell, "The Lesson of Ulysses," *Dante Studies* XCIX (1981), 113–131.

16. Singleton, *Commentary* 2, n. 132, p. 23.

17. Cf. Cassell, "The Lesson of Ulysses," 114: "The knowledge of the 'vizi umani' and the 'valore' can only be those committed and displayed by himself and his crew. Since he puts vice and worth on the same plane, he considers them both valid and undifferentiated as far as any universal hierarchy or eschatological end is concerned; he thereby denies the necessity of moral choice between the two. Ulysses urges his crew to sin."

18. G.W.F. Hegel, *The Phenomenology of Mind*, pp. 239–240.

19. Cf. John Freccero, "Dante's Prologue Scene," *Dante Studies* LXXXIV (1966): 5 [now in *Dante: The Poetics of Conversion*, ed. and intr. Rachel Jacoff (Cambridge, MA: Harvard University Press, 1986), p. 6]; see also Roger Dragonetti, *Dante pèlerin de la Sainte Face* (Gand: Romanica Gandensia, 1968), p. 17.

20. Freccero, "Dante's Prologue Scene," p. 18.

21. Ricoeur, "Manifestation et Proclamation," p. 61.

V. The Garden of the Negligent Princes

In the scene of Sordello's appearance in *Purgatorio* VI is the seed of the main action of a "return to Eden" that is fully organized into a dramatic representation in Cantos VII and VIII, in the valley of the princes. This scene stands in sharp opposition to a sequence of scenes that immediately precedes it whose main action is a hasty journey to Eden. The first reference to such a journey is made in lines 25–27, in connection with the pilgrim's doubt about the power of the prayers of the living made on behalf of the souls in Purgatory in order to speed "their way to blessedness." Another reference to a hasty return to Eden is in line 49: "My lord, let us go on with greater haste." This time it is the pilgrim himself who expresses a desire to speed his way to Paradise. His desire is kindled when Virgil points to Beatrice as the one who will conclusively solve his doubt and announces that he will see her "above, smiling and happy, on the summit of this mountain" (VI, 47–48).

But no sooner has the pilgrim expressed his desire for greater haste than he is reminded by Virgil of their limitations while crossing the distance that separates them from Beatrice and the Earthly Paradise. As in the Prologue scene, so now Virgil tempers the pilgrim's eagerness for "going the short way up the fair mountain" (*Inf.* II, 120) by calling attention to the necessity of the journey and to the fact that the climb will not be as rapid as he thought:

"Noi anderem con questo giorno innanzi,"
    rispuose, "quanto più potremo omai;
    ma 'l fatto è d'altra forma che non stanzi.
Prima che sie là sù, tornar vedrai
    colui che già si cuopre de la costa,
    sì che' suoi raggi tu romper non fai.

(*Purg.* VI, 52–57)

"We will go forward with this day," he answered, "as far as yet we may, but the fact is quite other than you suppose. Before you are there above you will see him return that is now hidden by the slope, so that you do not break his beams."

Virgil then shifts the focus from the thought of the journey to the journey itself by calling attention to the presence of one who will show the quickest way:

> "Ma vedi là un'anima che, posta
>   sola soletta, inverso noi riguarda:
>   quella ne 'nsegnerà la via più tosta."
>
> (Purg. VI, 58–60)

"But see yonder a soul seated all alone, who is looking towards us; he will point out to us the quickest way."

This scene is constituted by two acts (the second being, of course, virtual); they are antithetical, as the words "posta" and "tosta" clearly attest, with one expressing stasis and the other kinesis. Dante at once repeats and objectifies in a new synthesis what we have seen previously represented alternately as the assertion of haste and the counter-assertion of delay, or in other words of flight from the journey and of the necessity and reality of the journey. The crucial difference is now experienced and expressed through a dynamic interplay of discourse and action, of aspiration and event. The travelers Virgil and Dante, whose main goal is to find the quickest way to the summit of the mountain, stand in opposition to the one who is at rest, a rest which coincides with his act of gazing. The poet then underlines this contained vitality and equilibrium of stasis and kinesis:

> Venimmo a lei: o anima lombarda,
>   come ti stavi altera e disdegnosa
>   e nel mover de li occhi onesta e tarda!
> Ella non ci dicëa alcuna cosa,
>   ma lasciavane gir, solo sguardando
>   a guisa di leon quando si posa.
>
> (Purg. VI, 61–66)

We came to him: O Lombard soul, how lofty and disdainful was your bearing, and the movement of your eyes how grave and slow! He said nothing to us, but let us go on, watching only after the fashion of a couching lion.

The coexistence of opposites is expressed by *stavi* and *mover* (also by the latter with *tarda*), and by *gir* and *posa*. In the presence of the imposing figure of Sordello, as they enter his space the pilgrim and Virgil must necessarily modify their desire for a hasty journey.

The scenes that immediately follow represent the most creative stage of this encounter and of the dialectic that underlies it:

> Pur Virgilio si trasse a lei, pregando
>   che ne mostrasse la miglior salita;
>   e quella non rispuose al suo dimando,
> ma di nostro paese e de la vita
>   ci 'nchiese; e 'l dolce duca incominciava
> "Mantüa . . . ," e l'ombra, tutta in sé romita,
> surse ver' lui del loco ove pria stava,
>   dicendo: "O Mantoano, io son Sordello
>   de la tua terra!"; e l'un l'altro abbracciava.
>
> (*Purg.* VI, 67–75)

But Virgil drew on towards him, asking him to show us the best ascent; and he did not reply to his question, but inquired of our country and condition. And the gentle leader began, "Mantua—"; and the shade, all in himself recluse, rose toward him from his place there, saying "O Mantuan, I am Sordello of your city!"—and they embraced each other.

The dramatic tension is heightened as Virgil makes his way towards the soul who is "watching after the fashion of a couching lion." The word "pur" ("Pur Virgilio . . .") is especially effective in expressing the strength and the single-mindedness of Virgil's desire to find the quickest way, which makes him overcome the natural hesitation to enter the space of such a solemn, monumental figure.[1] Then the action takes an unexpected turn, pivoting on the point of rupture created by the juxtaposition of two conflicting actions, those of Virgil's appeal and of Sordello's "reply" with a question that ignores that appeal and shifts the focus to another perspective. The journey of our two pilgrims is thus delayed as they find themselves imitating—and hence to a certain degree surrendering to—the Other and his special mode of being. Kinesis temporarily gives way to stasis, external action is transformed into inner action, and movement becomes act.

As soon as it asserts itself, this act is in turn transformed into the external movement of gesture and action. If at first Sordello is characterized by contained vitality and by a certain tension and equilibrium between inner movement and outward stasis, suddenly he is then transformed from one who "was all in himself recluse" to one who "rises toward" another.[2] We now apprehend the nature of Sordello's inner movement and its secret motivation: the love that unites one citizen to another and is therefore the very foundation of the city. His innermost desire is as single-minded as our two pilgrims' desire to find the quickest way to Eden, and it manifests itself dialectically through his encounter with them and in opposition to their action and motivation. But more important, what at first we identified exclusively as a virtue (solemn monumentality, magnanimity) is in reality tainted by a certain degree of negligence. From the vantage point of the "new" scene in which Sordello suddenly shifts to an active role, we observe retrospectively that as Virgil and Dante drew near, he did not rise or move toward them to show the earnestness that he instead shows later. As Sordello "rises" from a state of inertia transformed from spectator to actor, he gives dramatic expression to the change that the souls of Anti-Purgatory must undergo before they can enter Purgatory proper. He embodies the ambivalence of the transitional stage and hence both the negative and the positive forces of delay in the journey to the Earthly Paradise. Here the pause and the delay at once echo and re-enact the former deficiency and sin that characterized the earthly existence of the negligent, and they constitute the salutary medicine that prepares them for the further transformation of the journey that lies ahead. But as before on earth, negligence combines with zeal, the only difference being that the conflict between the two forces is now played out as a drama that repeats and to some degree fulfills the earthly drama of the love for the *civitas* that had been hindered by negligence. Sordello had expressed this love in his political poetry, especially the *planh* or lament written on the death of Blacatz, in which he condemned the leading princes of Europe for their vices.

What is the creative force of this drama in the economy of the pilgrim's journey to the Earthly Paradise? Or, to put the question in terms of the problematic interpretation of the original myth of Eden, what role does this drama play—a drama whose center is the city, the realm of history—

in the general economy of a journey which has as its beginning and its end the garden? With his dramaturgy Dante helps us to formulate the answers. The delay in the pilgrim's journey to the garden, which Sordello helps to define and in some measure to bring about, makes it possible, by virtue of the space that it creates, to understand more deeply the meaning and value of the journey itself. This journey is deeply connected with the reality of the city and therefore with the state of happiness that human beings can attain in it as members of the *communitas*. By pausing to reflect on the city and therefore on the human journey on earth, the pilgrim is learning to return to Eden by correctly interpreting the original myth, the story of original innocence and the loss of that innocence, of the garden and of the fall from the garden which marks the fall into history and the foundation of human culture. Thus the pilgrim learns to discover in this delay—and in the creative, theatrical space that it provides for Sordello and Virgil—a true measure of the "quickest" or "best" way that he, with Virgil, was seeking earlier.

Before directing our attention to the scenes of *Purgatorio* VII and VIII, we should pause a moment to consider the creative force of the scene of the embrace between Sordello and Virgil. If we call to mind the earlier scenes that preceded, especially those that represented a desire for a hasty journey to the summit of Purgatory, we see more clearly how these scenes, with their respective actions and motivations, constituted an illusory return or a flight from the real scene and drama that the figure of Sordello first animates and defines in the special manner we have noted. In the scene of the embrace we see fulfilled, at least in part, Virgil's earlier admonition to Dante that the fact is quite other than he supposes—something he himself needs to experience, indeed as a *fact*, that is, an action, an event. As soon as Virgil utters the name of his city, "Mantüa," lingering almost imperceptibly on the word (as the dieresis clearly suggests), Sordello, aided or encouraged by this brief pause and by the evocative spirit that informs it, interrupts what was about to become a discourse. In a manner analogous to his previous neglect in replying to Virgil's question concerning the "best ascent," he now creates a *caesura* whose creative function we have already encountered many a time. This *caesura* which is the death of discourse constitutes the proper ground for action and its fullness. In fact the moment it comes into being, it transforms the expressive power of the word "Mantüa," merely by isolating it. This word, surrounded by silence, is rendered much more actual and direct—it is much closer to the "thing" that it signifies—than if it had been pronounced (and heard) as part of a phrase such as "Mantua me genuit," as Benvenuto imagined that Virgil would have said, or "Mantua fu la mia patria," as a modern commentator has suggested.[3] In the space produced by the caesura the word—what the poet a few lines later will call "dolce suon"—asserts its primal evocative power. Severed from discourse, it is now eminently *eventful*, and as such it provokes the action of the two Mantuans' embrace.

What gives special intensity to this scene is that Sordello sees not Virgil (whose identity will be revealed later) but a fellow citizen. There is thus a kind of purity in the manifestation of Sordello's love of the *civitas* (the purity of things seen in what we may call an absolute light). Dramatistically this purity coincides with a perfect scene-act, scene-agent, and agent-act ratio. To the scene of the city, evoked by the name "Mantüa," perfectly correspond the emergence and definition of the two agents as citizens and the act of embracing that manifests the love binding them. Another sign of the dramatic purity of this scene is in the absence of any comment, either by the narrator or by his characters, on the fact that theirs is a shadowy, vain embrace, like the one that the wayfarer experienced in some measure when he and Casella embraced (*Purg.* II, 76–78), which caused the poet to exclaim: "Ohi ombre vane, fuor che ne l'aspetto!" ("O empty shades except in aspect!"; II, 79). Another "vain" embrace, and an even more fitting example because it involves two shades, is the one between Virgil and Statius:

Già s'inchinava ad abbracciar li piedi
    al mio dottor, ma el li disse: "Frate,
    non far, ché tu se' ombra e ombra vedi."
Ed ei surgendo: "Or puoi la quantitate
    comprender de l'amor ch' a te mi scalda,
    quando'io dismento nostra vanitate,
trattando l'ombre come cosa salda."

(*Purg.* XXI, 130–136)

Already he was stopping to embrace my teacher's feet; but he said to him, "Brother do not so, for you are a shade and a shade you see." And he, rising, "Now you may comprehend the measure of the love that burns in me for you, when I forget our emptiness and treat shades as solid things."

We more deeply perceive the special power of the scene of Virgil's and Sordello's embrace the moment we observe that it constitutes the ground for the scenes that immediately follow. This moment of insight coincides with the rupture in the narration, when Dante, taking on the role of a *dramatis persona*, begins his famous invective against Italy:

> Ahi serva Italia, di dolore ostello,
>   nave sanza nocchiere in gran tempesta,
>   non donna di provincie, ma bordello!
> Quell'anima gentil fu così presta,
>   sol per lo dolce suon de la sua terra,
>   di far al cittadin suo quivi festa;
> e ora in te non stanno sanza guerra
>   li vivi tuoi, e l'un l'altro si rode
>   di quei ch'un muro e una fossa serra.
>
>   (*Purg.* VI, 76–84)

Ah, servile Italy, hostel of grief, ship without pilot in great tempest, no mistress of princes, but brothel! So eager was that noble soul, only at the sweet name of his city to give glad welcome there to his fellow citizen— and now in you your living abide not without war, and of those whom one wall and one moat shut in, one gnaws at the other!

Upon seeing Sordello suddenly transformed from a static to a kinetic figure, from one who is self-absorbed to one who is eager to manifest his love for his fellow citizen "only at the sweet name of his city," we along with Dante immediately see the larger scene of this life where not love but hatred reigns. No sooner has good come into view than it calls forth a vision of evil. And if we recall the paradisal scene announced earlier by Virgil— of Beatrice, "smiling and happy," at the summit of the mountain—which had kindled the pilgrim's desire to move "with greater haste," we see it retrospectively modified by the scene of this life's misery that the poet now evokes. Similarly, the pilgrim's eagerness to reach the garden of innocence and happiness now appears transformed (through dialectic opposition) by the poet's eagerness to expose the evil of the earthly city.

As Dante's invective unfolds, its deepest motivation emerges: the longing to reach the place of happiness at the summit of Purgatory analogous to the longing to see created (or restored) on earth the state of happiness which, in the *Monarchia* (III. xv. 7), is said to be figured in the Earthly Paradise. This longing is given special expression at the point of the invective when, after reproaching the Emperor Albert I of Austria for having abandoned Italy, Dante adds:

> ch'avete tu e'l tuo padre sofferto,
>   per cupidigia di costà distretti,
>   che 'l giardin de lo 'mperio sia diserto.
>
>   (*Purg.* VI, 103–105)

For you and your father, held back yonder by greed, have suffered the garden of the Empire to be laid waste.

The words "giardin" and "diserto" unmistakably signal the vital and always problematic presence of the myth of the Earthly Paradise, of which we caught a few glimpses in the preceding scenes. We now see in sharper focus what the pilgrim is gradually learning to discover and accept: one cannot think of the garden and not also think of it as the garden that has been laid waste—the garden becomes synonymous with its loss. To long for the garden of happiness and innocence without also turning one's attention to the desert of misery and sin is to long for a false garden—that of the "second innocence" of which we spoke earlier in this study. To abandon the problematic yet real present for a "perfect" but illusory future is itself ultimately a sin for in a sense "sin is nothing else but the failure to recognize human misery."[4]

Dante's invective dramatically represents the longing for the happiness "figured" by the Earthly Paradise as the longing to transform the desert into a garden in the here and now of this life. Thus the poet's vision at once departs from and perfects the pilgrim's nostalgia for Eden. This "leap" from one scene to another, from one economy to another, is further evidenced by the shift from an individual recovery of the garden (Dante the pilgrim who will see Beatrice "smiling and happy" at the summit of Purgatory) to a collective recovery of the garden, from a personal to a universal *renovatio*.

Another creative shift from one perspective or economy to another is in Dante's passionate appeal to the Emperor Albert and to Christ to come and see the state of anarchy and corruption in which Italy lies:

> Vieni a veder Montecchi e Cappelletti
>   Monaldi e Filippeschi, uom sanza cura:

color già tristi, e questi con sospetti!
Vien, crudel, vieni, e vedi la pressura
  d'i tuoi gentili, e cura lor magagne;
  e vedrai Santafior com'è oscura!
Vieni a veder la tua Roma che piagne
  vedova e sola, e dì e notte chiama:
  "Cesare mio, perché non m'accompagne?"
Vieni a veder la gente quanto s'ama!
  e se nulla di noi pietà ti move,
  a vergognar ti vien de la tua fama.
E se licito m'è, o sommo Giove
  che fosti in terra per noi crucifisso,
  son li giusti occhi tuoi rivolti altrove?

(Purg. VI, 106–120)

Come to see Montecchi and Cappelletti, Monaldi and Filippeschi, you man without care, those already wretched and these in dread. Come, cruel one, come and see the distress of your nobles, and heal their hurts; and you will see Santafiora, how forlorn it is. Come see your Rome that weeps, widowed and alone, crying day and night, "My Caesar, why do you abandon me?" Come see your people, how they love one another; and if no pity for us moves you, come to be shamed by your own renown! And if it be lawful for me, O Jove supreme that on earth wast crucified for us, are Thy just eyes turned elsewhere?

Once again we experience the tragic rhythm and the tragic vision that it engenders as we see disjunctively related the two scenes in which, respectively, Dante calls upon the Emperor Albert and Christ to see Italy's corruption. The rupture that both separates and joins the two scenes constitutes the creative space whereby the perspective inherent in one is transformed into the perspective of the other. We may bring to light a measure of this transformation by paying close attention to the analogical relation or ratio between the concrete elements of the two scenes. They both have in common a fundamental condition: the state of decay of Italy, the garden that has become a desert. The agents and "antagonists" are respectively Dante and the Emperor Albert, and Dante and Christ. Put in simple terms, the act that contributes to their identity is for Dante his longing to save the city, while for both the Emperor and Christ it is their lack of concern for the fate of the city (the poet has called the Emperor a "man without care" and similarly has asked Christ "are Thy just eyes turned else-where?"; VI, 107; 120). In both scenes Dante's voice is met with silence. His is a "vox clamantis in deserto." And his care for the city clashes with the indifference of both the earthly and the heavenly kings. Their delay corresponds to his eagerness for redemption. Thus if not only a greedy and negligent king but also God who is all powerful and just ("Jove supreme") does not see injustice and does not intervene to redress it, there is nothing left but terror and despair for those like Dante who thirst for justice.

The condition reflected in the scene the poet has created is eminently tragic. As he occupies the very center of this scene, he exhibits the unmis-takable traits of a man endowed with tragic vision. According to Richard Sewall:

The tragic vision impels the man of action to fight against his destiny, kick against the pricks, and state his case before God or his fellows. It impels the artist, in his fictions, toward what Jaspers calls "boundary-situations," man at the limits of his sovereignty—Job on the ash-heap, Prometheus on the crag, Oedipus in his mo-ment of self-discovery, Lear on the heath, Ahab on his lonely quarter-deck . . . The writing of tragedy is the artist's way of taking action, of defying destiny, and this is why in the great tragedies there is a sense of the artist's own involvement, an im-mediacy not so true of the forms, like satire and comedy, where the artist's position seems more detached.[5]

Wherein lies the creative force of Dante's tragic vision? How does it resolve or transform the tragic condition and the terror and despair that accom-pany it? If, glancing back to our text, we reply that the very shift from one scene to another—from human economy to God's economy, or more spe-cifically from the Emperor's silence to the silence of God—constitutes the transformation of that tragic condition into tragic vision, we run the risk of falsifying this vision by substituting for it a pious view that "would re-duce the fact of evil into something else or resolve it into some larger whole."[6] Dante himself seems to run this same risk when, soon after he has "accused" God of indifference or negligence, he adds:

O è preparazion che ne l'abisso
  del tuo consiglio fai per alcun bene
  in tutto de l'accorger nostro scisso?

(*Purg.* VI, 121–123)

Or is it preparation Thou makest in the depths of Thy counsel for some good quite cut off from our perception?

At first glance this seems to be the pious view described above. We can easily identify the reduction of the "fact of evil" into the "larger whole" of God's providence, of His *oikonomia*. Yet if we look closely, and more important, if we apprehend the form—not the individual scene or action, or the isolated utterance of a definition or "truth," but the whole sequence of scenes which are organized around a central idea or action—that tragic vision has hammered out we discover that Dante's vision is authentically tragic, and that the truth of his poetry is the truth of tragedy. "In tragedy, truth is not revealed as one harmonious whole; it is many-faceted, ambiguous, a sum of irreconcilables—and that is one source of its terror."[7] Significantly, Dante does not categorically state that what to humans appears to be God's indifference to the "fact of evil" is in God's perspective a "preparation" for "some good." He merely *asks* if this is a possibility or an alternative ("O è preparazion . . . ?"). The fact of evil and the terror that it provokes remain unresolved. It is equally significant that Dante's discourse does not end on this "optimistic" note of a possible, future transformation of evil into good. Rather, he returns (though implicitly) to the earlier spirit of indirect accusation or challenge regarding God's "absence" from the corrupt human world, adding:

> Ché le città d'Italia tutte piene
> son di tiranni, e un Marcel diventa
> ogne villan che parteggiando viene.
>
> (*Purg.* VI, 124–126)

For all the cities of Italy are full of tyrants, and every yokel who comes to play the partisan becomes a Marcellus.

The canto then comes to a close with Dante's famous invective against Florence (VI, 127–138). Throughout the part of *Purgatorio* VI we have studied, the accent clearly falls on Dante's doubled-edged cry to God. As he accuses Him of averting His eyes from the evil that ravages this world, he also trusts in Him and in His justice. Like Job, the tragic figure par excellence, he appeals to God against God and is moved by the same spirit of defiance and faith that we find in Job when he declares: "No wonder then if I cannot keep silence; in the anguish of my spirit I must speak, lament in the bitterness of my soul" (Job 7:11). And like the pleading of the ancient tragic hero, Dante's pleading remains unanswered.

Is there a way out? Can this condition be changed? And if it cannot, how can the terror and despair that accompany it be transformed or transcended? In other words, how can a tragic condition be transformed into tragic vision? We can answer, as we have done in part in the preceding pages of this study, that the very formulation of the tragic condition, and therefore the *poiema*, the representation that organizes the opposition or agon, makes it possible for the opposition to be "suffered"; and through this suffering (*pathema*) a new knowledge or vision is attained (*mathema*) which transcends the original tragic condition of unresolved conflict. We can apprehend the solution by transcendence as we experience the tragic rhythm created by Dante's shifting perspectives, by the movement from the human "restricted economy" to God's "unrestricted economy." Once the poet has defined the agon no longer as one between men (Dante and the Emperor Albert) but as one between humanity and God, and finally as one that appears to exist in God Himself (for he is just and yet averts his eyes from injustice), the circularity of reciprocity, of accusations and counteraccusations, of attacks and counterattacks by the two antagonists, is broken and transcended. God's silence now asserts itself as the true answer to the human questions about the "fact of evil." The "seed" of this answer can be found in the very words that earlier we heard Dante address to God:

E se licito m'è, o sommo Giove
    che fosti in terra per noi crucifisso . . .

(Purg. VI, 118–119)

And if it be lawful for me, O Jove supreme that on earth wast crucified for us . . .

Here God is portrayed as being both all powerful and meek, as "Jove supreme" and as Christ on the cross, as judge and victim, at once inflicting and suffering violence. In this paradoxical union of opposites, at the confluence of the two economies divine and human, lies the answer to the questions asked by Job or Dante. Why is there injustice? Why evil? And finally, why do You not come to destroy it?

To better define this "answer" which we have attempted to fashion in the presence of Dante's words, we may turn to C.G. Jung who commenting on Christ's cry from the cross of "My God, my God, why hast Thou forsaken me?" writes: "Here His human nature attains divinity; at that moment God experiences what it means to be a mortal man and drinks to the dregs what he made his faithful servant Job suffer. Here is given the answer to Job."⁸ This answer—no answer at all for the rationalist in us and among us—asserts itself as meaningful to one who accepts suffering and is thus open to tragic vision. Martin Buber helps us to define this vision when he writes:

The secret of God which stood over Job's tent (Job 29:4), before it grew terrifyingly into his suffering and questioning, can only be fathomed by suffering, not by questioning, and man is equally forbidden to question and to follow these secret ways of God. But God's handiwork, his revealed way of working, has been opened before us and set up for us as a pattern. . . . But where are the revealed ways of God's working revealed? Just at the beginning of the wandering through the desert: just at the height of Job's trial: Just in the midst of the terror of the other, the incomprehensible, ununderstandable works: just from out of the secret. God does not show mercy and grace alone to us: it is terrible when his hand falls on us, and what then happens to us does not somehow find a place beside mercy and grace, it does not belong to the same category as these: the ultimate does not belong here to the "attribute of stern justice"—it is beyond all attributes. It is indeed the secret, and it is not for us to inquire into it. But just in this quality of God's is his "handiwork" manifested to us. Only when the secret no longer stands over our tent, but breaks it, do we learn to know God's intercourse with us. And we learn to imitate God.⁹

By its very nature, this "answer-through-suffering" demands that we be open to hear it again and again, as often as we are compelled to cry like Christ "My God, my God, why hast Thou forsaken me?" and as we hear it in the depth of our being, we silence the wish to reduce "the fact of evil into something else," for we know—if only for an instant—that this fact is inseparable from the mystery and the tragic fate of God Incarnate, Who is at once infinitely removed from and at the very center of human suffering, just as the Father is infinitely distant and infinitely close to his Son on the Cross.¹⁰

In *Purgatorio* VII and VIII, Dante again attempts to formulate the never-ending agon of assertion and counter-assertion, question and answer, regarding evil and the terror it engenders. And again he does this as a dramatist, seeking meaning by setting a stage upon which his characters (and he is one of them) who share a common action and a common goal— to find "the best ascent" to the true garden and to God, "l'ortolano etterno" ("the Eternal Gardener"; *Par.* XXVI, 65)—give form to that action and bring nearer that goal both by the competition of their individual acts and by the mimetic exchange that at once binds and separates them, as each alternately acts upon and "suffers" the acts of the other.

This exchange and the action that it helps define are expressed by these words which Virgil addresses to Sordello:

"Non per far, ma per non fare ho perduto
   a veder l'alto Sol che tu disiri
   e che fu tardi per me conosciuto."

(Purg. VII, 25–27)

"Not for doing, but for not doing, have I lost sight of the high Sun that you desire and that was known by me too late."

As Virgil speaks of his loss of Paradise and the vision of God, attributing it to his "non fare," he also brings into focus Sordello's own "non fare" (a measure of which we have already captured in *Purgatorio* VI) and the corresponding delay in seeing "l'alto Sol"—a delay which coincides with a desire yet to be fulfilled. Once this desire has been defined as belonging to Sordello and his scene, it calls forth Virgil's own unfulfilled desire and his scene:

"Luogo è là giù non tristo di martìri,
   ma di tenebre solo, ove i lamenti
   non suonan come guai, ma son sospiri."

(Purg. VII, 28–30)

"A place there is below, not sad with torments but with darkness only, where the lamentations sound not as wailings, but are sighs."

"Sospiri" at once harks back both to "disiri," and therefore to Sordello's longing, and to the longing expressed by Virgil in Limbo ("sanza speme vivemo in disio," "without hope we live in hope and longing"; *Inf.* IV, 41). As we witness at once the mirror-like similarities that bind and the unbridgeable distance that separates Virgil and Sordello, we again apprehend the creative force of tragic rhythm, and we share Dante's tragic vision. With him, we see side by side Sordello's hopeful desire and Virgil's desire without hope to behold "l'alto Sol." And we also see that, conversely, Virgil *has known*, though late, that same "alto Sol" that Sordello, also late, will know at the end of his journey up the mountain of Purgatory.

Equally significant is Virgil's shift from the scene of hopeless longing, conjured up as he speaks of Limbo (VII, 28–36), to the following scene of hope—the hope for the true beginning of the purgatorial journey:

> "Ma se tu sai e puoi, alcuno indizio
>   dà noi per che venir possiam più tosto
>   là dove purgatorio ha dritto inizio."

(Purg. VII, 37–39)

"But if you know and can, give us some direction whereby we may come more speedily to where Purgatory has its true beginning."

Virgil thus transcends the original condition or scene which characterized him at the start, for the new scene he now enters (and helped create) stands in opposition to the scene of Limbo he evoked. He now moves and acts in the same space in which Sordello and Dante the pilgrim move and act as they are prompted by their longing to behold "l'alto Sol." Hence we see him at once as hopelessly lost and, at least virtually, very nearly as saved. He is "saved" for having accepted to play a role—as guide and companion in Dante's journey—that temporarily removes him from the ordered world of Limbo (with its seven walls and enclosed garden and its melancholy *gravitas*) and exposes him as pilgrim among pilgrims,[11] to an uncertain, problematic existence. We must again recall what Beatrice promised him in Limbo: "When I am before my lord, I will often praise you to him" (*Inf.* II, 73–74). As earlier in Chapter II, so now we find ourselves in the presence of two irreconcilable economies that paradoxically coexist, in the same way the economy of the justice embodied in the inscription above Hell's portal coexists with the economy of the love that, with Christ's death and descent to Hell, caused the "infernal ruin" and opened "the roads between heaven and earth" (*Par.* XXIII, 38).

   Then Virgil's eagerness to find the quickest way to Purgatory's true beginning clashes with the reality of the scene which he has just entered and that Sordello thus defines:

> . . . "Loco certo non c'è posto;
>   licito m'è andar suso e intorno;
>   per quanto ir posso, a guida mi t'accosto.
> Ma vedi già come dichina il giorno,
>   e andar sù di notte non si puote;
>   però è buon pensar di bel soggiorno.

Anime sono a destra qua remote;
   se mi consenti, io ti merrò ad esse,
   e non sanza diletto ti fier note."

                           (*Purg.* VII, 40–48)

. . . "No fixed place is set for us; it is permitted me to go up and round, and as far as I may go I will accompany you as guide. But see now how the day declines, and to go up by night is not possible, therefore it is well to take thought of a good resting place. There are souls on the right here, apart: with your consent I will lead you to them, and not without delight will they be known to you."

The "true beginning" of the purgatorial journey that Virgil seeks stands in sharp contrast to the limited and undefined journey of Sordello (who may go "up and around" but not where Purgatory proper begins) and of other souls who, with him, have "no fixed place." And even this journey (more a wandering than a true journey) is now not possible as darkness falls.

    The conflict between Virgil's longing for the scene that he envisages and Sordello's invitation to enter the scene that he has defined reaches its highest tension and acquires greater dramatic force in this exchange between the two poets:

"Com'è ciò?" fu risposto. "Chi volesse
   salir di notte, fora elli impedito
   d'altrui, o non sarria ché non potesse?"
E 'l buon Sordello in terra fregò 'l dito,
   dicendo: "Vedi? sola questa riga
   non varcheresti dopo 'l sol partito:
non però ch'altra cosa desse briga,
   che la notturna tenebra, ad ir suso;
   quella col nonpoder la voglia intriga."

                           (*Purg.* VII, 49–57)

"How is that?" was answered; "he who wished to climb by night, would he be hindered by others, or would he not climb because he had not the power?" And the good Sordello drew his finger on the ground, saying, "Look, even this line you would not cross after the sun is set. Not that aught else save the nocturnal darkness hinders the going up: that hampers the will with impotence."

We recognize the familiar dialectic of discourse versus action, and once again, at the point where the two intersect, we experience with Virgil (and with his silent disciple) the sudden shift from the reality as plotted by the mind's eye to the reality as perceived and organized through action.

As dramatist here Dante has made it possible for meaning to assert itself through life's very movement, through the progression and transcendence that come into being when Virgil's assumption (reflected in his question)—that either external forces or the lack of inner power may constitute a hindrance to his journey—is modified by Sordello's revelation that such hindrance is due to the direct effect of the nocturnal darkness on the will, in other words to the mysterious yet real correlation between the power of nature and the power of human will, or to put it in dramatistic terms, to the scene-act ratio. Sordello's action of drawing a line on the ground, by the directness and simplicity with which it calls attention to the world of concrete experience, gives full expression to this secret correlation. In a note on Sordello's writing on the ground, Singleton invites the reader to compare it with Jesus' writing as described in John 8:6, 8; but oddly he does not offer any interpretation of this correspondence. I welcome his invitation and what I consider the implicit challenge to extract some meaning from the suggested comparison. Although I am not sure that Dante intended the allusion to the passage from John (I suspect that he in fact did not), if we look at the entire scene from which Singleton isolated the action of Jesus' writing, we will find significant similarities—but only in terms of its dramatic form—with the scene that Dante has fashioned:

At daybreak he appeared in the temple again; and as the people came to him, he sat down and began to teach them. The scribes and Pharisees brought a woman along who had been caught committing adultery; and making her stand there in full view of everybody, they said to Jesus, "Master, this woman was caught in the very act of committing adultery, and Moses has ordered us in the law to condemn women like this to death with stoning. What have you to say?" They asked him this as a test, looking for something to use against him. But Jesus bent down and started writing on the ground with his finger. As they persisted with their question, He looked up and said, "If there is one of you who has not sinned, let him be the first to throw a stone at her." Then he bent down and wrote on the ground again. When they heard this they went away one by one, beginning with the eldest, until Jesus was left alone with the woman, who remained standing there. He looked up and said, "Woman, where are they? Has no one condemned you?" "No one, sir," she replied. "Neither do I condemn you," said Jesus. "Go away, and don't sin any more." (John 8:2–11)

From a dramatistic perspective, we immediately discover that the conflict between the Pharisees and Christ is analogous to the conflict between Virgil and Sordello, and that Christ, like Sordello, resolves it not intellectually, by engaging in lengthy explanations, but through an unexpected action. Both the Pharisees and Virgil are motivated by the logic of received opinion, of a "law"—the law of Moses for the former and the law of reason for the latter. And in their desire to apply that law coherently ("reasonably") to a particular situation, they both see things in terms of dualistic opposition. With their questions the Pharisees pressed Jesus to adhere either to Moses' law, that an adulteress should be stoned to death, or to the law of love which He teaches, that the woman should be forgiven. They know that no matter how He replies, He will incur a grave contradiction, either by repudiating the law of Moses or by repudiating His own law of love. How does Jesus reply? He replies by not replying, that is, by remaining silent. And he makes his silence speak through His action of writing on the ground. By its very directness and simplicity, and by the very space that it defines within the scene which at the start was characterized only by discourse, this action suggests that the solution to the conflict lies beyond discourse and the dualistic opposition that it engenders. By introducing an unforeseen break in their discourse, it also creates a space within the conscience of each of the accusers which makes it possible for them, if only temporarily, to receive Jesus' words. These reveal to them that, like the woman they are accusing, they are sinners.[12]

Similarly, by his action of drawing a line on the ground, Sordello unexpectedly introduces a break in Virgil's discourse, thus creating a space that forces him to shift his focus from the logic of dual opposition, according to which human actions are governed either by external or internal forces (and therefore by a strict determinism in either case), to the logic of experience, which affirms that the effect of darkness upon the will is mysterious yet real. In both the scenes of the Pharisees and Christ and that of Virgil and Sordello, the solution to conflict is brought about by a form that is essentially dramatic and by the assertion of tragic vision, for it achieves the transformation and transcendence of the linear logic of discursive reasoning (which like the logic of justice often leads to violence) by a "leap" into the realm of action. For the Pharisees and Virgil, this leap produces in them an acceptance of "things as they are." The Pharisees are made aware of the condition of sin which they share with the adulteress, and as a result violence is avoided. Similarly Virgil discovers the limits of the will (to fashion its own "journey") as he discovers directly and before predication, that like Sordello and the other souls he (and his disciple) cannot journey upward at night. Sordello's action of writing on the ground helps transform and transcend Virgil's logic which at first questioned the order that reigns in Purgatory, paradoxically revealing that the point where the journey of repentance and purification has its "true beginning" cannot be reached without "tarrying" in the valley of the princes.

A tangible proof of the motivational force of the scene, which represents a measure of the sacred, is Virgil's acceptance—without understanding ("quasi ammirando")—of Sordello's invitation to go to the place where are gathered those who would be known "not without delight":

> Allora il mio segnor, quasi ammirando,
>   "Menane," disse, "dunque là 've dici
>   ch'aver si può diletto dimorando."
>
> (*Purg.* VII, 61–63)

Then my lord, as though marveling, said, "Lead us therefore whither you say we may have delight in tarrying."

Interestingly, the tarrying that Virgil now accepts takes place within a setting that speaks of beauty and delight and, more deeply, of the problematic of the return to Eden:

> Oro e argento fine, cocco e biacca,
>   indaco legno lucido e sereno,
>   fresco smeraldo in l'ora che si fiacca,
> da l'erba e da li fior, dentr'a quel seno
>   posti, ciascun saria di color vinto,
>   come dal suo maggiore è vinto il meno.
> Non avea pur natura ivi dipinto,
>   ma di soavità di mille odori
>   vi facea uno incognito e indistinto.
>
> (*Purg.* VII, 73–81)

Gold and fine silver, cochineal and white lead, Indian wood bright and clear, fresh emerald at the moment it is split, would be surpassed in color, if placed within that valley, by the grass and by the flowers growing there, as the less is surpassed by the greater. Nature had not only painted there, but of the sweetness of a thousand scents she made there one unknown to us and blended.

"The artistry Dante expends on the verse," notes A. Bartlett Giamatti, "coupled with the pigments and plastic materials . . . and the extended metaphor of Nature as painter . . . give the valley the aura of an 'artifact'. . . . This very 'artificiality,' the sense that the valley is *too* overtly made, that too much care is expended on its visible aspects, provides the proper setting for those who tended the external and secular world to the detriment of higher goals."[13] We can expand the meaning of these remarks by adding that the artificial garden that Dante has created is the "proper setting" for the negligent princes because their worldly cares were essentially an expression of their nostalgia for an Eden-without-the-serpent. Like the scene we have just reproduced, this is a garden created to shut out the real world of sin and misery. It is the garden of the "second innocence" which represents the princes' negligence in healing the wounds of *civitas*. Once again, we can interpret this nostalgia for a "second innocence" as a false reading or re-enactment of the original myth of the Earthly Paradise.

The scenes that follow offer further evidence for our interpretation. As we turn to the tercet that comes immediately after the passage of the *locus amoenus* we have quoted, we experience a shift from a scene of the "second innocence" to a scene in which innocence and the recognition of sin are juxtaposed:

> "*Salve, Regina*" in sul verde e 'n su' fiori
>   quindi seder cantando anime vidi
>   che per la valle non parean di fuori.
>
> (*Purg.* VII, 82–84)

From there I saw, seated upon the green grass and the flowers, singing "*Salve, Regina*," souls who because of the valley were not visible from without.

As the souls sing *Salve Regina*, the well-known prayer to the Virgin Mary which in the journey of this life is recited at dusk, they introduce "scenes" that contrast sharply with the scene in which they now dwell. When they utter the words (which of course we "hear" only in our imagination) "Ad te clamamus exules filii Hevae" ("to Thee we cry, the banished children of

Eve"), they speak of both the exile of Adam and Eve and their own banish-
ment from the Earthly Paradise. Thus as they are gathered in a valley which
resembles the paradisal scene of innocence and bliss preceding the Fall,
they speak—though indirectly—of the garden which, with Adam and Eve,
they have lost.

The second scene the souls conjure up in their prayer is that of the "valley of tears": "Ad te suspiramus gementes et flentes in hac lacrimarum
valle" ("to Thee we send our sighs, mourning and weeping in this valley of
tears"). As we imagine them singing the words "in this valley of tears," we
are struck by the special force of the adjective "this" which, like "nostra" in
the first line of the *Comedy*, refers at once to the fictional scene and the
scene of our life. The scene of innocence and the scene of misery, the valley
of green grass and flowers and the valley of tears are now represented as
one. The single vision of the garden-without-the-serpent has been transformed into the double vision of the garden of innocence and sin, of bliss
and suffering. We thus see re-enacted a measure of the original myth of the
Earthly Paradise and the tragic vision that informs it. As we follow Dante's
staging of this myth in the valley of the princes, we must observe that the
souls' performance as they sing *Salve Regina* constitutes an integral part of
the main action of their journey to blessedness, although it paradoxically
coincides with "tarrying," with delay.

The last scenes of *Purgatorio* VII contain significant developments of
this action. A striking scene is the one that Sordello points out and interprets for Virgil and Dante:

> "Colui che più siede alto e fa sembianti
>   d'aver negletto ciò che far dovea,
>   e che non move bocca a li altrui canti,
> Rodolfo imperador fu, che potea
>   sanar le piaghe c'hanno Italia morta,
>   sì che tardi per altri si ricrea."
>
> (*Purg.* VII, 91–96)

"He who sits highest and has the look of having neglected what he ought
to have done, and does not move his lips with the others' song, was Rudolf the Emperor, who might have healed the wounds that were the
death of Italy, so that through another she is succored too late."

What gives prominence to the figure of Emperor Rudolf is not only that he "sits highest" but that he does not join the other souls in their song. As we see the two contiguous scenes of Rudolf's "look" of the negligent and of his lips that do not move "with the others' song," we know intuitively that one is the expression of the other, and that in reality (that of the "performance" as opposed to the reality of the narration in time) they are unified and yet remain distinct. And as our attention moves from one scene to the other, we apprehend disjunctively an important correlation between the Emperor's negligence in healing "the wounds that were the death of Italy" and his refusal to join in prayer the community of souls. In the light of what we have noted earlier, this refusal implies a rejection of the reality of sin and suffering which that prayer reasserts, as it speaks of exile from the garden and of dwelling in the valley of tears. Moreover, it implies a refusal to participate in the liturgical life, the sacred drama of the community whereby the mysterious and timeless reality of the great myths is re-enacted.

As the Emperor Rudolf sits "highest" among the other souls, seemingly fixed in the form that characterized his earthly existence, there may stir, however, under the overt gestures and acts, the inner action of his repentance. His silence, which at first speaks clearly of his negligence, may also constitute the creative space within which he can see himself as separated from the choral life of the community. And as he "suffers" this opposition, he may begin—if only imperceptibly—to transform negligence into zeal, thus transcending his original state.

We can capture a tangible measure of this subtle, secret movement of the soul towards the good as soon as we direct our attention to the scene that immediately follows that of the negligent, silent Rudolf:

> "L'altro che ne la vista lui conforta,
>   resse la terra dove l'acqua nasce
>   che Molta in Albia, e Albia in mar ne porta:
> Ottacchero ebbe nome . . . ."
>
> (*Purg.* VII, 97–100)

"The other, who appears to be comforting him, ruled the land where the waters spring that the Moldau carries to the Elbe, and the Elbe to the sea: his name was Ottokar . . . ."

As we see Ottokar, the king of Bohemia, comfort his former enemy Rudolf who had slain him in battle, we experience another shift of perspective which signals the transformation we glimpsed earlier. The dramatic form inherent in the juxtaposition of two scenes reveals the inner action of Rudolf's soul. What at first—with Sordello, Virgil and Dante—we could only interpret exclusively as a distinctive mark of the Emperor's negligence, we are now led to see in a new light by virtue of Ottokar's act of comforting his old enemy. Since such comforting can only be called forth by suffering, we can conclude that the look of negligence that first characterized the figure of Rudolf was that of negligence "suffered," as we hinted earlier, namely negligence seen in all its destructiveness as a sin that, as all sins, separates us from the community and God. Thus Rudolf's repentance coincides with the outward manifestation of his negligence. As he performs the role of the negligent, suffering the separation from the good, he repents. As Simone Weil has observed in essentially dramatistic terms that "We experience good only by doing it. We experience evil only by refusing to allow ourselves to do it, or, if we do it, by repenting of it. When we do evil we do not know it, because evil flies from the light."[14]

We have witnessed the first stage of the process of repentance and expiation that will have its "true beginning" when the souls enter Purgatory proper. This process is fundamentally one of change from the illusory and destructive aspiration to create their own garden of innocence to the recognition and acceptance of "the fact of evil" and of the misery caused by the distance that separates them from the true garden. This is analogous to the acceptance of Adam and Eve not only of their exile after their expulsion from the Earthly Paradise, but also of the journey through time and history (through "this valley of tears"). And as we have already observed at the beginning of this chapter, it is also the acceptance of "tarrying," of delay. We should also note that the drama which we see unfold in the Valley of the Princes is also the drama of the sacred. Through liturgy the sacred enters the profane space—the "scene" of the garden created by man and nature—and redefines it, bringing it in contact with the original myth (and its mystery) which speaks of both the garden and its loss, of the idyllic life and the life of conflict and toil.

Beginning with the opening lines of *Purgatorio* VIII, Dante again stages the drama of the return to the garden.

Era, già l'ora che volge il disio
  ai navicanti e 'ntenerisce il core

lo dì c'han detto ai dolci amici addio;
e che lo novo peregrin d'amore
   punge, se ode squilla di lontano
   che paia il giono pianger che si more;
quand'io incominciai a render vano
   l'udire e a mirare una de l'alme
   surta, che l'ascoltar chiedea con mano.

(Purg. VIII, 1–9)

It was now the hour that turns back the longing of seafaring folk and melts their heart the day they have bidden sweet friends farewell, and that pierces the new pilgrim with love if he hears from afar a bell that seems to mourn the dying day, when I began to annul my hearing and to gaze on one of the souls, uprisen, who was signing with his hand to be heard.

Especially striking here is the contiguity of two opposite scenes and therefore the tragic rhythm produced by the disjunctive relation of one to the other. Together in essence they constitute an assertion and a counter-assertion, or a question and an answer. The first scene speaks of the human journey away from home and the community, and of the resulting nostalgia. And as the reference to "peregrin" suggests, it speaks not only of a nostalgia for the earthly home, but also of a nostalgia for that "home" lost because of the Fall. Giovanni Cecchetti has aptly called this a "nostalgia of the future."[15] This scene speaks at once of a journey and of a *peregrinatio*, in other words of the universal human condition of separation from the original state of perfect communion with God and his creation, and of the nostalgia for that state, for the garden. This is also the condition of the souls of Anti-Purgatorio, for although they are saved, they have yet to begin their pilgrimage up the mountain of Purgatory.

As hinted earlier, this scene of exile and nostalgia can be interpreted essentially as a question: given this condition of exile—which is individual and collective, historical and mythical, and of the living and of the dead—how can it be transformed from a journey without a goal (similar to the "wandering" of the souls in Anti-Purgatorio) into a pilgrimage, more precisely, into an authentic return to the garden? Or, to say it in terms suggested by our text, how can the nostalgia that is born of "disio" be transformed into a nostalgia that is born of "amore"? As we formulate this question, we are prompted to ask yet another question: what is the nature of this love that "pierces" the pilgrim? And, with Francis Fergusson, we may ask: "Is it frightening or comforting? Good or evil?"[16]

The second scene of our text begins to "answer" these questions by speaking not of nostalgia for the garden but of an action that is present and whose very immediacy totally absorbs the pilgrim's attention. Interestingly, and in a sense paradoxically, the very moment the pilgrim's hearing is annulled as he gazes on the soul who signals the others to be attentive, he is open to another sound. Thus along with the pilgrim we experience a break in the movement of the soul which earlier we tentatively identified with the double nostalgia for the earthly home and for Eden, and therefore we discover that narrow space which makes it possible for us to witness a new scene and a new action. Disjunctively or metonymically, this may constitute, if only partially, an "answer" to the previous scene of nostalgia that for a moment filled our and the pilgrim's soul. In other words, in and *through* this *caesura*, we reach the degree zero of consciousness, and like the pilgrim, temporarily "deaf" to the sound of the bell that "seems to mourn the dying day," we are totally open, totally given to a new act and a new scene and hence to a new *creation*, like Adam, we might say, the instant before he opened his eyes in (and to) the garden. With the pilgrim, we learn to suspend our ordinary way of looking at things, to forget our nostalgias for paradise and correspondingly our laments for its elusiveness. With him, we learn to be patient and therefore hopeful that the next scene and the next act—which will suddenly enter our field of vision—will, if only partially or temporarily, shed some light on or "interpret" the scene of nostalgia which we "suffered" earlier. And as we have already hinted, like Dante the pilgrim we want to discover the nature and power of the love that "pierces" the soul; we are looking not for a definition but for an action.

Francis Fergusson has captured a measure of this "movement of the soul" which Dante calls "moto spiritale" (*Purg.* XVIII, 32), when he writes:

The literal scene with its sounds is only the signal for love (apparently from without) to pierce the Pilgrim. And he listens for it, not with the ear of the flesh, but with the whole being; he "looks" for something which is to be perceptible through the dusky scene around him. This is one of the many places in which Dante uses the shift from one physical sense to another to suggest a focus of attention which is not to be defined as sight, hearing, or any other single sense. He wants us to be poised, thus all attentive, for some clue to the meaning of the love that pierces the Pilgrim.[17]

Fergusson then adds:

The clue which appears is that pair of green-feathered messengers of heaven who come winging through the evening air and alight, on either side of the valley. It is not difficult to discover that they represent that "love" which prevails in the whole realm of purgation, the divine grace, the unearned gift, which prevents the Pilgrim from taking the wrong path until he reaches the *Paradiso Terrestre*. For the *Purgatorio* shows *one* view of human destiny, man as mysteriously capable—capable beyond what he can understand—of sane growth.[18]

Although I find this reading essentially correct and indeed very useful to our discourse, I must call attention to an important element that it ignores: what constitutes the counterpart, and therefore—dialectically—the necessary ground for this "clue" to come into being.

Returning to our dramatistic language of question and answer or of assertion and counter-assertion, we should not fail to identify the "correct" question and the *why* of its correctness, without which the corresponding answer or clue could not be called forth. This question coincides in a narrow sense with the hymn *Te lucis ante*, and in a large sense with the entire scene of which this action is the center:

> Ella giunse e levò ambo le palme,
>   ficcando li occhi verso l'orïente,
>   come dicesse a Dio: "D'altro non calme."
> "*Te lucis ante*" sì devotamente
>   le uscìo di bocca e con sì dolci note,
>   che fece me a me uscir di mente . . . .

(Purg. VIII, 10–15)

He joined and lifted both his palms, fixing his eyes on the East, as if he said to God, "For naught else do I care." "*Te lucis ante*" came from his lips so devoutly and with such sweet notes that it rapt me from myself.

To begin to understand the meaning and function of this "question" as the necessary condition for the "answer" or "answers" which the later scenes will provide, we must first consider how it relates to the earlier scene of homesickness and nostalgia. In other words, we must examine it as an answer to the preceding question before we look at it, in turn, as a question that seeks an answer in the scenes that follow. We are once again engaged in the search for the creative force inherent in the tragic rhythm produced by a sequence of scenes. Like the earlier scene of the soul who enjoins the others to be attentive, this scene is characterized by action, except that action now takes on the fuller form of spectacle or drama that is inseparable from ritual and myth. As we follow the articulation of this drama, we discover that it gives a number of answers to the scene of nostalgia which we have earlier "translated" into the question: how can humanity return to the true garden? Of course this question can also be formulated thus: what *is* our true home?

The first answer emerges from the simple yet highly charged gesture of the soul joining his palms. It suggests the gathering into oneself (thus overcoming the duality to which, with the Fall, all are subject) in preparation for prayer. This action may also be seen as an invitation to and a foreshadowing of the coming together of the community of souls in prayer. The pointing heavenward of the joined palms obviously speaks of the realm where God dwells—eternity—to which prayers are addressed. A similar meaning is expressed by the soul's action of fixing his eyes on the east, and therefore to the point where the day is born and from which, symbolically, Christ the *sol oriens* may come. These first actions, with their respective scenes and agents, assert a mode of being that lies beyond the nostalgia expressed by the scene of the "navicanti" and of the "novo peregrin." Through a few simple but powerful actions, Dante has shown us the gathering together, with perfect correspondence of the literal to the symbolic, of nature to spirit—the *re-orientation* of the soul and hence the discovery of its true goal and true "home." The melancholy scene of the "dying day" has now been transformed and transcended. The pilgrim captures an important measure of this transformation when he interprets the actions of the officiating soul as "words" that he "hears" him address to God: "D'altro non calme." Before intoning the hymn *Te lucis ante*, this soul has already entered into a dialogue with God through the concentration of his actions which, we can easily gather, have annulled all dispersions, all separations, and all nostalgias, that, like the "navicanti" and the "novo peregrin," he may have experienced earlier. The "novo peregrin" too is similarly transformed the moment in which he becomes an active spectator, as he is drawn through a spontaneous, sympathetic response, into the staging of those actions. Thus he cooperates in their creativity, more precisely, in their manifestation of the inner action or word which inaugurates the dialogue between I and Thou as it seeks a response from God.

As we pause before this scene and see one of the negligent souls of Anti-Purgatorio and our pilgrim come into focus as new beings—"new" if, again, we compare them to the figures of the "navicanti" and the "pere-grin" of the canto's opening scenes—without a word having been spoken, we may be reminded of the meaning and the power of what Martin Buber has called the "Primary word": "The primary word I-Thou can be spoken only with the whole being. Concentration and fusion into the whole being can never take place through my agency, nor can it ever take place without me. I become through my relation to Thou; as I become I, I say Thou. All real living is meeting."[19]

Then, with a deeper sense of recognition of the struggle of the "primary word I-Thou" to assert itself (thus making "real living" possible), we dis-cover another significant transformation of the scene of exile and nostalgia into a scene of choral unity by the power of words and song:

> "*Te lucis ante*" sì devotamente
>   le uscìo di bocca e con sì dolci note,
>   che fece me a me uscir di mente;
> e l'altre poi dolcemente e devote
>   seguitar lei per tutto l'inno intero,
>   avendo li occhi a le superne rote.

(Purg. VIII, 13–18)

"*Te lucis ante*" came from his lips so devoutly and with such sweet notes that it rapt me from myself. Then the rest joined him sweetly and de-voutly through the whole hymn, keeping their eyes fixed on the supernal wheels.

As we become part of the chorus of the souls in the Valley of the Princes and with them join the officiating soul—if not "singing through the whole hymn," at least in reading or recalling it—we observe that it harks back to and completes the *Salve Regina* which they sang earlier. And as we see side by side the scene that the two hymns respectively create, we notice that the two prayers are quite different. The *Salve Regina* is a prayer addressed to Mary "our Advocate" and speaks of human exile from the true garden and from the Creator, dwelling in "this valley of tears." The *Te lucis ante* is a prayer addressed directly to God and speaks not of exile and of the suffer-ing of our life but of the primordial, mysterious cause or ground of this suffering—of the evil which is "outside" us, the Ancient Adversary, the serpent. Significantly, this latter prayer sets the stage for God's healing of human wounds in terms of an agon between God and the serpent. Our adversary is thus seen as God's adversary. We are thus in the presence of another dimension of the tragic which we found earlier in the "scenes" of the *Salve Regina*. Equally significant is the fact that the hope expressed in this hymn—that the "blessed fruit" of Mary's womb, Jesus, be shown "unto us" "after this our exile"—in the *Te lucis ante* is "transformed" into the hope that "through Jesus Christ" God will "tread underfoot our ghostly foe" *now*, in the hour when we are more vulnerable to the temptation of the adversary. The focus in this "scene" is thus not on exile and on the accompanying nostalgia for Paradise or its equivalent (the longing for a future epiphany like Christ's advent *post exsilium*), but on Christ's coming *hic et nunc, during* our exile.

These reflections are hints and guesses that will turn into more explicit meaning in the other scenes of *Purgatorio* VIII. Before examining these, I must call attention to how Dante stages the souls' singing of *Te lucis ante*, and therefore to the creative force or "message" inherent in the very *performance* of the scenes we have reproduced above. The first tercet contains a significant measure of this power, which is expressed by the pilgrim's transformation provoked by the "devout" and "sweet" singing of the officiating soul: he is "rapt" from himself, thus experiencing directly that state of concentration and transcendence that a moment before he had "heard" the officiating soul express through his prayerful gestures ("D'altro non calme"). This power of performance and mimesis is reaffirmed in the second tercet, where we witness the coming into being of the community as a chorus by the mimetic response to the soul's sweet and devout singing (note how *"dolcemente e devote"* clearly "imitate" *"devotamente"* and *"con sì dolci* note" said of the one soul).

The significance of this power of performance—and therefore the specific function of spectacle, of "theater"—in the economy of expiation and redemption in the Valley of the Princes, is then underscored by this famous address of Dante to the reader:

> Aguzza qui, lettor, ben li occhi al vero,
>   ché 'l velo è ora ben tanto sottile,
>   certo che 'l trapassar dentro è leggero.
>
> (*Purg.* VIII, 19–21)

Reader, here sharpen well your eyes to the truth, for the veil is now indeed so thin that certainly to pass within is easy.

The "truth" of which the poet speaks here can only be that of the "letter"
or the representation and performance that is as immediately accessible to
the reader as it is to the pilgrim.[20] The emphasis is clearly on the meaning
or truth inherent to the "suchness" of things, that is, to what is perceived
directly before predication and hence dramatistically.

Dante invites us to accept and to value spectacle, drama, and the tragic
vision embedded in it, as the only mode of addressing the reality and mystery of evil, and specifically, of assessing God's role—as dramaturge and
actor—in the drama of both allowing the existence of evil and combatting
it. Furthermore, the invitation is to continue to find meaning and truth in
the larger drama of question and answer, of assertion and counter-assertion
and therefore in the tragic rhythm that they engender of which, with the
pilgrim, we so far have witnessed only a part. Having staged and performed man's condition of exile in a valley which is at once the *locus
amoenus* or "paradise" of the princes and the "valley of tears," and having
staged and performed the recognition of the mysterious yet real presence
of evil in and outside him, as well as his prayer that God intervene to "tread
underfoot our ghostly foe," Dante turns to us to sound a warning. As we—
along with the pilgrim and the chorus of souls of Anti-Purgatorio—await
a response or counter-assertion, he enjoins us not to reduce to discourse or
speculation the actions and scenes to which such a response will be made.
As a dramatist endowed with tragic vision, Dante wants not to prove but
to make visible, knowing that the easy "trapassar dentro"—the "passing
within" through the thin veil that separates events from meaning and spectacle from speculation and theory—brings about a reduction and a loss in
truth and meaning. As Paul Ricoeur observes:

It is of the essence of the tragic that it must be exhibited in a tragic hero, a tragic
action, a tragic dénouement. Perhaps the tragic cannot tolerate transcription into a
theory which—let us say it immediately—could only be the scandalous theology of
predestination to evil. Perhaps the tragic theology must be rejected as soon as it is
thought. Perhaps also it is capable of surviving, as spectacle, all the destructions
that follow its transcription into the plain language of speculation. This connection
with the spectacle, then, would be the specific means by which the *symbolic* power
that resides in every tragic myth could be protected.[21]

Thus as we approach the "spectacle" which the poet *saw* (and which he
wants us to see), we can be confident both that it will survive "all the destructions that follow upon its transcription into the plain language" of *our*

speculation, of *this* discourse, and that the "symbolic power" of the tragic myth of the Earthly Paradise which that spectacle re-enacts will be "protected."

> Io vidi quello essercito gentile
>   tacito poscia riguardare in sùe,
>   quasi aspettando, palido e umìle;
> e vidi uscir de l'alto e scender giùe
>   due angeli con due spade affocate,
>   tronche e private de le punte sue.
> Verdi come fogliette pur mo nate
>   erano in veste, che da verdi penne
>   percosse traean dietro e ventilate.
> L'un poco sovra noi a star si venne,
>   e l'altro scese in l'opposita sponda,
>   sì che la gente in mezzo si contenne.
> Ben discernea in lor la testa bionda;
>   ma ne la faccia l'occhio si smarria,
>   come virtù ch'a troppo si confonda.
> "Ambo vegnon del grembo di Maria,"
>   disse Sordello, "a guardia de la valle,
>   per lo serpente che verrà vie via."
>
> (*Purg.* VIII, 22–39)

Then I saw that noble army silently gaze upward as if expectant, pallid and humble; and I saw come forth from above and descend two angels with flaming swords, broken short and deprived of their points. Their robes were green as newborn leaves, which they trailed behind them, smitten and fanned by their green wings. One came and took his stand a little above us, and the other alighted on the opposite bank, so that the company was contained in the middle. I clearly discerned their blond heads, but in their faces my sight was dazzled like a faculty confounded by excess. "Both come from Mary's bosom," said Sordello, "to guard the valley, because of the serpent that will presently come."

In the first tercet we see the souls of the late repentant united in silence as before they were united in prayer and song. They are still a community, a "chorus." As such they constitute an essential component of the tragic play in which and through which the tragic myth continues to live and can be experienced anew. That they are performing a play is declared by the words "quasi aspettando," for "quasi" is the "as if" of spectacle, of theater. And of course equally theatrical are the words "palido e umile" which speak of fear and obedience (or acceptance) vis-à-vis the "response"—the "answer"— which may come from above to the "question" staged and performed earlier concerning our exile from Paradise and the threatening reality of the serpent, the "adversary."

Before moving on to interpret this "response" I must again call attention to the "chorus," not because I wish to repeat the commonplace that the choral life is emblematic of all of *Purgatorio* but rather to reveal its specific function within the economy of the drama that we are seeing unfold in the Valley of the Princes, a drama whose central action is the return to the garden. The very coming together of the community of souls as "chorus" through prayer, ritual, and song—in a word, through spectacle— constitutes the privileged form, and the privileged "agent," through which the individual may go beyond "localized," private, and inchoate fear and pity. The very "as if" of spectacle and performance invites the spectator to enter, through imitation and natural sympathy, the circle of the chorus and thus transcending oneself, or the "old" self, as the pilgrim goes beyond himself and is "rapt," along with the other souls of Anti-Purgatorio, in response to the devout and sweet notes of one soul. Here in the chorus, all dispersions of the self, all negligence and tarrying, all illusions—such as that of an easy return to the garden or an easy victory over the old adversary, as well as the longing for a true return to the garden in the face of the reality of evil—are made visible as constitutive elements of the tragic human condition. And through this "vision" they are reconciled. Thus the experience of the tragic produces tragic wisdom. The following remarks by Paul Ricoeur on the spectacle and the chorus in Greek tragedy are, *mutatis mutandis*, strikingly appropriate to our discourse:

There remains the tragic *spectacle* itself, to purify whoever yields himself to the sublimity of the poetic word. It is neither counsel in the Apollinian sense, nor an alteration of personality in the Dionysiac sense, except, perhaps, in a very remote sense—for example, in the sense that the spectacle fosters "illusion." Through the spectacle the ordinary man enters into the "chorus" which weeps and sings with the hero; the place of tragic reconciliation is the "chorus" and its lyricism. By entering into the tragic "chorus" ourselves, we pass from the Dionysiac illusion to the specific ecstasy of tragic wisdom. Then the myth is among us; it is we who are frightened and lament, because we have put ourselves into the scene. One must become a member of the chorus in order to yield himself to the feelings which are specifically those of the tragic reconciliation. The ordinary man knows only fear and the sort of bashful sympathy that the spectacle of misfortune calls forth; in becoming a member of the chorus, he enters a sphere of feelings that may be called symbolic and mythic, in consideration of the type of utterance to which they are appropriate.[22]

As we turn our attention to the "response" that comes from "above," we note that its form, like the "question" that called it forth, is eminently dramatic. The two angels with flaming swords who came down to "guard the valley" are reminiscent of the cherubim placed by God outside Eden after the Fall "to guard the way to the tree of life" (Gen. 3:24). But here they are sent to guard the valley against the adversary, the serpent, and they do this not as harsh judges whose actions cannot be separated from violence but as messengers of mercy, of love, for their swords are "broken short and deprived of their points." Further evidence of this action of "vanquishing by being vanquished"—of the Logos of Love—is given, of course, by the suggestion that these angels come "from Mary's bosom" and therefore come as figures or "masks" of Christ. And whereas the angel of Genesis marked the beginning of our exile from the garden, forbidding return to it, these angels intervene in the exile and help recover the garden. Significantly, this recovery is also a recovery of the original myth of paradise—which tells of innocence and bliss that are always threatened by the presence of the serpent, by the reality of evil—and is always problematic and hence always open to failure, as the scenes that follow the appearance of the two angels make manifest.

> Ond'io, che non sapeva per qual calle,
>   mi volsi intorno, e stretto m'accostai,
>   tutto gelato, a le fidate spalle.
> E Sordello anco: "Or avvalliamo omai
>   tra le grandi ombre, e parleremo ad esse;
>   grazïoso fia lor vedervi assai."
>
> (*Purg.* VIII, 40–45)

Whereat I, who knew not by what path, turned round all chilled and pressed close to the trusty shoulders. And Sordello continued, "Let us go down into the valley among the great shades, and we will speak with them: it will be well pleasing to them to see you."

The pilgrim's fear, provoked by Sordello's announcement of the imminent appearance of the serpent (VIII, 39), contrasts sharply with Sordello's unconcern (which is also unconcern for the pilgrim and his fear) and is accentuated by his interest in joining "the great shades." It has been observed that this characterization "may remind the reader of the 'great shades' of Limbo (*Inf.* IV, 83, 119)," and that "a certain correspondence between the two groups is surely intended by the poet."[23] I must add that this correspondence seems specifically intended to suggest a "return" to a garden that, like the one in Limbo, is a human creation. This return constitutes essentially a departure from the true garden and the true myth of Eden, whose representation in the Valley of the Princes is still "in the making." As it ignores the serpent (though only temporarily), thus annulling fear and the accompanying tragic vision, it reasserts the nostalgia for the "second innocence" and therefore delays the authentic return to the garden. Equally significant, this return to an artificial garden marks also a departure—again, only temporarily—from the life of the community at its best, from the "chorus" and its sacred "space." These two tercets are marked by the pattern of a movement, a rhythm—created by alternating scenes of zeal and negligence, of concentrated attention (and even rapture) and dispersion—which we have identified earlier in the Valley of the Princes and which informs the entire episode through the last scenes of *Purgatorio* VIII.

As we move through them, we find that the main actions of Dante's encounters (first with Nino Visconti and then with Currado Malaspina) are characterized, now in subtle and now in explicit ways, by shifts and breaks produced by the intersection of two perspectives. Indifferent to the imminent appearance of the serpent (and this is now also true of the pilgrim, who has been the only one to show fear at the mere mention of it), as these figures interact, exchanging courteous greetings—in a word, as they "tarry"—they also show a certain zeal, a certain attention to lasting, "eternal" concerns such as the pilgrim's privileged journey to God, which causes them to marvel. To cite another example, if like the other souls Nino Visconti has temporarily "stepped out" of the "chorus" and its highest concerns to enter into a dialogue with God and to take part in the re-enactment of the myth of the Earthly Paradise, he nevertheless shows a certain care for the community, for the "chorus," and an awareness of God's presence as he asks Dante:

> . . . "Per quel singular grado
> che tu dei a colui che sì nasconde
> lo suo primo perché, che non li è guado,
> quando sarai di là da le larghe onde,
> dì a Giovanna mia che per me chiami
> là dove a li 'nnocenti si risponde."
>
> (*Purg.* VIII, 67–72)

. . . "By that singular gratitude you owe to Him who so hides His primal purpose that there is no fording thereunto, when you are beyond the wide waters, tell my Giovanna that she pray for me there where the innocent are heard."

Yet true to the pattern mentioned above, this soul soon abandons the "general economy" of his purification—of the bond to his daughter, as well as of God's unfathomable judgment—to enter the "restricted economy" of mundane life as he casts a dark gaze (and judgment) on his wife Beatrice for having remarried after his death (VIII, 73–78).

The sarcastic note with which he ends his reproach of her inconstancy in love is a telling measure of how far he has deviated from the life of the "chorus" and its tragic wisdom:

> "Non le farà sì bella sepultura
> la vipera che Melanesi accampa,
> com'avria fatto il gallo di Gallura."
>
> (*Purg.* VIII, 79–81)

"The viper that leads afield the Milanese will not make her so fair a tomb as Gallura's cock would have done."

The reference to the "viper" of the Milanese banner cannot go unnoticed in the "larger" scene that Dante is constructing, in which another "viper" is soon to make its appearance. Nor can we ignore the ironic shift created by the "contiguity" of the two "vipers." We must not fail, however, to see the proportion or ratio that "binds" the two respective economies—of the evil of which the myth of the race speaks, and of the evil of partisan strife.

If Nino Visconti first appears to us as one who has forsaken the "general economy" of the "chorus," if he seems negligent, he also exhibits to a certain degree concern for the community. We may thus share the poet's view when he comments on Nino Visconti's words:

> Così dicea, segnato de la stampa,
>   nel suo aspetto, di quel dritto zelo
>   che misuratamente in core avvampa.
>
> (*Purg.* VIII, 82–84)

Thus, he spoke, his aspect stamped with the mark of that righteous zeal which in due measure glows in the heart.

Yet no sooner have we identified with Dante the "righteous zeal" of Nino Visconti than we are made aware of its limits by the sudden shift to this scene:

> Li occhi miei ghiotti andavan pur al cielo,
>   pur là dove le stelle son più tarde,
>   sì come rota più presso a lo stelo.
>
> (*Purg.* VIII, 85–87)

My greedy eyes kept going to the sky just where the stars are slowest, as in a wheel nearest the axle.

What can this sudden turn heavenward of the pilgrim's gaze represent if not a "zeal" of a higher order than that just commended in Nino Visconti? And does it not hark back to the gaze of the "chorus" of souls that sang *Te lucis ante*? Does not the pilgrim thus (mimetically) recapture the life of the "chorus" by reopening the eternal human dialogue with the cosmos and implicitly the Creator?

Significantly, Virgil, who for a long time remained silent, is now awakened into being by the pilgrim's "eloquent" gaze to play the role of the pilgrim's interlocutor, thus becoming God's "mask":

> E 'l duca mio: "Figliuol, che là sù guarde?"
>   E io a lui: "A quelle tre facelle
>   di che 'l polo di qua tutto quanto arde."

Ond'elli a me: "Le quattro chiare stelle
   che vedevi staman, son di là basse,
   e queste son salite ov'eran quelle."

(Purg. VIII, 88–93)

And my leader, "Son, what are you gazing at up there?" and I to him, "At
those three torches with which the pole here is all aflame." And he to me,
"The four bright stars you saw this morning are low on the other side,
and these are risen where those were."

The symbolism of the three stars, like that of the four stars "never seen
before save by the first people" (*Purg.* I, 24), will be revealed at the summit
of Purgatorio.[24] Here they mark a mysterious yet significant shift of cosmic
and spiritual dimension, from an old to a new vision, from that of Adam
and Eve ("the first people") to that of their progeny.

   Suddenly a new scene comes to life as Sordello draws Virgil to himself
to point to the coming of "our adversary" (VIII, 94–96). Thus for a moment Sordello's attention to the threatening presence of the serpent has
been reawakened, in contrast to his early indifference. The appearance of
the serpent, "perhaps such as gave to Eve the bitter food" (99), "through
the grass and the flowers" (100), calls forth the angels' intervention which
puts the snake to flight (103–108). The spectacle of the tragic myth of Eden
is resumed and the last act is performed. However, as Dante tells us that
through this entire scene ("through all that assault," 110) the shade of Currado Malaspina had not for an instant turned his gaze from him, we witness again the indifference to what we, along with the pilgrim, can only
consider the most essential part of that drama of which the "choral" scenes
of the *Salve Regina* and the *Te lucis ante* marked the inception. Since the
poet does not speak of any interest on the part of the other souls for the
same spectacle, we may assume that Currado's indifference or negligence
represents to a heightened degree their relative indifference or negligence.
By contrast, the pilgrim is shown to be the most attentive spectator, followed by Sordello, whose awareness of the spectacle, however, does not
betray any emotion.

   How can these souls, who earlier as members of a "chorus" invoked
God's intervention in their struggle with "our adversary," now turn their
gaze away from the "response" to their prayer and therefore the most crucial scene of the drama which they themselves began to shape and perform?
We may answer with Mark Musa:

No, they do not fear the serpent; they are not concerned about the outcome of the mock battle (this is surely made clear): they are incapable of being tempted, and for them the outcome of the battle between good and evil was already decided when they died. What did concern them (and we remember their total absorption in expectancy) was that important moment of the day when the angels would come as they had come before and would come again: a never-failing sign of God's grace, which means for them a reassuring reminder of their salvation. . . .

But the Pilgrim (Everyman) fears the serpent. He is afraid because he does not know from what direction ("per qual calle") it will come. He is reacting "symbolically" as the Christian in this life, who must be on guard against temptation which may come from any direction. . . . The contrast between the indifference shown by the souls in the valley to this drama, and the Pilgrim's avid interest in it, is the contrast between a soul that has been saved and a Christian still living in this world.[25]

In the light of the previous remarks on the function of spectacle and on the "chorus" in the economy of the return to "the Earthly Paradise," I find this answer unconvincing. If the souls of the late-repentant are incapable of being tempted because they are saved, does this justify their indifference to the presence and reality of evil? I would say, rather, that the more fully one is "saved," the greater one's awareness of evil (think, for example, of St. Peter's fiery invective against the corruption of the Church, in *Par.* XXVII, 19–60). And how can they be concerned with the sign of God's grace, the "reassuring reminder of their salvation," and yet separate it from the very act and efficacy of that grace—the vanquishing of evil? And what makes "a Christian still living in this world" necessarily more concerned with this drama? May he not be as indifferent to it as the late-repentant or negligent were in their life?

A more accurate answer, which I have already in part suggested throughout the preceding pages of this chapter, is that in the Valley of the Princes Dante gives expression to the problematic recovery of the true garden and its inherent tragic vision. Indeed, the late-repentant are saved, but they have not yet begun their journey of full repentance and expiation which, of course, is inseparable from the recognition of evil, of the "serpent," within each individual life and within the life of the community. In the Valley of the Princes—which is, as we have seen, at once a garden and a "valley of tears"—these souls begin to find the way back to the true garden which awaits them at the summit of Purgatory (and which prefigures the celestial garden), through their recreation or re-enactment of the central action of the myth of Eden and therefore through the "tragic spectacle" of which we spoke earlier. Yet the privileged, sacred space, the concentrated life of the "chorus," which with its lyricism brings about rapture, transformation, and the reconciliation of the tragic, may soon be abandoned and neglected for more "mundane" concerns. Nevertheless, having once experienced the fullness of the "choral" life and having shared, if only for an instant, the tragic vision which mysteriously brings together man and God, and "our" adversary, in an endless dialogue of conflict, these souls carry with them and infuse in those "lesser" concerns a measure of that life. And their very "departure" from the "chorus" is also already a kind of suffering that foreshadows the suffering of repentance and expiation that awaits them. In other words, like the Emperor Rudolph's indifference to the song of the "chorus" which we encountered earlier as a foretaste and an intimation of what is to come, these souls "suffer" again, and therefore re-enact the negligence that separated them on earth from the life of the "chorus" and tragic vision.

As for Dante the pilgrim, though he is in many ways like the shades of the late repentant, having survived the quasi-death of the "selva oscura," he is nevertheless the privileged traveler, the tragic hero whose vision—and therefore suffering—is keener. That he should be the one who more deeply experiences fear in the presence of evil is understandable, for he has seen evil in all its darkness and power in his journey through Hell. He has seen Dis. And as a tragic hero, he must be in the fuller sense the most intensely alive character, the most receptive to the passions of fear and pity. He is "our" mediator, the one who can lead us to the "chorus." And now he leaves behind Sordello and the other souls of the late-repentant to commence the journey to where Purgatory "has its true beginning," that is, where the life of ritual and spectacle begins to assert itself in all its fullness, culminating at the summit of the mountain, where the tragic myth of the Earthly Paradise is reenacted and made new.

Notes

1. Cf. Singleton, *Commentary* 2, n. 67, p. 122: "*Pur*: may mean either 'only' (i.e., Virgil advances, leaving Dante somewhat behind) or 'nonetheless' (i.e., in spite of this soul's 'distant' attitude), which seems more probable."

2. Ibid., n. 72, p. 123: "By this effective touch, the physical apartness is made a psychological apartness: the soul was 'in sé romita' ('in himself recluse') and now rises out of such condition *and* out of the *place* where it is (the physical place, vs. 73) to embrace Virgil."

3. Ibid., n. 72, p. 123.

4. Simone Weil, *The Simone Weil Reader*, p. 414.

5. Richard Seawall, *The Vision of Tragedy*, p. 5.

6. Ibid.

7. Ibid., p. 13.

8. C.G. Jung, *Answer to Job*, trans. R.F.C. Hull (Princeton, NJ: Princeton University Press, 1958), p. 46.

9. *The Way of Response: Martin Buber, Selections from His Writings*, ed. N.N. Glatzer (New York: Schocken Books, 1966), p. 37.

10. For an elucidation of what I am suggesting here by the words "mystery of evil" cf. Gabriel Marcel, *Tragic Wisdom and Beyond*, trans. Stephen Jolin and Peter McCormick (Evanston, IL: Northwestern University Press, 1973), pp. 145–146:

> We have to substitute the words "mystery of evil" for the words "problem of evil". . . . Mystery of evil—this means that it is useless and illusory to resort to some kind of dialectical artifice for integrating evil into a higher synthesis. . . . Many ways of facing evil have proven to be misguided. Only one way really remains, and that is the acceptance of paradox in Kierkegaard's sense, of a double affirmation whose tension must be maintained. Evil is real. We cannot deny its reality without diminishing the basic seriousness of existence and thus falling into a kind of nonsense, a dreadful buffoonery. And yet evil is not real absolutely speaking. We have to arrive not so much at a certitude, but rather a faith in the possibility of overcoming it—not abstractly, of course, by adhering to a theory or theodicy, but *hic et nunc*. And this faith is not without grace. It *is* grace. And what would we be, and what would the difficult journeying which is our very way of existing be, without the light which is so easy both to see and to miss, and which lights every man who comes into the world?

11. Cf. Virgil's words to the souls who had asked if they could be shown the way up the mountain: "Perhaps you think we are acquainted with this place; but we are pilgrims, like yourselves" (*Purg.* II, 61–63).

12. Cf. J.K. Kadowaki, S.J., *Zen and the Bible*, trans. Joan Rieck (London: Routledge & Kegan Paul, 1980), p. 49: "By His silence He calmed the violent emotions of His opponents and exposed the hypocrisy of their argument."

13. Giamatti, *The Earthly Paradise*, p. 99.

14. Simone Weil, *The Simone Weil Reader*, p. 383.

15. Giovanni Cecchetti, "Il 'peregrin' e i 'navicanti' di *Purgatorio* VIII, 1–6: Saggio di lettura dantesca," in *A Dante Symposium in Commemoration of the 700th Anniversary of the Poet's Birth*, ed. William De Sua and Gino Rizzo (Chapel Hill: University of North Carolina Press, 1965), p. 168.

16. Fergusson, *Dante's Drama of the Mind*, p. 25.

17. Ibid.

18. Ibid.

19. Martin Buber, *The Way of Response*, p. 45.

20. Cf. Rocco Montano, *Storia della poesia di Dante*, vol. II (Florence: Olschki, 1965), p. 72, n. 20:

> E' facile in questo caso, ci dice il Poeta, passare al significato allegorico, il velo costituito dal senso storico, letterale è tanto sottile che è facile (*leggiero*) *trapassar dentro*. E' però necessario considerar bene i fatti, egli ammonisce. Ed è

avvertimento che assai spesso i teologi facevano per la Bibbia contro i pericoli di un troppo precipitoso allegorizzare. . . . Gli interpreti credono che Dante invitando ad aguzzare gli occhi al vero, parli del vero morale, allegorico da cercare e non comprendono perché mai il poeta dice che il velo è sottile ed è facile trapassar dentro. Sembra una contraddizione. Ma tale non è. Il vero di cui parla è il vero letterale.

21. Paul Ricoeur, *The Symbolism of Evil*, p. 212.

22. Ibid., p. 231.

23. Singleton, *Commentary* 2, n. 44, p. 165.

24. See Singleton, *Journey to Beatrice*, pp. 159–183.

25. Mark Musa, *Advent at the Gates* (Bloomington: Indiana University Press, 1974), p. 107.

VI. The Earthly Paradise and the Recovery of Tragic Vision

If, as Fergusson has noted, the Earthly Paradise "corresponds to the *Anti-purgatorio* as the epiphany ending a tragic action corresponds to its prologue,"[1] in a larger sense, it is the epiphany of the tragic action whose prologue we found represented in *Inferno* I. In this final chapter I shall examine some of the most salient scenes of this epiphany which spans the last six cantos of the *Purgatorio*.

At the threshold of the Earthly Paradise, Virgil tells Dante:

> "Quel dolce pome che per tanti rami
>   cercando va la cura de' mortali,
>   oggi porrà in pace le tue fami."
>
> (Purg. XXVII, 115–117)

"That sweet fruit which the care of mortals goes seeking on so many branches, this day shall give your hungerings peace."

As we hear this promise of the pilgrim's imminent possession of the garden, there arise within us deep reverberations that tell of many other promises such as this. Beginning with the Prologue scene, we recall the promise of paradise coming first from the sunlit hill and then from "the hour of the day" and the "sweet season" which, coinciding with the time of creation, gave the pilgrim "cause for good hope of that beast with the gay skin" (*Inf.* I, 37–42). Thus he momentarily seemed to be transformed into prelapsarian man. And we recollect other scenes of unfulfilled promises of the garden, remembering the pilgrim's and our own hungers and longings for its "sweet fruit." We also think of the mythical tree whose fruit proved for Adam and Eve to be "bitter food," as Dante called it in *Purgatorio* VIII, 99. As we hear Virgil speak of "the care of mortals," our sense of solidarity with the pilgrim and with all the "exules filii Hevae" is reawakened, and we rediscover the common action and motivation that drives us on. Like a chorus, we take part in the drama of Dante's return to Eden. Indeed it is from the vantage point of the "chorus" that we have interpreted Virgil's words as both a true promise and an implicit recollection of unfulfilled or false promises of a return to the garden. We are aware that the pilgrim may not be conscious of this opposition as he is drawn to the "sweet fruit."

As we witness his response to Virgil's words and share his longing to enter the garden, we shift focus, and expectation outruns memory:

> Tanto voler sopra voler mi venne
>   de l'esser sù, ch'ad ogne passo poi
>   al volo mi sentia crescer le penne.
>
> (*Purg.* XXVII, 121–123)

Such wish upon wish came to me to be above, that at every step thereafter I felt my feathers growing for the flight.

In the very moment we see the pilgrim redouble his effort to reach the summit of the mountain, the image of flight arrests our attention and re-kindles our memory, and again we experience a shift of perspective as we find in this image echoes of other flights that we have encountered along the journey from Inferno to Purgatorio. Those that immediately come to mind are Ulysses' "folle volo" towards the dark mountain—none other than of Purgatorio (and Eden) (*Inf.* XXVI, 133–142), and the pilgrim's "flight of the mind" toward the illusory mountain of delight of the Pro-logue (*Inf.* I, 13–54). Again as "chorus," we wonder if, upon entering the garden, the pilgrim will leave behind all memories of unfulfilled promises of paradise, and all recollections of his past sins and misery (and the sins and misery of the race of Adam). Most important, we want to know how his "return" to the edenic state can be accomplished. And so we ask: is forgetfulness of evil possible? How will Dante interpret and represent the original myth of the Earthly Paradise and its tragic vision? Will this vision be a confirmation and expansion of our earlier glimpses of it? And will it reveal to us its creative power in a way that it will not only increase our understanding but will enable us to experience it directly, if imperfectly, as our own vision?

The scene of the pilgrim's entrance into the Earthly Paradise will help us to find the answers we seek:

Vago già di cercar dentro e dintorno
  la divina foresta spessa e viva,
  ch'a li occhi temperava il novo giorno,
sanza più aspettar, lasciai la riva,
  prendendo la campagna lento lento
  su per lo suol che d'ogne parte auliva.

(Purg. XXVIII, 1–6)

Eager now to search within and round about the divine forest green and
dense, which tempered the new day to my eyes, without waiting longer I
left the bank, taking the level ground very slowly over the soil that everywhere gives forth fragrance.

The opposition between the pilgrim's intense desire to search within and
around the "divine forest" and his slow movement across the meadow arrests our attention. It seems that the very spaciousness of this *campagna*, as
new as the pilgrim's freedom to "sit or walk about" (*Purg.* XXVII, 138),
produces an equally new effect on his desire, tempering its promptings just
as the dense, green forest tempers the early morning light for his eyes. In
contrast to the pilgrim's eagerness to reach the forest, which marked his
entire ascent of the mountain of Purgatory, there is now a new relation or
ratio between scene and act, between moving toward a goal with the desire
to possess it and merely seeing it, between action and contemplation. This
scene, which may remind one of the Latin proverb *festina lente*, clearly
speaks of a paradoxical union of opposites and therefore of a new-found
harmony. Also important is the suggestion that the pilgrim is alone. Indeed, not until the middle of the canto are we made aware of the presence
of Virgil and Statius. This temporary solitude of the pilgrim which the
poet invites us to imagine, together with the elements we have just noted
(not to mention the obvious presence of the *topos* of the *locus amoenus*),
speaks of a pristine time, of paradise.

For a moment we have the impression that here the pilgrim has begun
to taste the "sweet fruit" of paradise promised by Virgil. But as soon as we
resume our reading and follow the action of Dante's entrance into the forest, that foretaste of Eden appears precarious as a stream suddenly comes
into view:

Già m'avean trasportato i lenti passi
  dentro a la selva antica tanto, ch'io

non potea rivedere ond'io m'intrassi;
ed ecco più andar mi tolse un rio . . . .

(Purg. XXVIII, 22–25)

Now my slow steps had carried me on into the ancient wood so far that I could not see back to where I had entered it, when lo, a stream took from me further progress . . . .

The spacious meadow and the pathless forest are now marked by a distinct boundary. Gone, therefore, is the sense of freedom that characterized the pilgrim's entrance into the garden. Indeed his first reaction to this new element of the landscape is to consider it an insurmountable obstacle. He rapidly shifts his focus, however, turning his gaze to the river and the extraordinary purity of its waters:

Tutte l'acque che son di qua più monde,
    parrieno avere in sé mistura alcuna
    verso di quella, che nulla nasconde,
avvegna che si mova bruna bruna
    sotto l'ombra perpetüa, che mai
    raggiar non lascia sole ivi né luna.

(Purg. XXVIII, 28–33)

All the waters which here are purest would seem to have some defilement in them, compared with that, which conceals nothing, although it flows quite dark under the perpetual shade, which never lets sun or moon beam enter there.

The obstacle is thus suddenly transformed into something positive, a natural mirror which "conceals nothing." It therefore seems to promise, symbolically, truth and knowledge. Yet mysteriously the stream is perfectly transparent despite its darkness. The "perpetual shade, which never lets sun or moon beam enter there" brings to mind the dark wood of the Prologue "where the sun is silent" (Inf. I, 60), and where—equally mysteriously—the wayfarer encountered not only the absolute fear of death but also the "good" of "other things" (Inf. I, 8–9). What is the significance of this correspondence? We cannot say. Like the pilgrim, we see but without understanding, and we do not know the specific function or creative force of the present scene within the larger economy of his return to Eden. Yet through analogy, and therefore dramatistically, we may discern a few hints of meaning as we focus our attention upon the "selva antica" (the ancient forest) at the summit of Purgatory and recall, as the poet invites us to do, the "selva oscura" of *Inferno* I. We may view the relationship between these two scenes as similar to the one between the epilogue and the prologue of a tragic action. Specifically, we may begin to understand that, as I argued in the first chapter, we cannot identify the dark wood exclusively with the sinful life according to the conventional interpretation; we must see it instead as the symbol of the primordial human condition in which good and evil coexist inchoately and await differentiation and development. Indeed the point of inception of this differentiation and development coincides with the wayfarer's awakening to both the terror of death and the good of the "other things" found in the dark wood. And we may see more clearly that this process of differentiation constitutes the central action or drama we are watching unfold at the summit of Purgatory—a drama that is one with the drama of the poet's interpretation of the original myth of the Earthly Paradise. But these are only hints, or flashes of intuition, which also await differentiation and development. Having experienced with the pilgrim the dialectic of assertion and counter-assertion—and hence the tragic rhythm created by the opposition of urgency and delay, freedom and restriction, light and darkness, the manifest and the hidden, and the familiar and the *totally other*—we seek clarification and transcendence.

In the scenes of Dante's encounter with Matelda a significant measure of tragic rhythm and tragic vision is manifested. No sooner has the pilgrim observed the mysterious transparency of the stream than his eyes are drawn away from it by what lies beyond:

> Coi piè ristetti e con li occhi passai
> di là dal fiumicello, per mirare
> la gran varïazion d'i freschi mai;
> e là m'apparve, sì com'elli appare
> subitamente cosa che disvia
> per maraviglia tutto altro pensare,
> una donna soletta che si gia
> e cantando e scegliendo fior da fiore
> ond'era pinta tutta la sua via.
>
> (*Purg.* XXVIII, 34–42)

With feet I stayed and with my eyes I passed to the other side of the rivu-
let to look at the great variety of the fresh-flowering boughs; and there
appeared to me there, as appears of a sudden a thing that for wonder
drives away every other thought, a lady all alone, who went singing and
culling flower from flower, with which all her path was painted.

Again the poet creates a scene that is clearly marked by a dialectical opposition, with the stream constituting the boundary that at once separates
and binds two contrasting scenes and actions, or two different modes of
being. As it arrests the pilgrim's action and desire, it also becomes the
ground for "crossing the stream" by looking beyond it. From the fixed
point in which his freedom has come to a halt, he discovers a plurality of
things that delight—"the great variety of the fresh-flowering boughs." He
thus experiences a new freedom, the freedom of seeing. Yet as the fair
maiden appears with the same suddenness with which the stream had earlier entered his field of vision, this freedom is modified as his desire and
attention are again fixed upon a single object.

At once within and beyond the form of the medieval *pastorella*, this
scene sums up all the idyllic elements the pilgrim has so far savored as signs
of the paradisal state. Even more than in the preceding scenes, we are now
invited to think that perhaps this is the "sweet fruit" that all mortals seek
that today will satisfy all of the pilgrim's hungers. Like him, we may put
aside "every other thought" as we marvel at the presence of the fair
maiden—whose name, we will later learn, is Matelda—and imagine that
we have before us the embodiment of the innocence and bliss of paradise.
We experience a sudden shift of perspective, however, as we read these
words that the pilgrim addresses to Matelda:

> "Tu mi fai rimembrar dove e qual era
>   Proserpina nel tempo che perdette
>   la madre lei, ed ella primavera."
>
>   (*Purg*. XXVIII, 49–51)

"You make me recall where and what Proserpina was at the time her
mother lost her, and she the spring."

We recognize the underlying pattern of opposition between near and far,
presence and absence, and richness and indigence, as we discover that the
innocence the pilgrim sees represented beyond the stream is perceived not

in its fullness and integrity, but as innocence that is about to be lost. Peter Dronke has aptly observed: "[Matelda] herself is joyful . . . , and yet Dante, at the moment of seeing her, feels his thrill at her beauty mingled with sadness: to him she is like Persephone at the moment when the young goddess, and all the bliss of spring that she brings with her, must part from the world. This exultant beauty he perceives has the poignancy of imper-manence—it is a paradise, and implicitly, paradise lost."[2]

The scenes that immediately follow give further evidence of the pil-grim's inability to apprehend the true identity of the fair maiden: he sees her as a woman dancing, as a virgin who lowers her chaste eyes, and finally as a woman in love, whose eyes shine more intensely than those of "Venus, transfixed by her son against all his custom" (*Purg.* XXVIII, 53, 57, 65–66). He thus risks mistaking the mutable, fragmentary images arising from his time-aware self for the real innocence that the maiden embodies. His desire is therefore directed to an object that he himself has fashioned out of im-ages of innocence and innocence lost.

But can he rend the illusion that conceals from him the maiden's true identity? Or will she always remain inaccessibly "other"? As dramatist, Dante invites us to look for the answers in his staging of the action, and especially in the "suffering of the opposition" by the pilgrim (and the sym-pathetic reader), which on the one hand is built into the scene, and on the other the pilgrim himself brings to it as he transfers to the object before him his own duality and conflict. Let us first focus our attention on the scene as *he* sees and in a sense constructs it:

Tre passi ci facea il fiume lontani;
    ma Elesponto, là 've passò Serse,
    ancora freno a tutti orgogli umani,
più odio da Leandro non sofferse
    per mareggiare intra Sesto e Abido,
    che quel da me perch'allor non s'aperse.

(*Purg.* XXVIII, 70–75)

The river kept us three paces apart, but Hellespont where Xerxes passed it—ever curb on all human pride—did not suffer more hatred from Lean-der for its swelling waters between Sestos and Abydos than that from me because it did not open then.

We have now reached the point of highest tension in the opposition of the near and the far, the known and the mysterious, and, we may add, of desire and love. This is the crucial juncture, the point of convergence of meanings we have so far seen only as shadows and intimations of things to come. The sudden changes of perspective, the disjunctions we have come to know as distinctive traits of the pilgrim's return to Eden, acquire now a new poignancy. Of all the things he has so far encountered in the garden, none, like this maiden, has had the effect of filling his entire consciousness to the point of erasing from it every thought; and none has produced in him at once such an intense longing to possess the object of his desire and the anguish of being separated from it. Now we experience more deeply something that we saw adumbrated in the beginning when we watched unfold the first scenes of the pilgrim's entrance into the garden. The beauty of nature, the tranquillity of the idyllic landscape, and the appearance of the fair maiden have not brought him the desired peace. Despite all these promises of paradise, he finds himself excluded from it. And even the river, whose pure water and gentle movement had at first awakened his attention, promising by the power of its transparency the knowledge he secretly seeks, is now transformed in his eyes into something hateful, more hateful than the Hellespont was to Leander for separating him from his beloved Hero. And as we recall that Leander drowned in the Hellespont when he attempted to cross it one stormy night, and that after crossing the same strait to wage war against the Greeks, Xerxes and his army were defeated at Salamis, we see that by analogy the river of Eden is further transformed into a sign of interdiction and, if violated, of death.

Yet the Hellespont, with its menace of death, is also a bridle to all forms of human pride. The river of Eden correspondingly can thus be seen as a bridle to the pilgrim's pride, expressed in his desire to possess a maiden and a paradise of his own creation. An even more striking sign of the pilgrim's hubris is the reason for his hatred of the stream: that "it did not open," given the obvious allusion to Exodus 14:21–23, as the Red Sea opened for the Israelites. To equate his desire to possess Matelda (as Leander possessed Hero) with the Israelites' desire to reach the Promised Land, as willed by Yahweh, and to be angered because the waters of the stream did not part for him, clearly speaks of his arrogance—the arrogance of fallen humanity, or of Adam at the threshold of sinning.[3] Like Adam at that moment, he prefers illusion to reality, wishing to be what he is not and transforming the creative limit of his condition into a hated obstacle. As in the Adamic myth, limit which marks the finiteness of the created being suddenly appears in this scene as an interdiction.⁴ Unlike Adam, however, here the pilgrim does not shatter this limit and its inherent creativity. He does not cross the river, and he does not sin, although he is still marked by an *inclination* to sin, the *fomes peccati*,⁵ which is present even after repentance; and in the sense of a re-enactment of the myth of Eden, the pilgrim's condition is analogous to our primordial fragility as finite beings. At this point the pilgrim's deepest impulse is to recover the innocence that Adam possessed before the Fall, the innocence he now sees represented in the fair maiden only intermittently and obscurely. This innermost longing for the true Eden lives side by side with the desire to possess a false image of it.

The scene that immediately follows redefines this conflict:

> "Voi siete nuovi, e forse perch'io rido,"
>   cominciò ella, "in questo luogo eletto
>   a l'umana natura per suo nido,
> maravigliando tienvi alcun sospetto;
>   ma luce rende il salmo *Delectasti*,
>   che puote disnebbiar vostro intelletto."
>
> (Purg. XXVIII, 76–81)

"You are newcomers," she began, "and perhaps, why I am smiling in this place chosen for nest of the human race some doubt holds you wondering; but the psalm *Delectasti* gives light that may dispel the cloud from your minds."

As Matelda addresses not only the pilgrim, who had asked her to draw near, but also Virgil and Statius, we are made aware that he is not alone. This may seem of little significance, unless we recall that the preceding scene was marked by the pilgrim's solipsistic view of the fair maiden as a *pastorella* to be possessed, true to the genre that bears this name.⁶ The shift from the expected "tu" to the unexpected "voi" exposes that solipsism as it points away from it. But more significant is the shift from the pilgrim's scene of frustrated desire and hate to the joyous scene introduced by Matelda as she points to the psalm *Delectasti*. This shift marks the creative point of redefinition of the pilgrim's scene of duality and conflict on a new plane of experience. When Matelda states "You are new here," she is implying that the paradisal scene they see, with all its familiar or conventional features (natural and literary), does not coincide with the-thing-in-itself.

Despite all interpretations, it remains *totally other*. And when she speaks of their wonderment at her smile, she is essentially "translating" the pilgrim's and tacitly his companions' earlier scene of mutable perceptions of her and of the stream. This "translation" may be formulated thus: You may be wondering how someone who seems to embody innocence lost (like Proserpina) could possibly smile. In other words, this sign of joy may seem incongruous in the place where innocence and joy were lost.[7]

Having interpreted the three poets' inner action of unresolved conflict and doubt, she invites them to resolve it by reading the words of Psalm 91:5–6 (Vulgate):

> Because Thou didst delight me, Lord, in Thy work;
>   and in the works of Thy hands I will rejoice.
> How praiseworthy are Thy works, O Lord.[8]

By calling attention to this scene of delight in God's creation, Matelda is asserting a truth—the good of all things—that no memory of lost innocence, no hatred arising from fallen humanity's inordinate desires, and therefore the Fall itself, can obscure or annul.[9] The meaning and function of her smile are now manifest as an "answer" or "counter-assertion" to the earlier scene in which we saw Dante the pilgrim (and implicitly Virgil and Statius) move and act as "fallen man," or, as we have hinted, as Adam at the threshold of sinning, or, finally, as still weakened by the *fomes peccati* even after repentance and expiation.

Along with his companions Dante is thus invited by Matelda to see in her both the innocence and joy preceding the Fall and the innocence and joy that despite the Fall still exist in virtue of what can be termed the ontological good inherent in all creation (even in the "selva oscura," as we have already noted). Hence what at first had appeared as an irreconcilable opposition between innocence in and of itself and innocence either threatened or lost—between Matelda and Proserpina, and between Matelda and Venus—is now reconciled. But this is not a reconciliation that can be understood and explained through discourse. It can only be *narrated* or *represented*. For how can one understand and explain the coexistence of the good inherent in all creation—before and after the Fall—and human deviation from it through sin? As we witness Dante's interpretation and reenactment of one of the central scenes of the myth of Eden (that of Adam "at the threshold of sinning"), we discover this fundamental function or truth of the myth and its tragic dimension: that as a narration it does not ignore or annul evil, nor does it "reduce the fact of evil into something else." as it asserts the inexhaustible reality of good. Paul Ricoeur writes:

The myth tries to get at the enigma of human existence, namely, the discordance between the fundamental reality—state of innocence, status of the creature, essential being—and the actual modality of man, as defiled, sinful, guilty. The myth accounts for this transition by means of a narration. But it is a narration precisely because there is no deduction, no logical transition, between the fundamental reality of man and his present existence, between his ontological status as a being created good and destined for happiness and his existential or historical status, experienced under the sign of alienation. Thus the myth has an ontological bearing: it points to the relation—that is to say both the leap and the passage, the cut and the suture—between the essential being of man and his historical existence.[10]

Having just "dispelled the cloud" from the poets' minds concerning her smile, Matelda is called upon to resolve yet another conflict, which Dante thus enunciates:

"L'acqua," diss'io, "e 'l suon de la foresta
   impugnan dentro a me novella fede
   di cosa ch'io udi' contraria a questa."

(*Purg*. XXVIII, 85–87)

"The water," I said, "and the sound of the forest contend in me with a recent belief in a thing I have heard contrary to this."

The "thing contrary to this," which Dante learned from Statius when the mountain had quaked, is that above Purgatory's gate "this place is free from every change" (*Purg*. XXI, 43). Once again we witness the drama of received opinion that clashes with the truth of the new scene in which it is introduced. My first impression, and working hypothesis, is that here the pilgrim, like Adam at the threshold of sinning, not content with the *what* of things (the *quia* of *Purg*. III, 37), questions the order of the created world. Significantly, this questioning is focused on the problematic contiguity of the immutable and the mutable, of the timeless and time, and therefore on the line or limit which is like the river that separates the pilgrim from Matelda.

Matelda prepares the ground for her answer by beginning at the beginning. "The highest Good," she says, ". . . made man good and for good," giving him the garden "as an earnest of eternal peace" (XXVIII, 91–93).

But, she continues, man soon lost this place "through his fault," and "through his fault exchanged honest joy and sweet sport for tears and toil" (94–96). Then she adds that the mountain, on whose summit lies the Earthly Paradise, "rose thus high toward heaven" in order to protect man from the "disturbance which the exhalations of the water and of the earth . . . produce below" (97–102). Thus, before directly addressing Dante's question, Matelda implicitly enlarges the scope of that question, exposing its deepest motivation: on the one hand, as we have observed, to be given an explanation for what appears to be a contradiction—the presence in Eden of the "disturbance," and therefore of the disorder associated with the sublunar world of fallen man—and on the other hand, to seek justification from God for this contradiction in His creation. In other words, the context within which Matelda places Dante's question unveils his innermost, secret doubt concerning God's creation and our place in it, and specifically our responsibility for the Fall. And if we look even more deeply, we may see this doubt as something that may turn into an accusation directed at God. For if the place of original innocence is marked by change, and therefore by division and disorder, and it is not the privileged place that is differentiated from the world below, how can one speak of a "fall" from it? If the division and disorder we identify with fallen nature are essentially "scenic" traits of the Earthly Paradise, they can only be considered as the condition or ground for the Fall. Hence, how can man be culpable?

Matelda addresses and aims to resolve this doubt—which is deeply rooted in the pilgrim's heart and in the heart of all who ask: wherefore evil? Is Adam, and every human being, the initiator of evil or its heir? She both underscores and expounds metonymically the fact of man's original sin and radical culpability that she has categorically enunciated with the words "Per sua difalta . . . per sua difalta . . . ," by asserting the unalterable perfection of the garden. She points out that the revolving air set in motion by the Primum Mobile strikes the summit of the mountain, making the forest resound "because it is dense" (XXVIII, 103–108), and then she adds that the river, whose presence had suggested to the pilgrim that it may rain in the garden, "issues from a fountain constant and sure which by the will of God regains as much as it pours forth freely on two sides" (124–126).

Matelda's affirmation of the original good of all creation, the immutable perfection of the garden, and the radical human culpability, has resolved the opposition she has organized by setting Dante's question about the "disturbance" in Eden within the larger scene of creation and of innocence lost through sin. But this solution has obviously shifted all the burden of responsibility and culpability to man. Significantly, there is no mention here of the serpent, the Adversary that the pilgrim, with Virgil and Sordello, has encountered in the Valley of the Princes. There is no mention of temptation. Hence the tragic dimension which we have so far seen as a distinctive trait of the human condition now seems completely dissolved. If Adam is radically guilty—and we in him and after him—then his and our loss of the garden can only be seen as a just punishment. Hence no one can be considered a tragic figure. Only the suffering of the innocent is truly tragic.

But the moment we have extracted this meaning and conclusion from the scene of the Fall evoked by Matelda, can we be sure that we have fathomed its depth? Or should our discourse stop here as we face the irreducible fact of man's loss of Eden through his fault? It may perhaps be more fruitful to merely acknowledge this fact and immediately proceed, with Matelda, to the other scenes that she fashions and offers as corollaries to her first answers. This is what we are tempted to do—and indeed should do *as readers*—before and after analysis, that is, in the fullness and integrity of aesthetic experience whereby we silently enter the poet's world of creative intuition. But our task here is to stretch our discourse to its limits, abandoning it only when we think we have reached the point where the scene before us is most unyielding, in other words, when we come to the degree zero of speculation, the moment of blindness, the *caesura* that at once separates and binds the present scene to the one that immediately follows.

In the economy of the pilgrim's return to Eden, what is the function of acknowledging radical human culpability? In other words, how does this fact, and the very acceptance of it as such, help the recovery of the original state of innocence? And how does it constitute a correction of the original fault? In the light of the glimpses we have caught in the preceding pages, we may answer that Matelda's affirmation of original human culpability constitutes a restatement of the fact of evil as a constitutive element of the condition or "scene" of the Earthly Paradise. This is what Adam, at the threshold of sinning, and like him the pilgrim in the "edenic" scene of the Prologue, had refused to acknowledge before experiencing evil directly, dreaming instead of a "second innocence" of his own making. The only substantial difference is that in the scene evoked by Matelda the fact of evil is represented as existing not outside but within man himself. The moment the pilgrim sees and accepts this fact—that in Adam and in himself lies the potential for evil and, once committed, the ineluctable fact of his responsibility and culpability—he cannot accuse the serpent, nature, fate, or God. As we mentioned earlier, in this perspective the tragic is annulled.

Yet if we shift our focus from the piercing moment of the act of sinning, and therefore from sinning as a radical departure from good, to the primordial status of being good, like all creation, and in some proportion like the Creator, the *Summum Bonum*, we discover, with the anteriority of good, that in man there is not culpability alone, but a conflict between the ontological good of his being and the relative evil of his act, for evil cannot totally destroy good without also destroying itself.[11] It is indeed the disproportion in man between good and evil that prompts him to deny that evil is within him, and to assert instead that it is outside, that it is "other," for being fundamentally good, he can only perceive evil as something foreign. As we reflect on this *agon* within man, we are forced to consider his culpability not only in a moral sense, that of a transgression of a law, but also in an existential sense. Thus the suffering of being exiled from the innocence of the garden, which in the moral perspective takes on the meaning of just punishment, is a method or pedagogy whereby the lost harmony can be restored. In the existential perspective this suffering may be seen as either unjust or absurd, unless man believes—and this is the greatest of temptations—that the evil of his sin is nothing but the manifestation of his original evil *nature*.

As we experience this conflict, whether as spectators or as actors, the tragic emotions of fear and pity are awakened in us. The tragic, which we thought had dissolved, we now find reaffirmed in the very heart of man. We may catch a glimpse of a possible solution of this conflict as soon as we remember the original and (even after the Fall) unbroken bond between human good and the highest Good in whose image we are made, as Matelda invited the pilgrim to remember when she mentioned the psalm *Delectasti*.

In the other "scenes" of Matelda's corollaries of which we spoke earlier are embedded some of the answers that we and the pilgrim seek. The first of these scenes immediately follows the above-mentioned one of the forest that, struck by the circling air, resounds "because it is dense":

"e la percossa pianta tanto puote,
     che de la sua virtute l'aura impregna
     e quella poi, girando, intorno scuote;

e l'altra terra, secondo ch'è degna
   per sé e per suo ciel, concepe e figlia
   di diverse virtù diverse legna.
Non parrebbe di là poi maraviglia,
   udito questo, quando alcuna pianta
   sanza seme palese vi s'appiglia."

(Purg. XXVIII, 109–117)

and the plant, being struck thus, has such potency that with its virtue it impregnates the breeze, and this then in its whirling scatters it abroad; and the rest of the earth, according to its fitness in itself and in its sky, conceives and brings forth from diverse virtues diverse growths. It should, then, not seem a marvel on earth, this being heard, when some plant takes root there without visible seed."

Matelda's answer takes an unexpected turn, as it goes beyond what the pilgrim's question about the "disturbance" in Eden had originally intended to elicit. She again expands the discourse initiated by him by redefining the opposition between the changeable sublunary world and the unchanging world of Eden. She does this by introducing a third, mediating force—the circling air beneath the sphere of fire and above that of earth—which, striking the plants of the Earthly Paradise, helps to actualize their potential creative power and to transmit their "virtù" to the earth below. Thus while the two spheres remain separate and distinct—in a sense, as chaos and order, as the turbulent nature known to fallen man and the pristine nature known to prelapsarian man—they are nevertheless connected by a force which "leaps" across the boundary that divides them. Significantly, this force constitutes a kind of violence as it strikes the otherwise perfectly still forest. But paradoxically, as this violence is "suffered" by the plants of Eden, it has a creative effect. We recall that the pilgrim experienced a similar paradoxical union of opposites upon entering the garden:

Un'aura dolce, sanza mutamento,
   avere in sé, mi feria per la fronte
   non di più colpo che soave vento . . . .

(Purg. XXVIII, 7–9)

A sweet breeze that had no variation in itself was striking on my brow with the force only of a gentle wind . . . .

On the verbal level, and therefore that of representation and performance, Dante has interpreted the sweet, invariable breeze of Eden as a force that "wounded" ("feria"), but a force no more than a "blow" ("colpo") from a "gentle wind."

The other scene to which Matelda calls attention, by way of an explanation that is unforeseen by the pilgrim, is that of the rivers Lethe and Eunoe, which spring from the same source:

> "L'acqua che vedi non surge di vena
>   che ristori vapor che gel converta,
>   come fiume ch'acquista e perde lena;
> ma esce di fontana salda e certa,
>   che tanto dal voler di Dio riprende,
>   quant'ella versa da due parti aperta.
> Da questa parte con virtù discende
>   che toglie altrui memoria del peccato;
>   da l'altra d'ogne ben fatto la rende.
> Quinci Letè; così da l'altro lato
>   Eünoè si chiama, e non adopra
>   se quinci e quindi pria non è gustato . . . ."
>
> (*Purg.* XXVIII, 121–132)

"The water you see springs not from a vein that is restored by vapor which cold condenses, like a stream that gains and loses force, but issues from a fountain constant and sure which by the will of God regains as much as it pours forth freely on two sides. On this side it descends with virtue that takes from one the memory of sin; on the other side it restores the memory of every good deed. Here Lethe, so on the other side Eunoe it is called; and it works not if first it be not tasted on this side and on that."

This scene constitutes an answer that again goes beyond what the pilgrim's question had initially sought. It implicitly invites the pilgrim to enlarge the ground upon which that question had been originally formulated. As it further addresses the question of the "disturbance" in Eden, it also reveals the regenerative powers of the two rivers, earlier seen by the pilgrim as one river and as an obstacle to his newly acquired freedom. Moreover Matelda's scene, as it implicitly represents a true feature of the original myth of Eden, acts as a correction of the pilgrim's initial false perception and re-enactment

of that myth. What he had at first envisaged as the place of pristine innocence—that of the "dolce pome" whose total possession Virgil had promised him—is now once again manifested to him as the place of both
innocence and sin, and of innocence lost and innocence regained. The
myth which he is learning to discover (or re-discover) through action and
performance is, like the river that separates him from Matelda, eminently
dramatic, for it is constituted by the paradoxical union of opposites.

The final corollary of Matelda marks another creative opposition
whereby discontinuity and continuity are reconciled:

> "E avvegna ch'assai possa esser sazia
>   la sete tua perch'io più non ti scuopra,
> darotti un corollario ancor per grazia;
>   né credo che 'l mio dir ti sia men caro,
>   se oltre promission teco si spazia.
> Quelli ch'anticamente poetaro
>   l'età de l'oro e suo stato felice,
>   forse in Parnaso esto loco sognaro.
> Qui fu innocente l'umana radice;
>   qui primavera sempre e ogne frutto;
>   nettare è questo di che ciascun dice."
>
> (*Purg.* XXVIII, 134–141)

"And notwithstanding that your thirst might be fully satisfied even if I
disclosed no more to you, I will yet give you a corollary for grace, nor do
I think my speech will be less welcome to you if it reaches beyond my
promise. They who in olden times sang of the Age of Gold and its happy
state perhaps in Parnassus dreamed of this place. Here the root of mankind was innocent; here is always spring, and every fruit; this is the nectar
of which each tells."

We may thus summarize Matelda's "answer" to the pilgrim as follows: if
the beauty and perfection of the Earthly Paradise are, on the one hand,
"totally other," in contrast to the sublunary world of change in which fallen
man dwells, and if they are inaccessible—as Matelda is to Dante, despite
her nearness—on the other hand, man, after the Fall and even before the
"Word became Flesh" and entered history, may recapture a measure of the
lost garden by the power of poetry. The word "forse" marks at once
the distance that separates and the bridge that links the garden dreamed by

the poets of antiquity and the garden dreamed by our poet. To carry the analogy even further, as we have done in an earlier chapter, we may think of a similar separation and bridge between Parnassus and the mountain of the Earthly Paradise: dwelling in one is analogous to dwelling in the other.

An essential component of Matelda's answer is the fact that like the previous ones, it is a corollary or gift. Offered in the place which speaks in so many ways, as we have seen, of the Creator's gifts to man, before and after Adam's rebellion and subsequent exile from the garden, it appropriately bestows on the pilgrim (and his poets) a measure of God's superabundant grace. In the scene of Eden Matelda acts as one more "mask" of God. And through her gifts Dante seems to interpret and make new the Pauline paradox, ". . . but where sin abounded, grace did much more abound" (Rom. 5:21).

If we compare the scene of the pilgrim's first encounter with Matelda to the present scene, in a flash we grasp the expansion of meaning experienced by him as he moved through the intervening scenes, and we know that his "moto spiritale" has advanced. Yet in a sense nothing has changed, for the river still separates him from Matelda and the paradise he seeks—the "dolce pome." By moving and acting in scenes that repeatedly (and yet always unpredictably) reveal not the "why" of things but their "suchness" (*quia*), and by directly experiencing the tragic rhythm created by their sequence, with its alternating moments of blindness and insight, the pilgrim (and the sympathetic reader) has "suffered the opposition" which he has fashioned "in cooperation" with the constitutive elements of those scenes (agents, acts, and so on), and hence he has achieved a kind of transcendence—the transcendence of and through the tragic.

One more striking example of this transcendence is given at the very end of Canto XXVIII:

Io mi rivolsi 'n dietro allora tutto
    a' miei poeti, e vidi che con riso
    udito avëan l'ultimo costrutto . . . .

(*Purg.* XXVIII, 145–147)

I turned then right round to my poets, and saw that with a smile they had heard these last words . . . .

In the ancient poets' smile I see not only the luminous recognition of the correspondence or continuity between their "dreamed" garden and the present garden, but also the epiphany of the tragic action that had begun with Matelda's smile at the very center of the canto, where we heard her say, "Voi siete nuovi e forse perch'io rido . . . / maravigliando tienvi alcun sospetto" (XXVIII, 76, 79). This smile, which the three poets may at first have considered incongruous in the place where innocence and happiness were lost, is now shared by Virgil and Statius. They now appear to possess Matelda's innocence and joy. For a moment they seem to have entered the paradise that they and other poets of the ancient world had "dreamed in Parnassus." As we witness this "leap" of Matelda's smile across the river that separates her from our three poets, we are again made aware of the creativity inherent in Dante's dramaturgy. With the pilgrim, who stands between Matelda and the two ancient poets, we perceive at once the division and the unity of their respective worlds and scenes. And as we follow the trajectory of the smile that spans these scenes, we may also smile (as does perhaps our poet and pilgrim) as we experience an analogous proportion between our own "dream" of the garden and Matelda's garden (as "dreamed" by our poet).

Hence as we smile, experiencing what elsewhere Dante called "una corruscazione de la dilettazione de l'anima" ("a scintillation of the soul's delight"),[12] we momentarily transcend all contradictions and unresolved questions connected with a return to Eden that we encountered earlier along with our protagonist and his companions. And this delight or paradisal innocence and joy which we share with them (and with the fair maiden) owes its life to the "space" that Matelda's "forse" creates (*"forse* perch'io rido . . ."; *"forse* in Parnaso . . ."), in which Dante "stages" the action of "dreaming" the Earthly Paradise. Remove this "forse" from Matelda's discourse and the entire stage would collapse, and with it the neverending, never resolved and yet fruitful dialectic between the pilgrims' dream of the garden and the real garden of Matelda, between human creation and God's creation. And finally, with the dissolution of the tragic rhythm of cooperative competition, of the creative conflict of assertion and counter-assertion, the goal of knowing and defining Eden as the thing-in-itself would also dissolve. Without the theatrical space of "forse" introduced by Matelda, Dante would have given us a world of certitude, where all questions are answered. If she had said, "my smiling here causes you to doubt and wonder about the nature of this garden," and "the ancient poets who sang of the Golden Age in Parnassus dreamed of this place," she would have answered the pilgrim's questions (and the tacit questions of

Virgil and Statius), stifling all possibilities of transformation and transcendence. "To answer a question," writes Northrop Frye, "is to accept the assumptions in it, and thereby to neutralize the question by consolidating the mental level on which the question was asked. Real questions are stages in formulating better questions; answers cheat us out of the right to do this."[13] I will add that answers cheat us out of the right to live the *drama* of formulating better questions.

In the opening scenes of *Purgatorio* XXIX Dante at once reasserts and expands the meaning brought forth by the scenes of the preceding canto. He accomplishes this by placing side by side, in metonymic relation, scenes of different valences:

> Cantando come donna innamorata,
>   continüò col fin di sue parole:
>   *"Beati quorum tecta sunt peccata!"*
> E come ninfe che si givan sole
>   per le selvatiche ombre, disïando
>   qual di veder, qual di fuggir lo sole,
> allor si mosse contra 'l fiume, andando
>   su per la riva; e io pari di lei,
>   picciol passo con picciol seguitando.
>
> (*Purg.* XXIX, 1–9)

Singing like a lady enamored, she continued, at the end of her words, *"Beati quorum tecta sunt peccata!"* and, like nymphs who used to wend alone through the woodland shades, this one desiring to see and that to avoid the sun, she moved on, then, counter to the stream, going along the bank, and I abreast of her, matching her little steps with mine.

As the pilgrim hears Matelda intone the words of the beginning of Psalm 31, "Blessed are those whose sins are forgiven," he can no longer see her as a Proserpina or a Venus, or as a "woman dancing," as he saw her earlier. She does sing "like a lady enamored" and moves like "nymphs that used to wend alone through the woodland shades," thus evoking the dream-like, idyllic world of the mythical garden of innocence and bliss; but she now moves and sings in a scene that speaks of the Christian drama of sin and redemption. Thus the present scene at once reasserts the perspective of the preceding scene and departs from it.

Commenting on Matelda's singing *Beati quorum tecta sunt peccata*, Singleton writes: "Although the lady sings these words immediately after ending her words of *Purg*. XXVIII, 144, this 'beatitude,' dealing as it does with the removal of sin, represents an abrupt change in outlook, for it concerns not ancient poets or their dreams of a Golden Age, but the 'covering of sins' as through Christ that became possible. The words look, therefore, to what is now to come."[14]

Although I concur with this reading, which I have cited as an illustration of what I perceived as a departure, I am compelled to modify it by stating that we should more appropriately speak of *both* an "abrupt change" and an expansion of meaning, of a break and a continuity whereby the "dream" of the ancient poets is at once transcended and fulfilled. As we have already observed, Matelda's "forse" ("forse in Parnaso . . .") provides the "space" within which we may see both the overt aspiration of the ancient world for a Golden Age of justice and peace and their secret aspiration for a similar age or "garden" in which we may one day dwell because evil has been conquered.

Another measure of the creativity inherent in the disjunctive structure of Dante's representation is in the simile of the nymphs, through which he reasserts the correspondence or continuity between the pagan and the Christian myth of paradise. At first glance we may see only the correspondence.[15] Yet upon closer scrutiny we notice that there is a certain disproportion between the vehicle and the tenor. The former, as it tells of nymphs who move through woodland shades—"this one desiring to see and that to avoid the sun"—evokes a carefree scene of opposite desires. The latter, as it tells of one lady and her measured steps taken "counter to the stream," creates a scene markedly defined by the stream that is animated by a single, deliberate action and correspondingly by desire that is fixed on one goal.

These remarks acquire greater weight as soon as we recognize a familiar pattern in the simile of the nymphs. In the correspondence between the nymphs and Matelda we find echoes of the opposition and continuity between the scene that Virgil had invited the pilgrim to enter at the threshold of Eden saying to him, "take henceforth your own pleasure for your guide. . . . See the sun that shines on your brow, see the tender grass, the flowers, the shrubs . . . , you may sit or go among them" (*Purg*. XXVII, 131–138), and the actual scene that the pilgrim helped to create with his action—a scene that, as we have already noted, was marked both by his eagerness to reach the "divine forest" and "search within and round about" and by his slow, yet deliberate steps across the meadow. Dante has thus brought into

focus the interplay and the creative tension between two modes of "return-
ing" to the Earthly Paradise, or, in a sense, between two "paradises": one
characterized by a seemingly limitless spaciousness and freedom, the other
by space that is sharply defined and correspondingly, by freedom that is
commensurate to limit.

In the scene in which the pilgrim matches Matelda's steps with his own,
the opposition between the two "paradises" begins to be resolved and transcended. While echoing his slow steps across the plain when he first entered the garden, these small steps do not represent merely the pilgrim's
own desire and freedom, but under the sign of obedience, as they imitate
Matelda's steps, they now constitute the measured movement through
which he is learning to recapture by analogy the pristine innocence and
harmony that she embodies.[16] Significantly, here the imitation of action
bears the unmistakable signs of play and ritual. In ritual "we see . . . an
imitation of nature which has a strong element of what we call magic in it.
Magic seems to begin as something of a voluntary effort to recapture a lost
rapport with the natural cycle. This sense of a deliberate recapturing of
something no longer possessed is a distinctive mark of human ritual."[17]

The river still separates the pilgrim from Matelda, for there is no "natural" bridge between his fallen nature and her perfect nature, between his
fragmented, profane time and her sacred, edenic time. Yet by imitating her
small, measured steps, as in children's play, he resolves this opposition, at
least in part. He now begins to transcend the small circle of his inner, obsessive drives. His desire is no longer for flight, whether nostalgia for the
past, lost innocence, or nostalgia for a future "second innocence" of his
own creation. Although he does not share her space, through mimesis he
shares Matelda's action and thus "enters" her scene, and in a sense he is
united to her, but without possessing her.

If we now fix our gaze upon the river that marks the distance between
the pilgrim and Matelda, we perceive it—more keenly than before—not as
an obstacle to desire and freedom, but as a creative limit *for* desire and
freedom. And we also see that as the pilgrim's freedom and desire are one
with those of the maiden who embodies the original innocence of Eden,
he resembles Adam before the Fall when, obedient to God's will, he enjoyed his finite freedom without perceiving its finiteness as an obstacle or
an interdiction.[18] We recall that when the river unexpectedly entered the
pilgrim's field of vision as a barrier to his way to the "divine forest" and
then to Matelda, he felt hatred for it, for he saw it as the sign of an interdiction. We also recall that, in the context of a "return to Eden," he repre-

sented not only man after the Fall but also Adam at the threshold of sinning, that is, in that dizzy moment when the creative limit became for him a "hostile negativity," and when infinite desire, or the desire of desire—that desire which makes insupportable the finiteness of the created being—sprang up.[19] Within the scenic or theatrical space defined by the stream, the action of the "short steps" recaptures—as only the action and performance of ritual and play can recapture—the creativity of limit, with its power of "orienting" desire and freedom. For our pilgrim this "orienting" is both symbolical and literal, for, as he walks in unison with Matelda, he comes to face the East (*Purg.* XXIX, 10–12).

No sooner has Dante turned eastward than Matelda draws his attention to the approaching procession with the words, "My brother, look and listen!" (15). Marking a sudden shift from one scene to another, these words are an invitation to orient further his desire and freedom. He must now turn his attention away from Matelda. The new scene of the procession takes him out of his "old" self, appearing to him at first as the sudden manifestation of a phenomenon that is at once familiar and foreign, natural and supernatural:

> Ed ecco un lustro sùbito trascorse
>   da tutte parti per la gran foresta,
>   tal che di balenar mi mise in forse.
> Ma perché 'l balenar, come vien, resta,
>   e quel, durando, più e più splendeva,
>   nel mio pensier dicea: "Che cosa è questa?"
>
> (*Purg.* XXIX, 16–21)

And lo! a sudden brightness flooded the great forest on all sides, such that it put me in doubt if it were lightning; but since lightning ceases even as it comes, and this, lasting, became more and more resplendent, in my thought I said, "What thing is this?"

Like a new Adam, the pilgrim experiences the primal wonderment at the sight of light and its power to reveal the immensity of the forest. Yet the very moment this experience is heightened by the sound of a sweet melody that permeates the luminous air, he blames "Eve's daring" and says that, were it not for her disobedience, he would have "tasted those ineffable delights before—and for a longer time" (XXIX, 22–30). Again, he cannot savor the paradisal happiness without also resenting its loss. His is still the delight of the fallen. As he is "recovering" Eden, he is like Adam who, after the Fall, accused Eve, as she in turn accused the serpent. And as he reproves Eve for not having been "divota" (devout or loyal), he fails to acknowledge what he will soon acknowledge in the presence of Beatrice, that *he* has not been "divoto."[20] But this "lapsing" into the old blindness only partially and momentarily overshadows the pilgrim's delight in the newly found beauty of the garden, for he is soon "all enrapt" as he moves "among so many first-fruits of the eternal pleasure . . . , still desirous of more joys" (31–33).

In the scenes that immediately follow, Dante represents the movement or tragic rhythm of the pilgrim's gradual discovery of what proves to be always something more, always something "other," as the procession draws near. What at first appears to him as lightning he later perceives as a "flaming fire" that kindles the air "under the green boughs" (XXIX, 34–35); and then, when he gazes upon the source of this light, at first he perceives it as "a delusive semblance of seven trees of gold" (43–45). Finally as he draws near he sees the light as seven candelabra (46). Similarly, the "sweet melody" that first had struck him he later hears as a song, and then, more distinctly, as the chant "Hosanna" (51). But the moment he seems to have identified what has brought him so much delight, he still does not know the "thing-in-itself" and the meaning of its presence in the garden. And when he turns to fix his gaze upon the candlesticks (58–60), Matelda shatters the impasse of his seeing-without-understanding by pointing to what comes after them:

La donna mi sgridò: "Perché pur ardi
   sì ne l'affetto de le vive luci,
   e ciò che vien di retro a lor non guardi?"

(*Purg*. XXIX, 61–63)

The lady chid me, "Why are you so eager only for the sight of the living lights, and do not heed that which comes after them?"

Matelda's words constitute a *caesura*, which not only resolves the pilgrim's impasse, but also reveals and helps him avoid the more serious danger of losing himself in his single vision, a kind of idolatrous enjoyment of one object. He now discovers that the object which engaged his entire consciousness is only a fragment—a partial good—whose true meaning lies in its *relation* to what comes after it. Matelda's admonition is deeply connected with Dante's dramaturgy, and correspondingly, with the principle that has informed our reading: that meaning is engendered by the tragic rhythm produced by the scenes as they succeed each other.

The pilgrim reaps the fruits of the shift of focus provoked by Matelda when he sees the people who follow the candlesticks "as after their leaders" (XXIX, 64–66). Now he begins to discover the larger economy of the history of the Church, which the procession performs as a symbolic drama. We may assume that he is no less amazed to witness this drama in the idyllic setting of Eden than when he first saw the candlesticks. It is the reality of history that the new scene introduces in his consciousness, correcting, once again, his (and our) conventional view of paradise. With him we now catch another glimpse of the poet's creative intuition of the original myth of Eden: that—as we have in part already discovered—human history, from beginning to end, is deeply and mysteriously rooted in the garden, and that consequently any other garden dreamed by humans (ancient and modern) which excludes history, with its drama of good and evil, is an imperfect if not entirely false garden.

The scene that immediately follows the one we have just examined exhibits another significant shift of perspective:

L'acqua imprendëa del sinistro fianco,
   e rendea me la mia sinistra costa,
   s'io riguardava in lei, come specchio anco.

(*Purg.* XXIX, 67–69)

The water was taking in my image on the left, and like a mirror reflected to me my left side if I looked in it.

This scene stands in sharp opposition to that of the procession. As he turns his gaze away from history and the communal life that the procession embodies and focuses it on his image reflected in the stream, the pilgrim seems to revert to the single vision from whose dangers Matelda has just rescued him, but now he, or rather his image is the object of that vision. Even more than before he risks sharing Narcissus' fate: to transform the act of seeing from one that may bring true knowledge of the world and the self, to one that brings a deceptive knowledge and the blindness and fixity of death. Michelangelo Picone has aptly pointed out that in *Purgatorio* XXIX "the drama lived by Dante the pilgrim is that of finding the true image. . . . The constant danger which might compromise the quest is represented by

Narcissus, the hidden antagonist. It could be enunciated thus: to exhaust one's own gnoseological thrust upon a sublimated image of the self."[21]

The pilgrim does not succumb to the threat of narcissism, for he soon redirects his attention to the procession, sharpening his vision:

> Quand'io da la mia riva ebbi tal posta,
>   che solo il fiume mi facea distante,
>   per veder meglio ai passi diedi sosta,
> e vidi le fiammelle andar davante,
>   lasciando dietro a sé l'aere dipinto,
>   e di tratti pennelli avean sembiante . . . .
>
> (*Purg.* XXIX, 70–75)

When I was at a point on my bank where only the stream separated me, I held my steps in order to see better, and I saw the flames advance, leaving the air behind them painted, and they looked like moving paint brushes . . . .

From the vantage point of this new scene, if we now glance back at the scene where Narcissus is the "hidden antagonist," we may see it not only as one that is marked by danger, but as a scene in which, though precariously, the pilgrim's self-knowledge stands in creative, dialectical opposition to his awareness of the procession. And as we have already glimpsed in earlier scenes, we may now see the river as a barrier that not only separates, but also, by virtue of its specularity, mediates and joins: we can easily construe that in the river Dante sees mirrored, along (if not indeed commingled) with his image, the image of the flames of the candlesticks and of the procession.[22] We should also note that the "if" in the verse, "if I gazed into it, as in a mirror,"[23] is equivalent to "whenever," and thus it suggests that the pilgrim's gaze at his image is intermittent, and therefore not fixed like the narcissistic gaze. The present scene thus represents, *in parvo*, the action we have seen emerge in the preceding scenes: the problematic interrelation between humanity and history, the individual and the communal life, the personal and the general quest and mythology. This is the main action of the drama whose center is Dante's encounter with Beatrice.

Before examining a few salient scenes of this encounter, we must direct our attention to the closing lines of Canto XXIX:

E quando il carro a me fu a rimpetto,
   un tuon s'udì, e quelle genti degne
   parvero aver l'andar più interdetto,
fermandosi ivi con le prime insegne.

(*Purg.* XXIX, 151–154)

And when the chariot was opposite to me, a thunderclap was heard: and those worthy folk seemed to have their further march forbidden, stopping there along with the banners in front.

This scene brings into sharper focus the interrelation about which we commented above, revealing to us that the pilgrim becomes increasingly less a spectator (with a risk of the narcissistic single vision) than an actor: in strictly dramatistic terms, the procession by necessity comes to a stop when the chariot is directly opposite our pilgrim. Like Beatrice who is soon to appear, the procession has come for him. The people of the procession and Dante are connected by a common action and its underlying conundrum. Their "andar" like his "andar" (of *Purg.* XXVIII, 25), appears to him to be forbidden ("parvero aver l'andar più interdetto"). In other words, he sees it not as a creative limit but as an interdiction. Their obedience to the supernatural signal (the thunder), like Matelda's measured steps, implicitly constitute for him a model to imitate and a state of harmony to recapture.

The pilgrim's encounter with Beatrice marks the center of the episode that spans the last six cantos of *Purgatorio*; it also marks the center of the tragic action whose beginning we saw represented in the Anti-Purgatorio, but whose deepest roots can be traced to the Prologue scene. As such, it sums up and expands both the meaning that we have seen emerge through the scenes we have examined and the dramatic forms whereby that meaning has come to life. We now find at once reaffirmed and heightened the creative force of the tragic rhythm produced by the shifts and breaks in the action, as well as the creativity inherent in spectacle, with its patterns of ritualization and sacralization, in which history and myth and the personal and the choral coalesce. In short, we now witness a very special measure of the manifestation of that "idea of a theater" expounded by Francis Fergusson. Defining the *Commedia*, especially the *Purgatorio*, as the "most comprehensive and consciously elaborated pattern we have [of the idea of a theater]", Fergusson writes:

It includes in rhythmic relationship the modes of action and awareness which in modern theatrical forms are absolute and isolated. Dante presents his contemporaries with the photographic accuracy of Ibsen and Chekhov; and presents all of the social and political issues of his time. But the literal realities are also seen in the round: with all the dimensions of meaning, historical, moral, and final. . . . The perspectives of dream, of myth, and of the most wakeful reason, which we think as mutually exclusive, succeed each other in the movement of his poem but do not cancel each other out. His eye is always directly upon the life of the psyche in its shifting modes of being, its thought, its suffering, and its contemplation.[24]

When Beatrice appears to the pilgrim, the stage for a sacred drama has been set by the procession, and her persona has been at once announced and invoked by these words, all of them sung except for the last two utterances: *"Benedicta* tue / ne le figlie d'Adamo, e benedette / sieno in etterno le bellezze tue" ("Blessed art thou among the daughters of Adam, and blessed forever be thy beauties"; *Purg.* XXIX, 85–87) is a paraphrase of the words of Gabriel to Mary, later echoed by Elizabeth (Luke 1:28 and 42). *"Veni sponsa, de Libano"* ("Come from Lebanon, my bride"; XXX, 11) must refer to the Wisdom of God and not to the Church, the bride of Christ, for the Church is already represented by the chariot. *"Benedictus qui venis"* (XXX, 19), with the slight change of *venit* to *venis*, echoes not only the words of the multitude welcoming Christ's entrance into Jerusalem (Matt. 21:9), but also "blessed is he who comes in the name of the Lord" of Psalm 117 [118]:86. Finally, *"Manibus, oh, date lilia plenis"* ("Give lilies with full hand") is taken from *Aeneid* VI, 883.

As these words help to define the *dramatis persona* who is about to enter the stage, they point to her "otherness" and to the fact that her coming is a manifestation of a mystery, of the sacred. It is a hierophany. And as the pilgrim shares this action of expectation and invocation, participating in the life of the "chorus," he is preparing himself to meet Beatrice in a scene that belongs at once to his personal drama and mythology and to the drama and mythology of the community. In her presence he must strive to capture a measure of the Infinite that not only Beatrice but every human being since Adam and Eve has experienced upon the first contact with God at the moment of being created and by virtue of being made in His image. Thus he must learn to face the awesome grandeur, the terrifying reality of the "other"—the created being of the beloved—and of the absolute Other of Whom she is a *figura* and, given the context of a sacred drama, a "mask."

The pilgrim experiences the coming of Beatrice, alternately, under the sign of the familiar and the known, and under that of the new and unknown:

> Io vidi già nel cominciar del giorno
>   la parte orïental tutta rosata,
>   e l'altro ciel di bel sereno addorno;
> e la faccia del sol nascere ombrata,
>   sì che per temperanza di vapori
>   l'occhio la sostenea lunga fïata:
> così dentro una nuvola di fiori
>   che da le mani angeliche saliva
>   e ricadeva in giù dentro e di fori,
> sovra candido vel cinta d'uliva
>   donna m'apparve, sotto verde manto
>   vestita di color di fiamma viva.
> E lo spirito mio, che già cotanto
>   tempo era stato ch'a la sua presenza
>   non era di stupor, tremando, affranto,
> sanza de li occhi aver più conoscenza,
>   per occulta virtù che da lei mosse,
>   d'antico amor sentì la gran potenza.
>
>   (*Purg.* XXX, 22–39)

Sometimes I have seen at the beginning of the day the eastern region all rosy, while the rest of the heaven was adorned with fair clear sky, and the face of the sun rise shaded, so that through the tempering of vapors the eye sustained it a long while: so within a cloud of flowers, which rose from the angelic hands and fell down again within and without, olive-crowned over a white veil a lady appeared to me, clad, under a green mantle, with hue of living flame; and my spirit, which now for so long a time trembling with awe in her presence had not been overcome, without having more knowledge by the eyes, through occult virtue that proceeded from her, felt old love's great power.

This scene is clearly marked both by presence and absence, by seeing and not seeing. The pilgrim perceives only the outward manifestation of Beatrice, and thus does not really *see* her. Rather it is she who makes her

presence felt in his spirit by her "occulta virtù." The subtle movement of
the soul (its innermost action) from one mode of perception to another of
a higher order is expressed by the special ratio or proportion between the
vehicle and the tenor of the rising sun simile. If at first one seems to correspond perfectly to the other, each speaking of a radiant object which can
be seen because a shade or screen tempers its intensity, upon closer scrutiny
we find signs of significant differences between the two. Among those that
first strike our attention is the one between "I have seen" and "appeared to
me," and the one between the eye that "sustained . . . a long while" the face
of the sun and the eyes that, after a brief perception of her outward appearance, fail to give "more knowledge" of Beatrice to the pilgrim's spirit.
Yet this failure of the eyes to see Beatrice coincides with the pilgrim's inner
vision of her presence through her "occulta virtù," which rekindles the "an-
tico amor." First he sees Beatrice as sometimes he has seen the rising sun;
then, the moment she manifests herself as something "other" than the familiar and the expected, he no longer sees. Yet this not seeing, and therefore the absence of his conscious awareness constitutes the ground for his
perceiving the presence of Beatrice in the depths of his being—through
love. This new meaning that she reveals "within" is not something that he
has arrived at by himself: it is something *given*. "The meanings we are able
to discover," writes Thomas Merton, "are never sufficient. The true meaning has to be revealed. It has to be 'given.' And the fact that it is given is,
indeed, the greater part of its significance: for life itself is, in the end, only
significant in so far as it is given."[25]

The unutterable "nearness" of Beatrice in the pilgrim's spirit makes itself
known by her "occulta virtù" and becomes "utterable" through the fear
and trembling that it provokes in him. This is the moment when he turns
to his familiar guide, like "a little child that runs to his mother when he is
frightened or in distress" (43–45),

> per dicere a Virgilio: "Men che dramma
>   di sangue m'è rimaso che non tremi:
>   conosco i segni de l'antica fiamma."
>
> (*Purg.* XXX, 46–48)

to say to Virgil, "Not a drop of blood is left in me that does not tremble:
I know the tokens of the ancient flame."

But Virgil is gone. The pilgrim's cheeks, which Virgil had cleansed with dew on the shore of Purgatory, now "turn dark again with tears" (53–54), as dark—we are tacitly invited to recall—as when he had first come out of the infernal abyss. And even the garden, which "our mother lost," could not prevent this sorrow (52–53). Dante again experiences suffering and a deep sense of loss in the very place which earlier had brought him delight. And as he weeps for being deprived of the one to whom he gave himself "for salvation" (51), Beatrice addresses him with these words:

> "Dante, perché Virgilio se ne vada,
>   non pianger anco, non piangere ancora;
>   ché pianger ti conven per altra spada."
>
> (*Purg.* XXX, 55–57)

"Dante, because Virgil leaves you, do not weep yet, do not weep yet, for you must weep for another sword!"

As we hear Dante's name mentioned (the only time that this occurs in the *Commedia*), we know that we have come to a crucial moment in the drama of his return to Eden. The confluence in our protagonist of the fictional and the real or the mythical and the historical dimensions which we have witnessed since the beginning of the *Commedia*, is now brought into sharper focus. Of special significance to us is that the pilgrim's identity is formally declared in the tragic moment of loss and rejection—the loss of Virgil, who could have assuaged his fear and trembling provoked in him by the sight of the beloved, and the rejection implicit in the harsh words of Beatrice. As we have already observed many times, here our poet represents the pilgrim's spiritual progress through suffering—the suffering of the tragic opposition or the "dialectic of the tragic," to use the Burkean phrase. If at first we are startled by the stern words of Beatrice, considering them inappropriate and contrary to the pilgrim's and our expectation—for Virgil had promised him that Beatrice would come with smiling eyes (*Purg.* XXVII, 136)—upon closer examination, we discern that with those words Beatrice is helping Dante organize the "dialectical opposition" of the tragic.

A measure of the creative force of this dialectic lies in the harshness of Beatrice's words, which constitutes a *caesura* that interrupts the pilgrim's action of weeping for the loss of Virgil and, correspondingly, for the fact that he is now "alone" with his fear at the sight of Beatrice—his *timor amoris*—without his comforter and advocate (as Virgil had been, for example, in the presence of the stern Cato).[26] As she cuts through Dante's sorrow over Virgil's departure, pointing to a sorrow of another kind, she prepares the ground for the transcendence of his original state. If she had merely consoled him for the loss of Virgil, she would have nourished in him only pathos and pity, without creatively connecting them to ethos and fear. In short, she would have reduced them to sentimentality, depriving them of their power of regeneration. We recall that it was pathos and pity which first moved Beatrice to descend to Hell and enjoin Virgil to save Dante from the she-wolf; and her tears made the ancient poet more eager to go (*Inf.* II, 61–69; 116–117). But in the present scene pathos and pity are not needed to move the pilgrim to the act of repentance. As an earlier scene announced with signs that foreshadowed the coming of Christ at the end of time (*Purg.* XXX, 13–18: "As the blessed at the last trump will rise . . ."), she now comes as judge. And she also resembles an admiral who "goes to stern and bow to see the men that are serving on the other ships, and encourages them to do well" (XXX, 58–60).[27]

Further evidence of the creativity of Beatrice's sharp words is in this famous scene:

> Tutto che 'l vel che le scendea di testa,
>   cerchiato de le fronde di Minerva,
>   non la lasciasse parer manifesta,
> regalmente ne l'atto ancor proterva
>   continüò come colui che dice
>   e 'l più caldo parlar dietro reserva:
> "Guardaci ben! Ben son, ben son Beatrice.
>   Come degnasti d'accedere al monte?
>   non sapei tu che qui è l'uom felice?"
>
> (Purg. XXX, 67–75)

Although the veil that fell from her head, encircled with Minerva's leaves, did not let her be seen distinctly, royally and ever stern in her mien, she continued, like one who speaks and keeps back the hottest words till the last, "Look at me well: indeed I am, indeed I am Beatrice! How did you deign to climb the mountain? Did you not know that here man is happy?"

The figure of Beatrice is now enriched by new dimensions, as she is likened to Minerva, the goddess of wisdom, and to a king. Her harsh and accusing words appear all the more fitting and dramatically necessary as soon as we see in them signs or echoes of the expulsion rite of Ash Wednesday which we mentioned in connection with the episode of Cato, and which is especially evident in *Purgatorio* IX. As she utters the words "How did you deign to climb the mountain?" Beatrice resembles the figure of the bishop who, after the penitents' names had been inscribed on a list of those who asked to be reconciled with God and the Church (similarly, Dante's name has been "registered," as the poet states in *Purgatorio* XXX, 62–63: "when I turned at the sound of my name, which of necessity is registered here"), and after the ceremony of placing ashes on their heads, led the penitents out of the church saying: "Behold—we expel you today from the portals of Holy Mother the Church, because of your sins, just as Adam, the first man, was expelled from Paradise because of his transgression."[28]

As we see represented in Beatrice's scene the form of the rite of expulsion, with its power of repetition (and thus of making *present* in one concentrated act a crucial event of both the Adamic myth and of the personal story of Dante), we can no longer consider her harsh words inappropriate or obscure. And as we pause before this scene, we are struck by the force of Dante's dramaturgy. Beatrice asserts the reality of her being simply and directly on this side of or beyond discourse, asking Dante to look at her as she really is. There is something primal and eternal in her iterated affirmation of her being, of her being present *here and now*. Yet no sooner has she asserted her presence and named herself—symmetrically, we might say, with the earlier naming of Dante—than she reproaches him for having dared to climb the mountain, and therefore, we can infer, for having dared to come to see her there, face to face.

As Beatrice reveals herself to Dante only to expel him from her presence, she is again "organizing the opposition" which he must "suffer" in order that he may transcend his original fallen state, and thus become "degno" (worthy) of standing before her. He must experience the tragic rhythm of seeing and not seeing, of possessing and losing, so that he may see and possess but on a higher plane of existence. He must therefore learn to accept the distance that separates him from Beatrice, just as earlier he learned to accept the distance separating him for Matelda. He must suffer this distance, as Adam suffered his exile from Eden and from God, as the necessary way to return to Beatrice. Like Christ on the Cross, he must experience something like the infinite distance from the Father, he must feel *forsaken* by Him, as he now sees Him represented in Beatrice. He must "die" so that he may live. But since, guided by Virgil, he has already experienced separation and "death" by descending to Hell and has thus imitated Christ, and Beatrice, who as a *figura Christi* also descended to Hell, he is now asked to relive, as in a final act of a tragic drama, that separation and that "death" within the narrow space of ritual.

Dante reacts to Beatrice's cutting words by turning his gaze away from her:

> Li occhi mi cadder giù nel chiaro fonte;
>   ma veggendomi in esso, i trassi a l'erba,
>   tanta vergogna mi gravò la fronte.
> Così la madre al figlio par superba,
>   com'ella parve a me; perché d'amaro
>   sente il sapor de la pietade acerba.
>
> (*Purg*. XXX, 76–81)

My eyes fell down to the clear fount, but, seeing myself in it, I drew them back to the grass, so great shame weighed on my brow; so does the mother seem harsh to her child as she seemed to me, for bitter tastes the savor of stern pity.

Unlike Narcissus, Dante gazes into his image reflected in the stream only for a brief moment. This is a moment of recognition of the true self: not the exalted, idealized self that Narcissus saw mirrored in the fount, but the sorrowful and humbled self. "Mirror and water, signifying pride and death in the story of Narcissus, become the instrument of humiliation and regeneration in the story of Dante the pilgrim."[29] Another measure of the creative movement of the pilgrim's soul, though almost imperceptible and still under the negative sign of separation and conflict, is expressed by the simile of the mother who seems harsh to her child. While it tells of the pilgrim's bitter taste of Beatrice's severe words, it also points to the transformation that those words are secretly producing in him, for in their harshness he may also begin to see pity—which the poet renders with the oxymoron "pietade acerba." Yet despite these intimations of the pilgrim's regeneration, separation and conflict still prevail, and in the scene that immediately follows are indeed intensified and more sharply defined as the angels intervene on behalf of Dante:

Ella si tacque; e li angeli cantaro
   di sùbito *"In te, Domine, speravi"*;
   ma oltre *"pedes meos"* non passaro.

(*Purg.* XXX, 82–84)

She was silent; and the angels of a sudden sang, *"In te, Domine, speravi,"*
but beyond *"pedes meos"* they did not pass.

Beatrice's silence provides the space for the new scene that the angels bring
to life. Like a chorus in a Greek tragedy, they represent the main action of
the drama—Dante's recovery of Eden—and accordingly, in cooperative
competition with Beatrice, they help "organize the opposition" whereby
that action can be developed. Thus as the pilgrim's advocate they represent—in opposition to Beatrice, "mask" of God the Accuser and Judge—
the figure of God the Merciful, the One Whom, with the psalmist, they
address with the words, "In you, o Lord, I put my trust," stopping at the
words "my feet" (Ps. 30:2–9 of the Vulgate).[30]

    The words "pedes meos" immediately arrest our attention, for, to men-
tion only the most recent occurrence, they call to mind the scene in which
the pilgrim matched Matelda's "little steps" with his (*Purg.* XXIX, 8–9).
They acquire greater significance as soon as we read the entire phrase from
which the poet extracted them: "statuisti in loco spatioso pedes meos"
("you have given my feet a spacious place"). The scene created here harks
back to the scene of another spacious place, that of the meadow of *Purgatorio* XXVIII, 5, in which the pilgrim experienced what to us seemed a kind
of limitless freedom, as he walked, "lento lento," toward the "divine forest"
of Eden—a freedom which was soon brought to a halt by the stream. And
as we recall what we said about freedom and the "creative limit" inherent
in Adam's prelapsarian state, one which Dante the pilgrim is learning to
recover, we now see the same conundrum reasserted and more sharply defined by the conflict between the pilgrim—who, with the "chorus" of angels as his advocate, seeks God's mercy—and Beatrice, who represents God
as the Accuser and Judge. We must add that as the angels "remind" God
(again, through Beatrice) of His mercy and His bestowal of freedom on
man by placing him in a "spacious place"—such as the place where Dante
now stands (as Adam once stood)—they imply that, in a sense, in Him
there is a conflict between God Who gives freedom and is merciful and
God Who sets limits and is a harsh judge. Thus, like Job, the angels plead
to God against God. Of course, this conflict or contradiction is only the

created being's *temporal* reading and dramatization of the paradoxical union of opposites that pertains to God. But Dante, like all mortals, cannot experience such *conjunctio oppositorum*: he is unable to see mercy in harshness, in other words, as the poet announced in the simile of the mother and child, to see God's wrath enacted by Beatrice as a "pietade acerba." Nor can he understand and experience the limit defined by God's "Thou shalt not"—as Beatrice now defines the pilgrim's scene of confession and repentance—other than as an obstacle and an interdiction. Yet he can experience a measure of the creativity of limit and of the Love that wounds in order to heal, by their effects upon his soul—effects which only ritual and drama, with their power of analogy, can produce.

It is this power that transforms Dante's soul, changing his fear into pity:

> ma poi che 'ntesi ne le dolci tempre
> >   lor compartire a me, par che se detto
> >   avesser: "Donna, perché sì lo stempre?"
> lo gel che m'era intorno al cor ristretto,
> >   spirito e acqua fessi, e con angoscia
> >   de la bocca e de li occhi uscì del petto.
>
> > > > > (*Purg.* XXX, 94–99)

but when I heard how in their sweet notes they took my part, quite as if they had said, "Lady, why do you so confound him?" the ice that was bound tight around my heart became breath and water, and with anguish poured from my breast through my mouth and eyes.

As a chorus the angels interpret Dante's innermost and unexpressed action by singing the words of the psalmist. Thus they enable him to discover this action and to look at it with some detachment, as if it belonged to another. From this new perspective which he shares with the angels, he is moved to pity for himself. The transformation of fear into pity occurs at the point when he in turn interprets the action of the "chorus," reading in their words a reproach directed at Beatrice (and God) for her excessive harshness. And as he deems himself undeserving of this harshness, seeing himself as the object of divine wrath, he experiences the unmistakable condition of the tragic. He is not yet able to transcend this condition by living through the tragic and by accepting it, or more precisely, by recognizing his guilt while at the same time considering himself a victim of a mysterious iniquity—of evil that, like the serpent in Eden, is always *already there*. This is the transcendence of tragic vision or tragic wisdom, which for the pilgrim, as for most of us, remains the goal to be realized.

However, the pilgrim (and the sympathetic reader) has moved closer to that goal by his participation in the life of the "chorus." As he beheld the "spectacle" and the "performance" through which the angels, in a single voice, sang his fear and hope—and the fear and hope of all who, like the psalmist, stand before God—, he experienced those same passions not merely as his own "feelings," but as passions that are raised up to the symbolic and mythic sphere. This is the place of tragic reconciliation. It is here that he has transcended his original terror, transforming it into pity. And as his frozen heart has melted into "breath and water," he is now more disposed to hear Beatrice's accusation and to transform his tears of self-pity into tears of remorse as he confesses his sins and his sinfulness. In other words, he is now open to experience more deeply the dialectic of the tragic by "suffering the opposition" that Beatrice and the chorus of the angels have "organized" for him.

Somewhat like our poet who, constrained by "lo fren de l'arte" ("the curb of art," *Purg.* XXXIII, 141), brings the *Purgatorio* to a close, so I, aware of the "curb" of my "art," must now conclude this work. I find no better way to do this than to point out that between the scenes of confession and purification, culminating in the ritual of Dante's immersion in the Lethe (XXXI, 13–102), and the final scene of restoration and renewal marked by his immersion in the Eunoe (XXXIII, 127–145), Dante witnesses a series of epiphanies that contrast sharply with visions of violence that are either retrospective or apocalyptic. Thus he experiences a new measure of tragic irony after his confession of sin, and after Lethe has washed away all memory of it, and after he has crossed over to the "blessed shore" (XXXI, 97) of Eden proper, where God placed Adam after He had created him (Gen. 2:8, 15). In the garden he finds not innocence and peace, but the terrifying scenes of a tragic drama in which the myth and history of the race are represented through the power of symbol as one action: the tragic conflict of good and evil.

When Dante sees the eagle (of the Roman Empire) strike like lightning the tree (of the knowledge of good and evil) that the griffin (representing Christ, the "second Adam") has just transformed from a barren to a leafy tree bearing flowers, and then witnesses the eagle's attack on the chariot (of the Church), he is again face to face with the irreducible fact of evil, namely the evil that he has not introduced in the world—evil that is *already there*. There are other symbols of evil: the fox (of heresy) that leaped into the chariot but was quickly put to flight by Beatrice (XXXII, 118–123); the dragon, later called "serpent" (34)—echoing the serpent of Gen. 3:1–5 and "the old serpent" of Rev. 12:9—which emerged from the earth and tore out part of the bottom of the chariot, making off with it (130–135); and the chariot's transformation into a seven-headed monster, modeled on the monster of Rev. 13:1 and symbolizing the corrupt Papal Curia (142–147). The final symbol of evil is the ungirt whore (again, the corrupt Church) who appears to Dante sitting upon the chariot-turned-monster and exchanging kisses with a giant (the French monarchy), and who, turning her lustful eye to Dante, provokes the giant's jealousy and rage, so that he beats "her from head to foot" and then drags the chariot-beast into the wood (148–160).

As Dante witnesses these scenes—especially the last one into which he is drawn by the harlot's lustful eye—he seems to be the victim of a terrible irony, for no sooner has he lost all memory of sin than he encounters it again, with all its mysterious and yet familiar, its primal and contemporary terror. Yet the fact that now he is no longer culpable redefines his relation to evil. As one who has recovered his innocence, through confession and expiation of sin, he begins to reveal to us what until now we found to be true only in part: he is the "victim" of evil and is thus distinctly a tragic figure. "The tragic *representation*," notes Paul Ricoeur, "continues to express not only the *reverse side* of all confession of sins, but the *other pole* of human evil; the evil for which I assume responsibility makes manifest a source of evil for which I cannot assume responsibility. . . . It might be said that the avowal of evil as human calls forth a second-degree avowal, that of evil as non-human. Only tragedy can accept this avowal of the avowal and exhibit it in a spectacle, for no coherent discourse can include that Other [i.e., the Adversary]."[31]

As one who suffers evil, Dante resembles Job, who stands in sharp opposition to the justly exiled Adam whom the pilgrim has until now imitated. "The evil that is *committed* leads to a just exile; that is what the figure of Adam represents. . . . The evil that is *suffered* leads to an unjust deprivation; that is what the figure of Job represents. The first figure calls for the second; the second corrects the first."[32] But while we see Dante as Job who suffers unjustly, we must also see him as Job who, as he appeals to God against God, in the end accepts His will. In other words, we must see foreshadowed in Job, and represented in Dante, the figure of the "Suffering Servant" Whom the Second Isaiah celebrated in the four "Songs of the

Servant of Yahweh" (Is. 42:1–9; 49:1–6; 50:4–11; 52:13–53:12).[33] This is the "third figure" that could transcend the Adam-Job contradiction, by making "of suffering, of the evil that is undergone, an *action* capable of redeeming the evil that is committed."[34]

It is perhaps ("forse," Matelda would say) this "third figure" whom Beatrice had tacitly invited Dante to imitate, when, before witnessing the tragic representation we rapidly sketched above, she told him:

> "Però, in pro del mondo che mal vive,
>   al carro tieni or li occhi, e quel che vedi,
>   ritornato di là, fa che tu scrive."
>
> (*Purg.* XXXII, 103–105)

"Therefore, for profit of the world that lives ill, hold your eyes now on the chariot, and what you see, mind that you write it when you have returned yonder."

Beatrice's command to write what he sees gives authenticity, retrospectively (for us readers) and prophetically (for the pilgrim), not only to Dante as poet, or as dramatist, but also to Dante as a tragic figure. It is as all of these personae that he, again and again, enters the stage of our imagination and stands before us, the community, to speak, move, and act, in order that we may be saved. From this perspective, Dante's journey, from the "selva oscura" of this life to the "selva antica" of Eden, appears to us at once as the just exile for the evil committed and the unjust suffering for the evil that he has not committed—a suffering which, freely accepted, redeems that evil. By the drama's power of analogy Dante has become for us, if only partially and imperfectly, what Beatrice has been for him: the Suffering Servant, and therefore the one whose suffering—again, as poet and pilgrim—has turned into a *gift* "in pro del mondo che mal vive."

Notes

1. Fergusson, *Dante's Drama of the Mind*, p. 181. Part of this chapter is forthcoming under the title of "Dante's Encounter with Matelda: A Dramatistic Reading of *Purgatorio* XXVIII," in *Lectura Dantis Newberryana*, ed. Paolo Cherchi and Antonio C. Mastrobuono (Evanston, IL: Northwestern University Presss, 1991)

2. Peter Dronke, "Dante's Earthly Paradise: Towards an Interpretation of *Purgatorio* XXVIII," *Romanische Forschungen* 82, 4 (1970), 478. Emerson Brown, Jr. offers a similar interpretation in his "Proserpina, Matelda and the Pilgrim," *Dante Studies* LXXXIX (1971): 44: ". . . Since he [the pilgrim] can remember his fallen

state, [he] is incapable of thoroughly grasping eternal innocence. He sees innocence not entire and of itself but only as innocence-before-the-fall. He sees Matelda
and thinks of Proserpina." While sharing the cited reading of Professor Dronke, I
disagree with his conclusion (p. 480): "Dante's surge of feeling for Matelda is indeed sensual, but also spontaneous and liberating, devoid of any sense of sin or
guilt. That is precisely why his encounter with her is his experience of the earthly
paradise . . . . What he celebrates at this moment . . . is instinctive love, that 'natural
love [which] is always without error' (*Lo naturale è sempre sanza errore* [*Purg.*]
XVII, 94)." This "natural love" is "without error" if, with Virgil, we see it (in the
light of reason or natural philosophy) as the-thing-in-itself. But can we (or does
Dante suggest that we can) separate this love from "rational love" ("amore d'animo") in the fullness and integrity of man's existence? When Dante the pilgrim faces
Matelda, he experiences the *conflict* between the two loves, intermittently turning
his will and desire now to the innocence she embodies and now to a false image of
it, a "malo obietto" (*Purg.* XVII, 95), that is, a false image of her that he himself
has fashioned. If there were no error or inclination toward evil in the pilgrim, who
has only just entered the Earthly Paradise, what function or meaning would his
later immersion in the Lethe and Eunoe have other than that of a purely formal rite
of purification and restoration? Cf. Caron Ann Cioffi, " 'Il cantor de' bucolici
carmi': The Influence of Virgilian Pastoral on Dante's Depiction of the Earthly
Paradise," *Lectura Dantis Newberryana*, vol. I, ed. Paolo Cherchi and Antonio C.
Mastrobuono (Evanston, IL: Northwestern University Press, 1988), p. 103: "The
intrusion of frenzied love into the pastoral landscape is a large thematic focus in the
second, sixth, eighth, and tenth *Eclogues* of Virgil, poems which I believe directly
influenced Dante's portrayal of Eden as the *locus* of his own frustrated desire. In
Virgil, as in Dante, spiritual discord is manifested primarily in the perversion of
harmonious love."

3. Needless to say, my interpretation differs substantially from Singleton's
(*Commentary* 2, p. 676, n. 75): "It is evident (though not explained) that Dante feels
somehow that he must not attempt to cross the narrow stream, much as he desires
to do so. It is as if he would cross over only if the water should be opened for him,
as the Red Sea was to the Israelites."

4. Cf. Dietrich Bonhoeffer, *Creation and Fall; Temptation: Two Biblical Studies*,
trans. John C. Fletcher and Kathleen Dowham (New York: Macmillan, 1959), pp.
77–78: "[The] division in *tob* [good] and *ra* [evil] must first of all express itself in
Adam's relation to Eve. Eve, the other person, has been to Adam the bodily form
of the given limit whom he acknowledged in love, i.e., in the undivided unity of
his devotion and whom he loved in her very nature as limit, i.e., *because* she was
human and yet 'another person.' Now that he has transgressed the limit, he knows
for the first time that he was limited. At the same time he no longer accepts the
limit as the grace of God the Creator but hates it, looking upon it as the envy of
God the Creator. In the same act he has transgressed the limit that the other person
had embodied for him. Now he no longer sees the limit of the other person as
grace but as the wrath, the hatred, the envy of God. This means that he no longer
sees the other person in love. He sees him over against himself, at variance with
himself. Now the limit is no longer grace, holding man in the unity of his creaturely

and free love; it is discord. Man and woman are divided." The reader will easily recognize the similarities between this division and duality and the division and duality manifest in the scene of Dante who is separated from Matelda by the stream.

5. Cited by Brown, "Proserpina, Matelda and the Pilgrim," p. 48. See St. Thomas Aquinas, *Summa Theologiae*, Ia IIae, q. 74, a. 3, ad 2, Latin text, English translation, introduction, notes, appendix and glossary, John Fearon, O.P. (New York: Blackfriars, 1969), pp. 102–103: "Perpetua corruptio sensualitatis est intelligenda quantum ad fomitem, qui nunquam totaliter tollitur in hac vita; transit enim peccatum originale reatu, et remanet actu." (The perpetual corruption of sensuality should be understood to mean the spark which kindles desire, which is never completely extinguished in this life; though the stain of original sin can be taken away, the effects remain.)

6. Cf. Dronke, "Dante's Earthly Paradise," p. 482: "Suddenly we become aware again of Vergil and Statius, who all the while must have been standing loyally nearby. Dante the character had caught us wholly into his own passionate absorption—we have forgotten the two poets as completely as he forgets them. . . . Dante, when she recalled the presence of his poet-friends to him, has been reminded only too clearly that the scene is not set for a pastourelle."

7. In Singleton's *Commentary* 2, pp. 676–677 we read: "There is no reason why Dante or the two poets should marvel that this lady smiles and rejoices in such a beautiful spot." This reading, it is easy to see, ignores the simple fact or truth of the letter, that "such a beautiful spot" is at once the place of innocence possessed and innocence lost, of joy and misery. Cf. Natalino Sapegno's commentary, *La Divina Commedia*, vol. II, *Purgatorio* (Florence: La Nuova Italia, 1956), p. 318, n. 80: "Nell'animo dei poeti poteva giustificarsi un sentimento di stupore, nel veder Matelda ridere in un luogo che rievoca la memoria della prima colpa e della conseguente caduta dell'umanità; ma la donna risponde che essa ride, perché esulta nella contemplazione delle meraviglie create da Dio . . . ."

8. As quoted in Singleton, *Commentary* 2, n. 80, pp. 677–678.

9. Singleton's n. 80 quoted above, p. 678, has a reference to Peter Abelard's *Expositio in Hexaemeron* (col. 762D) which helps strengthen my reading: "Peter Abelard had found that this particular psalm, and indeed the same verses referred to by Matelda, were relevant to the matter of the original condition of man in Eden. In his treatise on the work of the Creation, *Hexaemeron*, when he enters into the 'moral' interpretation of the events of Genesis, Abelard writes a commentary on those delights which man, *even now in his fallen condition*, may experience in the created universe, in all the creatures which have been made for him . . . ." (Italics mine)

10. Ricoeur, *The Symbolism of Evil*, trans. Emerson Buchanan (New York: Harper & Row, 1967), p. 163.

11. Cf. Etienne Gilson, *The Spirit of Mediaeval Philosophy*, trans. A.H.C. Downes (New York: Scribner's Sons, 1940), p. 122: "Since evil is but the corruption of a good and cannot possibly subsist at all save in this good, it follows that inasmuch as there is evil, there is also good. Certainly, we have travelled very far from that degree of order, beauty and measure which God bestowed on the world in creating it, but if sin had abolished all good it would have abolished all being along with

the good and the world would no longer exist. In this sense we may say that evil could not eliminate nature without eliminating itself, since it would have no subject left to inhere in, there would be none of which it could be affirmed."

12. *Convivio* III. viii, 11. English trans. Jackson, *Dante's Convivio*, p. 154.

13. Northrop Frye, *The Great Code: The Bible and Literature* (New York: Harcourt Brace Jovanovich, 1983), p. 196.

14. Singleton, *Commentary* 2, n. 3, p. 692.

15. Cf. Singleton, ibid., nn. 4–6, p. 493: "The simile may seem inappropriate at first, until we see that its function is to bring over into this canto something of the focus of the lady's last words of the preceding canto, which touched on ancient poets and their myths, *their* pastoral themes corresponding to those of modern poets." I must add that the function of this simile is also to reveal the differences between the two perspectives.

16. Cf. Dragonetti, *Dante pélerin de la Sainte Face*, pp. 244–245: "Les vers suivants [*Purg*. XXIX, 7–9] expriment, dans la tension, le devenir d'un accord entre l'être de Matelda et l'être de Dante . . . C'est seulement à partir d'un tel accord que la nature devient une théophanie d'ordre poétique." We recall that, by contrast, in the Prologue scene, the pilgrim's steps were those of *homo claudus* ("the firm foot was always the lower"; *Inf.* I, 30). For an elaborate discussion of the pilgrim as *homo claudus*, see John Freccero, "Dante's Firm Foot and the Journey Without a Guide," *Harvard Theological Review* LII, 3 (1959), 245–281, now in J. Freccero, *Dante: The Poetics of Conversion*, ed., intr. Rachel Jacoff (Cambridge, MA: Harvard University Press, 1986).

17. Northrop Frye, *Anatomy of Criticism* (Princeton, NJ: Princeton University Press, 1957), p. 119.

18. Cf. Ricoeur, *The Symbolism of Evil*, p. 250: "For an innocent freedom [of prelapsarian man] this limitation would not be felt as an interdiction; but we no longer know what that primordial authority, contemporaneous with the birth of finite freedom, is; in particular, we no longer know what a *limit* that does not repress, but orients and guards freedom, could be like; we no longer have access to that creative limit. We are acquainted only with the limit that constrains; authority becomes interdiction under the regime of fallen freedom. That is why the naïve author of the Biblical story projects into the state of innocence the sort of interdiction that we experience 'after' the fall; the God who says Yes—'Let there be light: and there was light'—now says No—'As for the tree of the knowledge of good and evil, thou shalt not eat of it.' "

19. Ibid.:

Dizziness begins with alienation from the commandment, which suddenly becomes my "Other," whereas it had been my "Orient." Floating at a distance from me, the commandment becomes insupportable; the creative limit becomes hostile negativity and, as such, problematic . . . . At the same time as the meaning of the ethical limit becomes hazy, the meaning of finiteness is obscured. A "desire" has sprung up, the desire for infinity; but that infinity is not the infinity of reason and happiness . . . , it is the infinity of desire itself; it is the desire of desire, taking possession of knowing, of willing, of doing, and of being. . . . It is in relation to this 'desire' that finiteness is insupportable, the finiteness which consists simply in being created being.

20. Cf. Peter Dronke, "The Procession in Dante's *Purgatorio*," *Deutsches Dante Jahrbuch* 53/54 (1978–1979): 23:

While it is possible to adduce not only misogynistic poets but authoritarian theologians, such as Augustine and Aquinas, who argued that Eve's blame in the Fall was greater than Adam's—that is, this could be a perfectly serious and tenable view in Dante's time—I cannot help feeling that, in its dramatic context in the *Purgatorio*, Dante's *zelo* concerning Eve comes a little strangely at this moment, and that it may be "good" (*buon*) in the sense of "abundant" rather than of "morally admirable." Does Dante's zealous reproach of Eve come to appear in a somewhat different light in the next canto, when Beatrice reproaches Dante: Dante who has failed to be *divoto* to her, straying from the heavenly ideal that she, a woman, embodies—Dante who has come to the brink of losing heaven for himself? Was it really a good moment for indulging in righteousness—however genuinely felt—at a woman's expense?

21. Michelangelo Picone, "Dante e il mito di Narciso: Dal *Roman de la rose* alla *Commedia*," *Romanische Forschungen* 89 (1977): 394–395. (Translation mine.)
22. Allen Mandelbaum has captured this implication when he translates: "The water, to my left, reflected flames, / and it reflected, too, my left-hand side / if I gazed into it, as in a mirror." *The Divine Comedy of Dante Alighieri, Purgatorio*, a verse translation with introduction by Allen Mandelbaum, notes by Laury Magnus, Allen Mandelbaum, and Anthony Oldcorn, with Daniel Feldman (Toronto: Bantam Books, 1984), p. 269.
23. Mandelbaum's trans., ibid.
24. Fergusson, *The Idea of a Theater*, p. 227.
25. Thomas Merton, *The New Man* (Toronto: Bantam Books, 1961), p. 5.
26. Cf. Joy Hambuechen Potter, "Beatrice Ammiraglio: *Purgatorio* XXX, 58–66," in *Italiana*, ed. Albert N. Mancini, Paolo Giordano, and Pier Raimondo Baldini (River Forest, IL: Rosary College, 1988), p. 100:

Beatrice appears, Dante again falls in love with her, as he had done in his *dolce stil novo* days; he is frightened of this love (which, by using Dido's words to describe it, he signals as tinged by sensuality); he turns to Virgil for protection and/or comfort, but, in the presence of his love, Virgil (i.e., reason, which he had trusted to help him towards redemption) is not there and cannot protect him; Dante weeps. If the text is read in this way on this level, Dante is weeping not only for his loss of Virgil but for his own fallen state, and this state is illustrated in a very personal manner.

27. For an illuminating discussion of this dimension of Beatrice see Joy Potter, pp. 97–108.
28. Quoted by Tucker, "Dante's Reconciliation in the *Purgatorio*," p. 78. I must note that the author sees the correspondence to the expulsion ceremony of Ash

Wednesday only in *Purgatorio* IX and then compares the reconciliation ceremony of Holy Thursday to the events represented in *Purgatorio* XXIX, XXX, and XXXI.

29. Picone, "Dante e il mito di Narciso," p. 395. (Translation mine)

30. Cf. Anthony K. Cassell, "Failure, Pride, and Conversion in *Inferno* I: A Reinterpretation," *Dante Studies* XCIV (1976): 5: "If the significance of the line from the Psalm remains opaque to the reader of the present day, we will do well to seek what the line signified in the tradition which Dante inherited. St. Augustine's exegesis particularly can be most revealing, for he makes the 'spacious place' a place of justice and contrasts the feet of the just with the limping foot of the unredeemed [*Enarratio II in Psalmum XXX*, 15; *PL*, 36, col. 238–239]." See also pp. 6 ff. for an insightful discussion of the "piè fermo" ("limping foot") of *Inferno* I, to which, by contrast, the image of the "pedes meos" harks back.

31. Ricoeur, *The Symbolism of Evil*, pp. 313–314.

32. Ibid., p. 324.

33. As cited in ibid.

34. Ibid.

Works Cited

Peter Abelard. *Expositio in Hexaemeron.*

Meyer Howard Abrams. "The Deconstructive Angel," in *Contemporary Literary Criticism,* ed. and intr. Robert Con Davis. New York and London: Longman, 1986.

The Divine Comedy of Dante Alighieri, Inferno, trans. with intr. by Allen Mandelbaum, notes by Allen Mandelbaum and Gabriel Marruzzo, with Laury Magnus. Berkeley: University of California Press, 1980; Toronto: Bantam Books, 1982.

The Divine Comedy of Dante Alighieri, Purgatorio, a verse trans. with intr. by Allen Mandelbaum, notes by Laury Magnus, Allen Mandelbaum, and Anthony Oldcorn, with Daniel Feldman. Toronto: Bantam Books, 1984.

Dante Alighieri. *The Divine Comedy,* trans. with a commentary by Charles S. Singleton, 3 vols. Princeton, NJ: Princeton University Press, 1970–1976.

Dantis Alagherii Epistolae, intr., trans., notes by Paget Toynbee. Oxford: Oxford University Press, 1920; rpt. with preface and additional bibliography by Colin Hardy, 1966.

Mowbray Allan. "Does Dante Hope for Virgil's Salvation?" *MLN* (Jan. 1989).

St. Thomas Aquinas. *Summa Theologiae,* Latin text, English translation, introduction, notes, appendix and glossary by John Fearon, O.P. New York: Blackfriars, 1969.

———. *Super libr. de Causis.*

Aristotle's "Poetics," trans. S.H. Butcher, intr. by Francis Fergusson. New York: Hill and Wang, 1961.

Erich Auerbach. *Literary Language and Its Public in Late Latin Antiquity and in the Middle Ages,* trans. Ralph Manheim. London: Routledge & Kegan Paul, 1965.

St. Augustine. *Confessions,* trans. William Watts. Loeb Classical Library. London: W. Heinemann, 1912.

Gaston Bachelard. *The Poetics of Space,* trans. Maria Jolas. Boston: Beacon Press, 1969.

Hans Urs von Balthasar. *Theo-Drama: Theological Dramatic Theory,* trans. Graham Harrison. San Francisco: Ignatius Press, 1988.

Piero Boitani. *The Tragic and the Sublime in Medieval Literature.* Cambridge: Cambridge University Press, 1989.

Dietrich Bonhoeffer. *Creation and Fall; Temptation: Two Biblical Studies,* trans. John C. Fletcher and Kathleen Dowham. New York: Macmillan, 1959.

Franca Brambilla Ageno. "Annotazioni a passi della Commedia." *Studi danteschi* XLII (1965).

Irma Brandeis. *The Ladder of Vision.* Garden City, N.Y.: Doubleday and Co., 1960.

Emerson Brown, Jr. "Proseprina, Matelda and the Pilgrim." *Dante Studies* LXXXIX (1971).

Martin Buber. *The Way of Response: Martin Buber, Selections from His Writings*, ed. N.N. Glatzer. New York: Schocken Books, 1966.

Kenneth Burke. *A Grammar of Motives*. New York: Prentice-Hall, 1945.

———. *Language as Symbolic Action*. Berkeley: University of California Press, 1966.

———. *The Philosophy of Literary Forms*, 3rd ed. Berkeley: University of California Press, 1973.

Glauco Cambon. "Francesca and the Tactics of Language," in his *Dante's Craft: Studies in Language and Style*. Minneapolis: University of Minnesota Press, 1969.

Anthony K. Cassell. "Failure, Pride, and Conversion in *Inferno* I: A Reinterpretation." *Dante Studies* XCIV (1976).

———. *Lectura Dantis Americana: Inferno I*, foreword by Robert Hollander. Philadelphia: University of Pennsylvania Press, 1989.

———. "The Lesson of Ulysses." *Dante Studies* XCIX (1981).

———. "Ulisseana: A Bibliography of Dante's Ulysses." *Italian Culture* III (1981).

Giovanni Cecchetti. "Il 'peregrin' e i 'navicanti' di *Purgatorio* VIII, 1–6: Saggio di lettura dantesca." In *A Dante Symposium in Commemoration of the 700th Anniversary of the Poet's Birth*, ed. William De Sua and Gino Rizzo. Chapel Hill: University of North Carolina Press, 1965.

Caron Ann Cioffi. " 'Il cantor de' bucolici carmi': The Influence of Virgilian Pastoral on Dante's Depiction of the Earthly Paradise." *Lectura Dantis Newberryana*, vol. I, ed. Paolo Cherchi and Antonio C. Mastrobuono. Evanston, IL: Northwestern University Press, 1988.

Gianfranco Contini. "Un'interpretazione di Dante." In his *Varianti e altra linguistica*. Turin: Einaudi, 1970.

Roger L. Cox. *Between Earth and Heaven: Shakespeare, Dostoevsky, and the Meaning of Christian Tragedy*. New York, Chicago, San Francisco: Holt, Rinehart and Winston, 1969.

Ernst Robert Curtius. *European Literature and the Latin Middle Ages*, trans. Willard R. Trask. New York and Evanston, IL: Harper & Row, 1953.

Dante Della Terza. "*Inferno* V: Tradition and Exegesis." *Dante Studies* XCIX (1981).

Jacques Derrida. *Writing and Difference*, trans., intr., and notes Alan Bass. Chicago: University of Chicago Press, 1978.

———. "Structure, Sign, and Play in the Discourse of the Human Sciences." In *Contemporary Literary Criticism*, ed. and intr. Robert Con Davis. New York and London: Longman, 1986.

John Dobbins and Peter Fuss. "The Silhouette of Dante in Hegel's *Phenomenology of Spirit*." *Clio* 11, 4 (1982).

Roger Dragonetti. *Dante pèlerin de la Sainte Face*. Gand: Romanica Gandensia, 1968.

Peter Dronke. "Dante's Earthly Paradise: Towards an Interpretation of *Purgatorio* XXVIII." *Romanische Forschungen* 82, 4 (1970).

———. "The Procession in Dante's *Purgatorio*." *Deutsches Dante Jahrbuch* 53/54 (1978–1979).

Mircea Eliade. *Myths, Dreams and Mysteries*, trans. Philip Mairet. New York and Evanston, IL: Harper & Row, 1967.

———. *The Sacred and the Profane*, trans. Willard R. Trask. New York: Harcourt, Brace & World Inc., 1957.

T.S. Eliot. *Four Quartets*. New York: Harcourt, Brace & World, Inc., 1943.

Francis Fergusson. *Dante's Drama of the Mind: A Modern Reading of "Purgatorio."* Princeton, NJ: Princeton University Press, 1953.

———. *The Idea of a Theater*. Princeton, NJ: Princeton University Press, 1949.

Franco Ferrucci. *The Poetics of Disguise*. Ithaca, NY and London: Cornell University Press, 1980.

Fernando Figurelli. "Il canto I dell'*Inferno*." *Inferno: Letture degli anni 1973–76. Casa di Dante in Roma. Nuove Letture*. Rome: Bonacci, 1976.

Kenelm Foster, O.P. *God's Tree*. London: Blackfriars Publications, 1957.

———. *The Two Dantes and Other Studies*. Berkeley and Los Angeles: University of California Press, 1977.

John Freccero. "Dante's Firm Foot and the Journey Without a Guide." *Harvard Theological Review* LII, 3 (1959), 245–281, now in J. Freccero, *Dante: The Poetics of Conversion*, ed. and intr. Rachel Jacoff. Cambridge, MA: Harvard University Press, 1986.

———. "Dante's Prologue Scene." *Dante Studies* LXXXIV (1966), now in *Dante: The Poetics of Conversion*.

Northrop Frye. *Anatomy of Criticism*. Princeton, NJ: Princeton University Press, 1957.

———. *The Great Code: The Bible and Literature*. New York: Harcourt Brace Jovanovich, 1983.

A. Bartlett Giamatti. *The Earthly Paradise and the Renaissance Epic*. Princeton, NJ: Princeton University Press, 1966.

R.B. Gill. "The Forms of Christian Tragedy." *Bucknell Review* 26, 2 (1982).

Etienne Gilson. *The Spirit of Mediaeval Philosophy*, trans. A.H.C. Downes. New York: Scribner's Sons, 1940.

René Girard. *Things Hidden since the Foundation of the World*, trans. Stephen Bann and Michael Metteer. Stanford, CA: Stanford University Press, 1987.

———. "The Mimetic Desire of Paolo and Francesca," in his *"To double buisiness bound," Essays on Literature, Mimesis, Anthropology*. Baltimore and London: Johns Hopkins University Press, 1978.

———. *Violence and the Sacred*, trans. Patrick Gregory. Baltimore: Johns Hopkins University Press, 1984.

Egidio Guidubaldi. "*Paradiso* XXXIII: Rassegna di ponti semantici analizzati con J. Lacan." In *Psicoanalisi e strutturalismo di fronte a Dante*, Atti dei mesi danteschi 1969–1971, vol. II. Florence: Olschki, 1972.

Cyrus Hamlin. "On Tragedy: A Review of Current Research." *Recherches Sémiotiques/Semiotic Inquiry* 4, 1 (1984).

O.B. Hardison, Jr. *Christian Rite and Christian Drama in the Middle Ages*. Baltimore: Johns Hopkins University Press, 1969.

Anna Hatcher and Mark Musa. "The Kiss: *Inferno* V and the Old French Prose Lancelot." *Comparative Literature* 20 (1968).

G.W.F. Hegel. *The Phenomenology of Mind*, trans., intr., and notes J.B. Baillie, 2nd ed. London: George Allen & Unwin, Ltd.; New York: Macmillan, 1955.

Hegel's Philosophy of Mind, Part III of the *Encyclopedia of the Philosophical Sciences* (1830), trans. William Wallace and A.V. Miller. Oxford: Clarendon Press, 1971.

Martin Heidegger. *Being and Time*, trans. John Macquarrie and Edward Robinson. Oxford: Basil Blackwell, 1980.

Friedrich Hölderlin. *Werke und Briefe*, ed. Friedrich Beißner. Frankfurt: Insel, 1969.

Robert Hollander. *Allegory in Dante's "Commedia."* Princeton, NJ: Princeton University Press, 1969.

———. *Il Virgilio dantesco: Tragedia nella "Commedia."* Florence: Olschki, 1983.

Amilcare A. Iannucci. "Ulysses' 'folle volo': The Burden of History." *Medioevo romanzo* III (1976).

Rachel Jacoff and William A. Stephany. *Lectura Dantis Americana: Inferno II*. Philadelphia: University of Pennsylvania Press, 1989.

Roman Jakobson and Morris Halle. *Fundamentals of Language*. The Hague: Mouton, 1956.

Karl Jaspers. *Tragedy Is Not Enough*, trans. Harald A.T. Reiche, Harry T. Moore, and Karl W. Deutsch. Boston: Beacon Press. 1952.

Jerusalem Bible, ed. Alexander Jones. Garden City, N.Y.: Doubleday and Co., 1975.

Pascual Jordan. "Die Stellung der Naturwissenschaft zur religiösen Frage." *Universitas* (Jan. 1947).

Pierre-Jean Jouve. *Lyrique*. Paris: Mercure di France, n.d.

James Joyce. *A Portrait of the Artist as a Young Man*. New York: Viking Press, 1964.

C.G. Jung. *Answer to Job*, trans. R.F.C. Hull. Princeton, NJ: Princeton University Press, 1958.

J.K. Kadowaki, S.J. *Zen and the Bible*, trans. Joan Rieck. London: Routledge & Kegan Paul, 1980.

Henry Ansgar Kelly. *Tragedy and Comedy from Dante to Pseudo-Dante*. Berkeley: University of California Press, 1989.

Karl Kerényi. "Theos e Mythos," trans. from German into Italian, in *Il problema della demitizzazione*, ed. E. Castelli. Padua: Cedam, 1961.

Walter Kerr. *Tragedy and Comedy*. New York: Da Capo Press, 1985.

Philippe Lacoue-Labarthe. "The Caesura of the Speculative," trans. Robert Eisenhauer. *Glyph* 4 (1978).

Susanne Langer. "The Tragic Rhythm." In *Feeling and Form*, ed. Susanne Langer. New York: Charles Scribner's Sons, 1953.

Liber Sacramentorum, Patrologia Latina, vol. LXXVIII, ed. Hugo Ménard.

Dietrich Mack. *Ansichten zum Tragischen und zur Tragödie*. Munich: Fink, 1970.

Allen Mandelbaum, trans. *The Aeneid of Virgil*. New York: Bantam Books, 1961.

Gabriel Marcel. *Tragic Wisdom and Beyond*, trans. Stephen Jolin and Peter McCormick. Evanston, IL: Northwestern University Press, 1973.

Jacques Maritain. *Creative Intuition in Art and Poetry*. Cleveland and New York: World Publishing Co., 1954.

Louis L. Martz. "The Saint as Tragic Hero. *Saint Joan* and *Murder in the Cathe-*

dral," in *Tragic Themes in Western Literature*, ed. Cleanth Brooks. New Haven, CT: Yale University Press, 1955.

Franco Masciandaro. "L'amor torto' di Francesca e il 'diritto amore' di Cunizza." *Pacific Northwest Council on Foreign Languages, Proceedings* XXIX (1978).

———. "The Good in Dante's *selva oscura*: A Dramatistic Reading." In *Studi di Italianistica in onore di Giovanni Cecchetti*, ed. Paolo Cherchi and Michelangelo Picone. Ravenna: Longo, 1988.

———. "Notes on the Image of the Point in the *Divine Comedy*." *Italica* LIV, 2 (1977).

———. "The Paradise of Paolo and Francesca and the Negation of the Tragic: A Dramatistic Reading of *Inferno* V (97–138)." In *Italiana*, ed. Albert N. Mancini, Paolo Giordano, and Pier Raimondo Baldini. River Forest, IL: Rosary College, 1987.

———. *La problematica del tempo nella "Commedia."* Ravenna: Longo, 1976.

Giuseppe Mazzotta. *Dante Poet of the Desert: History and Allegory in the "Divine Comedy."* Princeton, NJ: Princeton University Press, 1979.

Thomas Merton. *The New Man*. Toronto: Bantam Books, 1961.

Eugenio Montale. "Arsenio." *Ossi di seppia*, 8th ed. Milan: Mondadori, 1966.

Rocco Montano. "Il folle volo di Ulisse." *Delta*, n.s., II (1952).

———. *Storia della poesia di Dante*, vol. II. Florence: Olschki, 1965.

Mark Musa. *Advent at the Gates*. Bloomington: Indiana University Press, 1974.

Bruno Nardi. "La tragedia di Ulisse." In his *Dante e la cultura medievale*. Bari: Laterza, 1949.

Friedrich Nietzsche. *The Birth of Tragedy*, trans. Walter Kaufmann. New York: Random House, 1967.

Susan Noakes. "The Double Misreading of Paolo and Francesca." *Philological Quarterly* 62 (Spring 1983).

Oedipus at Colonus. Greek Tragedies, vol. 3, ed. David Green and Richmond Lattimore. Chicago: University of Chicago Press, 1960.

Georgio Padoan. *Il pio Enea e l'empio Ulisse: Tradizione classica e intendimento medievale in Dante*. Ravenna: Longo, 1977.

Antonino Pagliaro. *Nuovi saggi di critica semantica,* 2nd, rev. ed. Messina-Florence: G. D'Anna, 1963.

Giorgio Petrocchi. *Profilo di un'opera: L' "Inferno" di Dante*. Milan: Rizzoli, 1978.

Michelangelo Picone. "Dante e il mito di Narciso: Dal *Roman de la rose* alla *Commedia*." *Romanische Forschungen* 89 (1977).

Renato Poggioli. "Tragedy or Romance? A Reading of the Paolo and Francesca Episode in Dante's *Inferno*." *PMLA* 72, 3 (1957).

Joy Hambuechen Potter. "Beatrice Ammiraglio: *Purgatorio* XXX, 58–66," in *Italiana*, ed. Albert N. Mancini, Paolo Giordano, and Pier Raimondo Baldini. River Forest, IL: Rosary College, 1988.

Jean Pucelle. *Le Temps*. Paris: Presses Universitaires, 1972.

Ezio Raimondi. "Rito e storia nel I canto del *Purgatorio*." In his *Metafora e storia*. Turin: Einaudi, 1970.

R. Jahan Ramazani. "Heidegger and the Theory of Tragedy." *Centennial Review* 32, 2 (Spring 1988).

Paul Ricoeur. "Herméneutique des symboles et réflexion philosophique." In *Il problema della demitizzazione*, Archivio di Filosofia, ed. Enrico Castelli. Padua: Cedam, 1961.

———. "Manifestation et Proclamation." In *Il sacro*, Archivio di Filosofia, ed. E. Castelli. Padua: Cedam, 1974.

———. *The Symbolism of Evil*, trans. Emerson Buchanan. New York: Harper & Row, 1967.

Lawrence V. Ryan, "*Stornei, Gru, Colombe*: The Bird Images in *Inferno* V." *Dante Studies* XCIV (1976).

George Santayana. "Tragic Philosophy." In *Essays in Literary Criticism of George Santayana*, select., ed. Irving Singer. New York: Scribner, 1956.

Natalino Sapegno. *La Divina Commedia*, vol. II, *Purgatorio*. Florence: La Nuova Italia, 1956.

John A. Scott. *Dante magnanimo: Studi sulla "Commedia."* Florence: Olschki, 1977.

Richard Sewall. *The Vision of Tragedy*, 2nd ed. New Haven, CT: Yale University Press, 1980.

Maria Simonelli. "Bonaggiunta Orbicciani e la pzoblematica dello stil nuovo (*Purg.* XXIV)." *Dante Studies* LXXXVI (1968).

Charles S. Singleton. *Journey to Beatrice*. Baltimore: Johns Hopkins University Press, 1958.

George Steiner. *The Death of Tragedy*. New York: Hill and Wang, 1963.

Dunstan Tucker, O.S.B. "Dante's Reconciliation in the *Purgatorio*." *American Benedictine Review* XX (1969).

Giuseppe Ungaretti. "Il Canto I dell'*Inferno*," in *Letture dantesche*, vol. I, ed. Giovanni Getto. Florence: Sansoni, 1968.

Antoine Vergote. "La peine dans la dialectique de l'innocence, de la transgression et de la réconciliation." In *Il mito della pena*, Archivio di Filosofia, ed. E. Castelli. Padua: Cedam, 1967.

Barbara Vinken. "*Encore*: Francesca da Rimini: Rhetoric of Seduction—Seduction of Rhetoric." *Deutsche Vierteljahrsschzift und Geistesgeschichte* 62 (1988).

Simone Weil. *The Simone Weil Reader*, ed. George A. Panichas. New York: David McKay, 1977.

Warman Welliver. *Dante in Hell: The "De Vulgari Eloquentia,"* with introduction, text, translation, and commentary. Ravenna: Longo, 1981.

Tibor Wlassics. *Dante narratore: Saggi sullo stile della "Commedia."* Florence: Olschki, 1975.

W.B. Yeats. "The Gyres." In *The Collected Poems of W.B. Yeats*. Toronto: Macmillan, 1956.

Index

This book has been set in Linotron Galliard. Galliard was designed for Mergenthaler in 1978 by Matthew Carter. Galliard retains many of the features of a sixteenth century typeface cut by Robert Granjon but has some modifications which gives it a more contemporary look.

Printed on acid-free paper.